D0646953

HITLER'S GENERALS

A **S**ALAMANDER BOOK

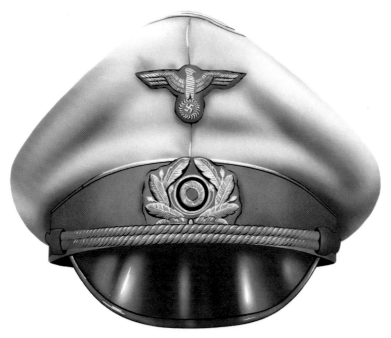

HITLER'S
GENERALS

A Salamander Book

Published by Salamander Books Ltd,
8 Blenheim Court
Brewery Road
London N7 9NT
United Kingdom

© Salamander Books Ltd 1977, 1998

Printed and bound in Spain

This edition distributed by
Random House Value Publishing, Inc.,
201 East 50th Street,
New York, NY 10022.

http://www.randomhouse.com/

ISBN 0-517-20164-X

No part of this book may be
reproduced or transmitted in any form
or by any means electronic or
mechanical including photocopying,
recording or by any information
storage and retrieval system,without
the prior permission in writing from the
publisher.

9 8 7 6 5 4 3 2 1

All correspondence concerning the
content of this volume should be
addressed to Salamander Books Ltd.

Editorial Consultant: Brigadier Shelford Bidwell
Editor: Christopher Chant
Designer: Chris Steer
Picture Research: Jonathan Moore
Maps: Richard Natkiel

Filmset by SX Composing, England

Color reproduction by
Metric Reproduction Ltd, England,
Paramount Litho Co, England and
Autographic Lithoplates Ltd, England

9 8 7 6 5 4 3 2 1

Printed and bound in Spain

The Consultant

Brigadier Shelford Bidwell *is a military historian with a particular interest in World War II. A Fellow of the Royal Historical Society, he is also an authority on contemporary defence questions and former Deputy Director of the Royal United Services Institute for Defence Studies. He is the author of five books, four on historical subjects and one on modern warfare, and is the Editor of a major work on modern artillery weapon systems. He was a major contributor to the Salamander titles, "The Soviet War Machine" and "The Encyclopedia of Land Warfare in the 20th Century."*

The Authors

Christopher Chant *is a highly experienced editor and a contributor to a number of authoritative and comprehensive partwork publications devoted to the history of both world wars. He is a specialist in modern military history, and has an intense interest in aviation history, particularly that of World War I. He is the author of numerous articles and reviews in specialist publications, and has had eight of his books published. He has also contributed to and edited several compendium volumes, and assisted in the preparation of many books, including the Salamander titles "The Illustrated Encyclopedia of Tanks and Fighting Vehicles" and "The Encyclopedia of the World's Warships."*

Richard Humble *is an editor and author of historical studies who has specialised in military history for the past 12 years. A former editor and managing editor of two extensive series publications on the history of World War II, his own books on the subject include studies of the German and Japanese surface fleets as well as Hitler's generals, and he has contributed to several other publications.*

William Fowler *read English and Moral Sciences at Cambridge University. He was Assistant Editor of a weekly partwork on World War II and has had several articles published on various aspects of that war. He is currently assisting in the preparation of a major partwork on weapons and warfare, and was a contributor to Salamander's "The Encyclopedia of Land Warfare in the 20th Century." He is a member of the Royal United Services Institute for Defence Studies.*

Jenny Shaw *read Politics and Geography at the University College of Wales and War Studies at King's College, London. She was Assistant Editor of a weekly partwork on World War II and has had several articles published on various aspects of that war. Her present position as Deputy Editor of the Journal of the Royal United Services Institute for Defence Studies allows her to combine her main interests of military history and current defence questions.*

Contents

The Western Front

The Eastern Front, June 1941-February 1943

The Political Front

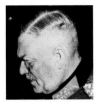

Foreword

General Collins, a 1939 graduate of West Point, commanded a battalion of Field Artillery in World War II. Landing with the Seventh US Corps on Utah Beach in Normandy he fought with the First US Army at the meeting with the Russians on the Elbe. He remained in Europe for two years after the war with the Intelligence Division of the principal US Headquarters in Germany.

He returned to Europe to serve with NATO in the 1951–54 period and later was in Washington on the Department of the Army Staff. A linguist himself, General Collins was placed in charge of the US Army's Language Training Program in 1959 and later consolidated the language training of all the US Armed Services.

In Germany again in 1967 where he commanded the Artillery with the Fifth US Corps he returned to the US in 1969 and was made Chief of Military History for the Department of the Army in 1970.

Success in battle depends on many things—not the least of which is the relative strength of the combatants. But the leaders of the contending sides can, and frequently do, upset the outcome suggested by a simple calculus of opposing military power. The leaders of battles are generals, and it is to the study of those of the Third Reich that this book is addressed.

Generals take their name from the concept that when an officer is advanced from regimental command he leaves the infantry or cavalry or whatever his branch of the military service has been. He is a 'General Officer' deemed capable of employing troops of all branches and not merely in the use of any single arm. The title also connotes superior rank and a wide sphere of authority and responsibility. Indeed the term 'General' is used in such applications in civil activities, such as Postmaster General or Attorney General. But generals are human; they are not a monolithic group. They have their strengths and weaknesses, their likes and dislikes. Their training and their intellect unavoidably affect their effectiveness in battle. The generals of the Third Reich were also hampered by their dual allegiance. On the one hand, their oath of loyalty to Hitler, the *Fahneneid*, bound them personally to the *Fuehrer;* on the other, the code of the German officers, and more particularly of the German generals, charged them with the safety of the state. The collision between these two loyalties certainly affected the actions of some key officers— exemplified by the death of Field-Marshal Rommel by his own hand.

In addition, the generals of the Third Reich laboured under other handicaps, many of which, it must be admitted, were not peculiar to Germany alone. Rivalry among them based on social position was not uncommon; the aristocratic *Junkers* of the old school did not suffer kindly the antics of the commoners promoted for battlefield achievement. Neither of these groups was enchanted with the posturing and incompetence of many of the generals

appointed for their political reliability and devotion to Hitler.

And then there was the friction caused by the new methods of warfare. For example, the use of great armoured formations as independent entities was slow to be accepted by those who regarded the tank as a mobile pillbox supporting the infantry. This in turn led to decisions which affected the conduct of the war. The successful British evacuation of Dunkirk was due in no small measure to lack of appreciation by the German high command of the mobility of armour.

Personal ambition, as is common in most fields of endeavour, did not pass by the generals. Hitler, whose military knowledge was but skin deep, yet whose early strategic triumphs in Poland and in Russia had convinced him of his own military genius, meddled interminably in the details, both large and small, of operations. This greatly impeded actions of commanders at all levels when Hitler's orders did not fit the local situation or when—as was so evident late in the war—they were touched with irrationality. Yet all Hitler's generals were expendable and none were more aware of this than the generals themselves. To argue, to contradict, to complain, to fail to carry out an impossible order, to be defeated even in a minor engagement, all were reasons for dismissal. The fact that a few of these dismissals did not stick —Rundstedt kept getting retired and then recalled to meet a fresh emergency—was no great comfort to those cashiered nor to those who survived for that matter. Advancement came to depend on not crossing Hitler more than on battlefield success.

How the generals who served Hitler for better or worse coped with these cross currents as well as with their enemies is set forth in these pages. Displayed in the context of the battles and campaigns they fought, their capabilities and strengths, their mistakes and triumphs are depicted in all the stark realism of a portrait by Goya. You will enjoy the telling of their stories as well as refreshing your memories of the perilous days of World War II.

Brigadier General James Lawton Collins, Jr. Chief of Military History for the Department of the US Army

General Collins' comments in this foreword in no way constitute or imply Department of the Army or Department of Defense endorsement of this publication.

The German Army and the Nazi Party, 1932-1939

The history of the relationship between the Nazi party and the *Reichswehr,* as the army of the Weimar Republic was named, in the late 1920s and early 1930s is a strange one, marked throughout by a multitude of ambivalent attitudes. On the one hand, many of the *Reichswehr*'s officers were of aristocratic lineage, and possessed an inherited disdain for the 'jumped-up corporal' Adolf Hitler who sought to take over the running of Germany; they also, moreover, distrusted anything that smacked of socialism, and feared the power of Hitler's private army, the *Sturmabteilung* or SA, under its repulsive and boorish commander, Ernst Roehm. On the other hand, many of the younger officers of the *Reichswehr* saw the advantages of a Nazi accession to power. The restrictions and conditions of service imposed upon the *Reichswehr* by the Treaty of Versailles in 1919 meant that the lot of the junior officers was a sad one: 'The actual purpose of the *Reichswehr* as a citadel of the military idea and as the basic nucleus of the future war of liberation pales. The need of earning bread becomes all important. Soldiers turn into officials, officers become candidates for pensions. What remains is a police troop. People know nothing of the tragedy of the four words: "Twelve years as subalterns".' Thus younger officers, disaffected by the stultifying round of training with inadequate resources and the appallingly slow rate of promotion, saw the opportunities that the Nazis represented, and attempted to spread its doctrines through the officer corps. The words above were written by a lieutenant serving a gaol sentence in 1930 for such illegal activities.

The attitudes of senior officers also reflected much the same feeling. The high command, in the Bendlerstrasse in Berlin, were basically against the Nazis as a threat to Germany's political stability and their own positions in the politico-military establishment. Many of the slightly lower ranking generals, however, commanding *Wehrkreise* (military districts) and divisions, were attracted by the Nazi idea, seeing in it advancement for themselves and for the army. Chief amongst this latter group was Lieutenant-General Werner Eduard Fritz

von Blomberg, commander of *Wehrkreis* I in East Prussia between 1930 and 1933, and head of the German military delegation to the Disarmament Conference in Geneva from 1932. Chief of the faction opposed to the Nazis were General Kurt von Schleicher, the *Reichswehrminister* or Minister of Defence from July 1932, and General Kurt Freiherr von Hammerstein-Equord, the *Chef der Heeresleitung* or Commander-in-Chief of the Army from October 1930.

The aged president of Germany, Field-Marshal Paul von Beneckendorff und Hindenburg, was faced by almost insuperable problems in late 1932. The Nazis had decided that the time was ripe for their bid

Right: **An expectant crowd awaits the arrival of the Nazi Party's leaders at a rally typical of these mass outpourings of hysterical energy before World War II.**

Below right: **Hitler addresses the massed ranks of *Sturmabteilung* (SA) troopers from the podium. The SA was broken as an effective force in the 'Night of the Long Knives'.**

Below: **Hitler makes a triumphal entry into the Czech town of Karlovy Vary (Karlsbad) in the ceded Sudetenland during September 1938.**

12

for absolute power, and had succeeded in toppling the government by means of a crippling transport strike in uneasy conjunction with the Communist party, the Nazis' sworn enemies. The new government accepted by Hindenburg had as its *Kanzler* (Chancellor or Prime Minister) Schleicher, who attempted to split the Nazi party into two manageable halves by offering the posts of Vice-Chancellor and Minister-President of Prussia to Gregor Strasser, the head of the party's political organisation and the only possible rival to Hitler as head of the Nazis. Strasser urged that Schleicher's offer should be accepted to avoid the possibility of further elections for a new *Reichstag* assembly, which might lose the Nazis some seats. Hitler refused, and Strasser quit the party. Schleicher's miscalculation had thus left Hitler in an even stronger position, especially as Schleicher's government was only a minority one, and must resign as the Chancellor could not form a coalition.

The only two possibilities as successors to Schleicher were Hitler and Franz von Papen, an ex-chancellor. Schleicher devoted his last days in office to ensuring the succession of the one he considered the right man. And although he would have preferred Papen, as did Hindenburg, his choice was forced to fall upon Hitler. The reasons for this were twofold: he thought that accession to power would mellow Hitler's more objectionable traits and policies, especially as he expected to be appointed *Reichswehr-minister*, a position in which he could keep a check on Hitler; the second reason was a military one. The transport strike of the previous November and December had taught the *Reichswehr* an important lesson

in its limitations. Poland was known to be prepared to launch a pre-emptive war against Germany should the opportunity arise, and so forces had to be concentrated to meet such a threat. This left an insufficient number of men to run the strike-bound transport system and cope with any armed resistance the strikers might offer, collectively or individually. Thus the governmental crisis of January 1933 offered Schleicher no choice. The Polish threat still persisted, and were Papen offered the chancellorship, there was every likelihood of Hitler and the Nazi party starting an armed revolt. The *Reichswehr* would not be able to cope with this, and therefore Schleicher decided that *faux de mieux* Hitler would have to be the next chancellor. Hitler was informed of Schleicher's *volte-face* by Hammerstein, but did not at first believe it, and set preparations to deal with an army *Putsch* or coup in hand.

Accession to power

The results are well known. On 30 January 1933 Hitler became the new chancellor of Germany, and the Nazi *Machtuebernahme* or assumption of power was accomplished. That the army was centrally involved is now evident, with all its disastrous consequences. Schleicher's folly in January 1933 was compounded, moreover, by his naive and totally erroneous belief that even had his assessment of Hitler turned out to be wrong, the army could then remove the new chancellor. And although the army had not had to use force to ensure Hitler's advancement to the chancellorship, Hitler himself later that year conceded that 'if the army had not stood on

our side, we should not be standing here today'. Schleicher began to sense how badly he had miscalculated when Blomberg rather than himself was appointed *Reichswehr-minister* in the new government.

Hitler's dealings with the *Reichswehr* were at first circumspect and grateful. The new chancellor thanked the army for its help in his rise to power, and led it to believe that it would continue in its traditional position in the German state, with considerable growth once the political climate was right. All these were just what the generals wished to hear. Hitler was also careful in his international position. He played along at the Geneva conference, insisting that Germany be treated as a major power, and only pulled out of the conference when it urged definite levels of disarmament. This again pleased the generals. Finally he abolished the rights of civil courts over military personnel, and also abolished the system, dating back to the military councils of the immediate postwar months of 1919, of elected representatives of the enlisted men, with all its overtones of socialism.

Although the appointment to key positions of outright Nazis such as Blomberg had not met with the wholehearted approval of the army and the president, this had been counterbalanced by the appointment of highly respected men such as Lieutenant-General Ludwig Beck (to the position of *Chef des Truppenamts* or Chief of the General Staff in October 1933). But the question of Hammerstein's replacement as commander-in-chief on his retirement in February 1934 proved a clearer indication of what lay ahead. Hitler, and of course Blomberg, wished this appointment to go to

the Nazi Colonel Walther von Reichenau, who had been head of the *Reichswehr* Ministerial Office since February 1933. This proposal met with violent opposition within the army and from Hindenburg, and despite Blomberg's threat to resign unless Reichenau was appointed, the position went to Lieutenant-General Werner Thomas Ludwig Freiherr von Fritsch. Reichenau had to be content with promotion to Major-General and the control of the Armed Forces Office, as the enlarged Ministerial Office was named.

The only chance that the army ever had to remove Hitler was in the early years of his rule, but the complacency engendered by its minor success in the Reichenau affair and its apparent victory in the purging of the SA caused the army to let its chances slip by without action. The purging of the SA was the direct result of the ambitions of Ernst Roehm to advance both the organisation and himself in the new Germany. He was disgusted by Hitler's dalliance with the army when it had long been his ambition to absorb it into the SA, which would then become Germany's major armed force. Hitler was aware of Roehm's ambitions, and wished to halt them. The problem was how to do so without offending the army and Hindenburg. In an effort to gain time, and to placate Roehm, Hitler invited the latter to join the cabinet. Once in the cabinet, however, Roehm produced his plan for the integration of the army and SA, presumably under his own leadership. The army was appalled, and even Blomberg and Reichenau would have nothing to do with the scheme. Blomberg in particular, who had been attempting to woo Hitler away from the

SA to the army, now redoubled his efforts, and some time late in June 1934 told Hitler that unless he took steps to clear up the SA problem, Hindenburg might declare martial law and ask the army to do so. Blomberg then stated that if Hitler took immediate steps to set the party's house in order, the army would not interfere. This offer, combined with the importuning of *Reichsfuehrer*-SS Heinrich Himmler and Hermann Goering, both of whom had for some time been very concerned with Roehm's ambitions, finally decided Hitler to act.

The orders went out to Himmler's SS units, and the results are well known. On 30 June 1934, variously known as the 'Blood Purge' and the 'Night of the Long Knives', Roehm and most of his senior colleagues were murdered by SS troopers. Himmler also took the opportunity to dispose of other 'hostile' elements, such as General von Schleicher and Gregor Strasser. Hindenburg, who was to die in little more than a month, was misinformed of the occasion and raised no objection; the army, with a few exceptions, was well pleased with the elimination of the SA as a real threat to its armed supremacy. Yet the army's compliance in what was only a large-scale series of political murders marked the real beginning of its decline from the high moral standards on which it had always prided itself. From this time onwards Hitler was consistently able to dominate his generals.

On 1 August 1934 President Hindenburg died, and Hitler immediately amalgamated the offices of President and Chancellor in himself as *Fuehrer und Reichskanzler*. And then there occurred a quite extraordinary event. Apparently without urging from

Above left: **Hitler's three senior military commanders attend a party rally in September 1936. On the left is War Minister von Blomberg, in the centre General von Fritsch, C-in-C of the Army and on the right Grand Admiral Raeder, C-in-C of the Navy.**

Above: **Hitler and a group of SA luminaries at a 1929 parade.**

Hitler, on 2 August every officer and man of the *Reichswehr* swore the following oath: 'I swear by God this sacred oath, that I will yield unconditional obedience to the *Fuehrer* of the German *Reich* and *Volk*, Adolf Hitler, the Supreme Commander of the *Wehrmacht*, and, as a brave soldier, will be ready at any time to lay down my life for this oath.' The event presumably took place on the instigation of Blomberg, to elicit a suitable reply from the new *Fuehrer*. This was forthcoming on the 20th of the same month, when Hitler wrote to Blomberg, thanking him for the oath and continuing: '...so will I at all times regard it as my highest duty to intercede on behalf of the stability and inviolability of the *Wehrmacht*, in fulfilment of the testament of the late Field-Marshal [Hindenburg]; and, in accordance with my own desire, to fix the army as the sole bearer of arms in the nation.' Thus for a promise of its sovereignty, which the SS was already violating, the leaders of the army sold themselves and their men by oath to a man, rather than to the state. It was an oath that was to drag them and their state down to total ruin by 1945.

As he was consolidating his position as supreme ruler of Germany, Hitler was already increasing the size of the armed forces, in direct opposition to the terms of the Treaty of Versailles. Serious expansion began with the German withdrawal from the disarmament conference in Geneva in October 1933, and during 1934 the basis of an additional 24 divisions was set up, the replacement of cavalry by armoured forces was given Hitler's enthusiastic support, and a start was made in building up the small, and totally illegal, *Luftwaffe*. Although the generals had doubts about the speed with which the army was to be increased, they were on the whole pleased that at last they would have the money and the scope to exercise their long-cherished plans to expand the army into the greatest army in the world. Yet Hitler was not satisfied with his current expansion plans, and in March 1935 he announced to a shocked Europe that Germany would no longer be bound by the military terms of the Treaty of Versailles. At the same time he announced that universal conscription was to be introduced, to produce a peacetime strength of 36 divisions, and that Germany had a powerful air force in the form of the *Luftwaffe*. The Western powers, who had imposed the '*Diktat*' of Versailles on a defeated Germany only 16 years before, did precisely nothing to try to prevent the rearming of Germany.

Army problems

Although it was easy for Hitler to announce a vast increase in the size of the army, it was difficult for the generals to implement this quickly. One of the main reasons for this was the acute shortage of officers. It is often claimed that the expansion of the German army in the 1930s was easy, as the 100,000 men of the *Reichswehr*, all long-service men, were an ideal cadre for growth. This is only partially true, however, for the reason that whilst a great many of the *Reichswehr's* men could profitably be promoted, it was usually to non-commissioned rank. And here the German army of the Nazi period excelled, for its NCOs were experienced and well-trained men. The position was also quite good at the other end of the scale, with the senior commanders. Although the Great German General Staff had been forbidden by the Treaty of Versailles, it continued to operate under the *nom de guerre* of the *Truppenamt* or Troop Department. Thus there was a continuity of senior command, together with its doctrines, practices and experience, which could undertake the limited expansion needed of it with facility.

The position was radically different with junior- and middle-ranking officers, however. The *Reichswehr* had had some 4,000 officers, of whom 450 were medical or veterinary officers. Of the remaining 3,550, some 500 were transferred to the newly-revealed *Luftwaffe*, leaving only 3,050

Hitler and an entourage of SA men. The ambitions of Ernst Roehm, the SA's leader, soon caused friction between this body and Himmler's SS which, with tacit army agreement, 'purged' the SA of its 'corrupt' leadership in the infamous 'Night of the Long Knives'.

officers for an army that was to grow to 52 divisions by 1939. Many NCOs were commissioned, and 1,000 policemen trained in military methods were drafted, but the army still had to find and train over 25,000 more officers in the six years up to the beginning of World War II. That it did so, and also produced a large number of first-class junior commanders, is a great tribute to the efforts of the senior commanders and the abilities of the junior commanders. This great expansion is also the reason for the comparative youth of German commanders up to battalion level, and why a young officer who would have commanded only a company in the British and American armies might command a battalion or even regiment in the German army.

There was also another side to the greatly increased need for young officers. With opportunities for promotion being so open, ambitious young men tried to ensure their swift advancement by adopting Nazism. This had little significance at first, but as more Nazi sympathisers reached the middle ranks, there emerged a tendency for pro-Nazi officers to be given promotions in ever greater numbers, with the concomitant problems of commanders having reached their positions on political, rather than military, merit. At the same time, officers who had the temerity to reveal themselves

little or no promotion, any military ability they may have had not withstanding.

The influx of so many new officers, many of them with very dubious backgrounds, helped to break down the cohesive strength of the German officer corps, making it less likely that any action against Hitler could have been undertaken. At the same time the growth of the army with conscripts, most of whom were Nazis or Nazi sympathisers, meant that even had the officer corps decided to take action against Hitler, the men might well have refused to follow them. The

Nazis' hold on the conscripted men was also strengthened by weekly indoctrination sessions.

Hitler, ever an astute judge of character, was very careful in how quickly he forced the army along. Although the generals had been taken aback by the size of the army Hitler desired, they had gone along with him; the same applied to the large-scale introduction of armoured forces in homogeneous units; and they had even acquiesced in the matter of the ratio of 'tooth' to 'tail' forces, in which Hitler had held out for greater 'tooth' fighting units and smaller 'tail' logistics and communications units than was customary. But Hitler realised that he would have to tread carefully about when he committed his new army to action for the first time, as most army officers considered that the efficiency of the army had been adversely affected by an expansion well over the triple one normally considered the maximum. Fritsch had exemplified the generals' opinions when he issued dire warnings of what might have happened had other states decided to deal with Germany in 1934 after the abortive *Putsch* in Vienna.

Hitler's spur

The army, Hitler decided, would take more pushing in 1936, and he decided to re-occupy the Rhineland, which had been demilitarised by the Treaty of Locarno in 1925. The *Fuehrer* gave his generals only five days in which to plan the operation, which they did after great protests. Virtually the whole of the army had to be used for the operation, which took place on 7 March 1936. The generals were ready for an immediate withdrawal in the event of French or British armed intervention, as Germany could not deploy any reserves. Yet Hitler stood firm, France and Britain did nothing, and the operation was a total success. In purely military terms the generals had been

Above: **The efficient nucleus of the Third Reich's army under training. In this photograph of the *Reichsheer* period, a group of senior non-commissioned officers (*Unter-offizieren*) are receiving tactical instruction from an officer on a sand table. With the expansion of the army by the Nazis, these men were soon turned into officers, or given highly responsible tasks as instructors.**

Right: **The *Reichsheer* puts on a tactical exhibition. Forbidden heavy weapons and tanks by the Treaty of Versailles, the German Army kept abreast of current developments in the military art by clandestine liaison with Soviet Russia's new army and military industries. For training purposes, dummy tanks were built on car chassis.**

right, but Hitler's amazing intuitive combination of political and military opportunism had prevailed. For the first time in 'combat', the *Fuehrer* had showed himself the 'strategic superior' of his staff generals, and his moral ascendency over his 'pusillanimous' commanders continued to grow, as did his belief in his *schlafwandlerische Sicherheit* or sleepwalker's assurance when it came to matters relating to foreign affairs.

Hitler's next venture was the despatch of small forces, with an assortment of the latest German equipment, to help the Nationalist cause of General Francisco Franco against the Republicans in the Spanish Civil War. Once again the generals complained that the despatch of all the equipment left the forces at home with great shortages, with dire results should any military action have to be undertaken. But Hitler insisted, and in the event was proved

The German Army, 1932-1939

right. His forces greatly aided Franco, and at the same time learned much of vital importance both about the equipment and about tactics. That some incorrect conclusions were also drawn was the fault of the generals, not of Hitler.

Despite the fears of his commanders, all went well, and Hitler turned his thoughts to his next conquest. There were still grave problems with the expansion of the army, not least of which was Hitler's insistence that no sooner had a formation reached a high level of efficiency than it should be divided into two, each half going to form the cadre of a new division. Thus although the army continued to grow swiftly, there was no efficient and inviolate nucleus that could fight at a moment's notice should the need arise. Fears about Germany's strategic position were also raised at this time, January 1937, by General Ludwig Beck, *Chef des Generalstabs des Heeres* or Chief of the Army General Staff since July 1935. The nation, Beck pointed out, was surrounded by potential enemies who might, individually or collectively, cut off Germany's

access to a great number of essential raw materials and foodstuffs. Although Germany had made great strides under the leadership of Hitler, Beck continued, there were virtually no stockpiles of basic foodstuffs for animals and humans, nor were there stockpiles of the strategic materials for war, such as oil, rubber, tungsten, copper, tin, platinum, nickel, iron ore, chemicals etc. Beck was absolutely right, and the closing years of the war were to prove it. Germany's civilians starved, and her armed forces were immobilised for lack of fuel, tires to run on, and shortages of high-quality explosives.

Strategic visions

Hitler was not overly concerned, however, and in November 1937 he confided his strategic plans to his senior military and political subordinates: 'The aim of German policy is to make secure and to preserve the racial community and to enlarge it. It is, therefore, a matter of living space [*Lebensraum*]', which was to be acquired by force in central and eastern Europe. First of all

Above: **The growth of the German Army after Hitler's renunciation of the 'shackles' of the Versailles Treaty was steady and impressive. But this growth could not be restricted only to men and equipment – also needed were logistical and administrative expansion to house, feed, clothe, pay and generally cope with the new forces. Here a regiment is seen marching into its new barracks on the outskirts of Berlin. Although little new building was needed, the buildings of imperial days for the most part sufficing, most of the barracks had to be converted and modernised.**
Right: **A striking poster for the German Youth Festival of 23 June 1934. Astute propagandists and mass psychologists in the early days, the Nazis were always at great pains to try to indoctrinate the growing generation of Germans into true belief of the Nazi doctrine.**

Austria and Czechoslovakia had to be taken over, and it was his 'unalterable resolve to solve the problem of Germany's space by 1943–1945 at the latest'. To say that his audience was dumbfounded would be an understatement. Even Goering objected to the plan, but Hitler was determined that now all should obey him. He had already decided that there must be a showdown with the army, and this may have prompted the timing of the meeting, recorded for posterity by Colonel Friedrich Hossbach, the *Fuehrer*'s military adjutant and later an army commander on the Eastern Front.

Hitler was strengthened in his resolve to have it out with the army once and for all by the campaign of slanders being waged against Fritsch by Himmler and his subordinate Reinhardt Heydrich, the head of the *Sicherheitsdienst* or SS Security Service. The two SS men constantly urged it upon Hitler that the completely apolitical Fritsch was the leader of a group of army generals plotting to overthrow Hitler. This, combined with a memorandum submitted by army chaplains, with Fritsch's approval, condemning the Nazi perversion of Christianity, so infuriated Hitler that he resolved to deal with his high command.

The army unwittingly played into the *Fuehrer*'s hands. Blomberg, who had reached the rank of Field-Marshal in April 1936, had recently married for a second time in January 1938. It was now revealed that the *Frau Generalfeldmarschall* had been convicted for prostitution and for posing for obscene photographs. Beck persuaded Fritsch that Blomberg would have to be dismissed from his post as Minister of Defence. Fritsch thereupon approached Hitler and persuaded him that Blomberg had to be sacked. But who was to replace Blomberg? The obvious answer was Fritsch, but here Himmler and Heydrich appeared, like two *diaboli ex machina,* and informed Hitler that Fritsch was a homosexual, 'proving' it by producing a paid informer. Fritsch resigned on the spot. Hitler had thus rid himself of what he imagined were two trouble-makers. But how was the army high command now to be reorganised? The answer was revealed on 4 February, when the retirements of Blomberg and Fritsch were announced. (Fritsch, it is worth noting, was subsequently cleared of all the allegations against him by a special army court of inquiry.) General Wilhelm Keitel, the head of the *Wehrmachtsamt* or Armed Forces Department, had been authorised to canvas candidates. He finally settled on General Walther von Brauchitsch, the commander of Army Group 4, who promised to try to bring the army into closer line with Nazi ideology. Brauchitsch took up his position as Commander-in-Chief of the Army or *Oberbefehlshaber des Heeres* with the rank of Colonel-General.

Of more far-reaching significance was the announcement that Hitler himself was to take over Blomberg's functions: 'Henceforth I will personally exercise immediate command over the whole armed forces. The former *Wehrmachtsamt* in the War Ministry becomes the *Oberkommando der Wehrmacht* (High Command of the Armed Forces), and comes immediately under my command as my military staff.' Salt was rubbed into the

army's wounds caused by the final assumption of supreme power by the *Fuehrer* and the effective downgrading of the general staff, by the appointment to the head of the OKW of the nonentity Keitel, with promotion to Colonel-General in October. The army's last chance of freeing itself and Germany from Hitler had passed. If Fritsch had called upon the army to support him in January, there is every chance that a large portion of it may have done so. But now the chance had been lost, as Fritsch himself admitted in June 1938. As Hitler explored the possibilities of his new office, Brauchitsch set energetically to work to remove from important positions any potentially seditious officers.

The German army, which for centuries had been a power unto itself, and virtually a state within a state, had at last lost its autonomy, and was now merely another adjunct of the Nazi state. John Wheeler-Bennett puts it neatly in his *Nemesis of Power:* Hitler 'had outmanoeuvred, defeated, humiliated and dragooned the German army'. And this was only the beginning.

Two weeks after delivering his strategic appreciation to his commanders in November 1937, Hitler was visited by Lord Halifax, Nevile Chamberlain's Foreign Secretary. From what Halifax had to say about the need for a peaceful solution to Europe's problems, Hitler realised that British

military strength no longer lay between him and his immediate objectives. He therefore speeded up his plans. First Austria was to be joined with Germany by an *Anschluss* or union. In February 1938 Hitler told the Austrian chancellor, Kurt von Schuschnigg, that unless the Austrian Nazi party were legalised and given a major share in power immediately, the German army would invade Austria to implement Hitler's conditions. After a series of delaying moves, during which Hitler ordered his armies to be prepared to march on 9 March, Schuschnigg resigned on the 11th, being replaced by Dr. Arthur Seyss-Inquart, the Austrian Nazi leader, who immediately sent out a pre-arranged telegram asking for German help. The generals had feared that the occupation would be chaotic, and they were very nearly right, the armoured formations in particular running into grave difficulties. Beck, now extremely worried about the subservient rôle of the army in German policies, had objected strongly to the whole venture, and Hitler determined that he would have to be replaced. But before he could do so, Beck resigned, totally embittered about the army's refusal to assume what he thought were its true responsibilities: 'If . . . [the generals'] advice and warnings are not listened to, then they have the right and the duty before their people and before history to resign their commands. If they all act with a

determined will, the execution of an act of war becomes impossible. In this way they save the fatherland from the worst possible fate, from destruction.

'Any soldier who holds a leading position and at the same time limits his duty and task to his military charge, without being conscious of his supreme responsibility to the nation, shows lack of greatness and of understanding of his task.'

Another victim

Beck resigned on 18 August 1938, and was succeeded as Army Chief-of-Staff by General Franz Halder on 1 September. Halder had acquired an intense aversion for Hitler's ideas in the 'Blood Purge' of 1934, and at first followed Beck's policies of trying to moderate Hitler's progress towards war. But the West's capitulation to Hitler at Munich partially converted him to Hitler's opinions, and thereafter he mellowed towards Hitler quite considerably.

The *Fuehrer*'s next target was Czechoslovakia, starting with the Sudetenland. He demanded that these German-speaking areas be handed over to Germany; and despite Czech protests that with help from France and Great Britain they could handle the German army severely, Edouard Daladier and Nevile Chamberlain meekly handed Germany this important strategic

frontier region of Czechoslovakia at Munich in September 1938. Hitler had told his generals to be prepared to invade Czechoslovakia if necessary, and the latter, although complying with the orders, had very grave reservations about the German army's ability to deal with the formidable Czech border defences, a miniature 'Maginot Line', but a far more powerful and well-planned one than the French *bête noire*. The loss of the Sudetenland sealed the fate of Czechoslovakia, and with it was lost a potentially able ally of the Western powers – and all for Hitler's assurance that it was his 'last territorial demand in Europe', so ensuring Chamberlain's devout wish for 'peace in our time'.

Yet Hitler was already thinking ahead. In May 1939, only two months after the occupation of the rump of Czechoslovakia on 15 March by German troops, Hitler informed his generals of his intentions of invading Poland, which might bring France and Great Britain finally to war, in turn necessitating the seizure of Belgium and Holland to prevent the British and French from occupying them. And on the eve of the signing of the Russo-German Non-Aggression Pact in Moscow on 23 August, Hitler told his generals that Russia would inevitable have to be crushed. There were no strenuous protests, just weary acceptance that the *Fuehrer*'s will be done. The German

Above left: A pensive *Fuehrer* at a march-past. Behind Hitler, in a cap, is War Minister von Blomberg, later forced out of the army by Hitler for having married an ex-prostitute. On the right is General von Fritsch, Commander-in-Chief of the Army, who was 'retired in February 1938 on trumped-up charges of homosexuality. With these two officers out of the way, Hitler was at last free to organise the army high command for his own purposes.

Above: German boys learn how to shoot. Apart from political indoctrination, the Nazis placed great emphasis on teaching German youth the rudiments of military life. Thus there sprang up, in addition to the *Hitlerjugend* or Hitler Youth, large numbers of youth organisations devoted to the paramilitary pursuits of shooting, gliding and other out-door physical activities.

officer corps, and in particular its generals, had been emasculated by Hitler and had abandoned any attempts to control the type of war it would have to fight. All that was left was to fight an unwanted war as best it could – and its best, as will be seen, was very good.

The Regalia and Uniforms of Hitler's Generals

The dress and equipment of Germany's generals reflect in some respects the fortunes of war of their armies. In the prewar and early war years they rode in recognisable staff cars or command vehicles and wore striking red-striped breeches and riding boots. By the end of the war they travelled in little *Kubelwagen* jeeps clad in the functional uniforms issued to the men at the front.

In 1939 the basic uniform of an officer of the rank of *Generalmajor* or above consisted of a greeny-grey tunic with four pleated pockets and a stand and fall collar. He wore darker grey breeches and high black boots. A grey cap, trimmed with gold piping, had a gold chin strap cord and a shiny black peak.

A feature which distinguished all officers from men was a brown belt with a twin-claw buckle. Generals had the national emblem woven in gold thread on their tunic, gold oak-leaves on a red background on their collars, and twisted gold and silver cord epaulettes with a series of silver 'pips' or stars up to the crossed batons of a *Generalfeldmarschall*. An exception to this rule were the six general officers who held the honorary rank of regimental '*Chef*' or Colonel-in-Chief. Rundstedt, who was the *Chef* of 18 *Infanterie-Regiment,* wore the epaulettes of *Generalfeldmarschall* and the parade-quality collar patches of an infantry officer.

The theatres and units with which generals served affected their dress and uniforms. In 1940 Eduard Dietl, the popular commander of the 3rd Mountain Division at Narvik, wore the long baggy trousers and heavily studded boots of the mountain troops. In place of the issue cap he wore the distinctive *Bergmuetze* with the *Edelweiss* badge on the left side.

A year later, in North Africa, the Germans adopted a uniform designed by the Tropical Institute in Berlin. Though the extremes of temperature at night meant that they needed greatcoats, or the fine-grain grey leather coats that officers were permitted to buy, all *Afrika Korps* personnel wore the comfortable open-neck tunic when the weather was hot. Rommel favoured his grey European service cap, though generals like Thoma and Ravenstein wore the characteristic *Afrika Korps* cotton drill cap, edged with gold piping.

The savage winters of Russia meant that officers and men alike adopted the extemporised cold-weather uniforms worn in the

Hitler talks to a staff officer at the 1935 Celle manoeuvres, with Blomberg and Fritsch in attendance. Note the oak-leaf insignia worn on each side of the collar by all officers of general rank.

A general in typical parade dress. He is wearing the standard uniform cap, with general officers' gold cap cords and gilt cap cord buttons. Note the riding boots (with spurs) and breeches worn with the parade dress tunic. The throat decoration is the *Pour le Mérite,* a World War I award.

A general dressed for the field. He is wearing the standard marching boots, and the field-grey greatcoat worn by all ranks. The greatcoats of generals were distinguished by the application of bright red facings to the lapels. Round his neck this officer is wearing the Knight's Cross of the Iron Cross.

first winter campaign. The issue greatcoat was trimmed with fur and reinforced with leather, or entire coats were made of sheepskin. In place of their caps they wore heavy fur or felt caps with ear-flaps. Later in the war, when the two-piece reversible quilted winter uniform became available, this was worn by all ranks.

One of the privileges of rank enjoyed by senior officers was the freedom to wear their own style of an issued uniform. Rommel had his own tropical uniform, which later became an accepted style of dress for the Mediterranean. Lieutenant-General Count von Schwerin wore a tailored M1944 battledress style blouse and long trousers, with the addition of general's epaulettes and collar patches and re-styled pockets.

When wearing camouflaged uniforms the Army, like the *Waffen*-SS, had a range of special rank insignia. For generals these consisted of a series of yellow stripes on a black background, surmounted by crossed oak-leaves and acorns. These stripes were sewn to the upper sleeves of the camouflaged smocks or jackets.

Few medals

Waffen-SS officers, however, had an entirely different system of collar patch insignia, though their epaulettes were almost identical to those of the Army. An SS *Oberfuehrer* or Brigadier-General had two stylised oak-leaves on his collar, whilst an *Oberstgruppenfuehrer* or Colonel-General had three oak-leaves and three pips.

Unlike the Army, the SS had been wearing camouflaged uniforms since the beginning of the war. Many of their senior officers were younger than men of equivalent rank in the Army, and in the spirit of the *Waffen*-SS affected an aggressive style in neat camouflaged uniforms and battered service caps or helmets with camouflaged covers.

The German attitude to medals and awards may seem unusual to some readers. There was only one true campaign medal, the 'Frozen Meat Medal', for men who had served on the Eastern Front during the winter of 1941–1942. When awards were given for campaigns they took the form of cuff-titles or arm-shields. The cuff-titles included ones for the attack on Crete and the campaign in North Africa, whilst those for the defence of Metz in 1944 and of Kurland in 1945 were designed but never issued.

The arm-shields, in white or yellow metal, began with one awarded to troops who served at Narvik in 1940, but the majority were awarded for operations on the Eastern Front, including Kholm in 1942, the Crimea in 1941–1942, and the Kuban in 1943. There was also a range of pin-backed badges awarded to men who had been wounded or participated in infantry, tank, or 'General Assault' attacks. Many of these were worn by generals who, liking to be up with their lead units to exercise personal control of the battle, had become involved in tank or infantry actions.

Among the decorations for valour were the range of Iron Cross medals. Originally instituted in 1813 by King Friedrich Wilhelm of Prussia, they were renewed in

Top left: Lieutenant-General Walter Lucht, general officer commanding the 336th Infantry Division, discusses the situation with one of his battalion commanders. The general is wearing a reversible coat and earmuffs, and the battalion commander a fur cap. Note the Infantry Assault Badge worn by the junior officer.

Bottom left: Marshal Cavallero, the Italian Chief-of-Staff, stands with his arms akimbo as he talks to two German officers. Note the major differences in uniform worn by the Germans: short boots and puttees compared with lace-up knee boots, and conventional cap compared with tropical pith helmet. The latter was soon abandoned in favour of the cloth peaked cap.

Above: Blomberg, Fritsch, Goering and Raeder at a 1937 parade.

Left: Hitler shakes hands with Field-Marshal Keitel, who is holding his marshal's baton in his left hand.

all the subsequent European wars. Though they were intended to be a 'Decoration for Merit in front of the enemy' they came to be awarded to generals who had conducted successful operations, and later as diplomatic sweeteners to officers in Axis armies. The Iron Cross, with the exception of two special awards, reached its zenith with the Knight's Cross with Oak-Leaves, Swords and Brilliants, while at the bottom was the Iron Cross, Second Class. Generals who had won the Iron Cross in World War I were entitled to wear a bar when they won it in World War II. It consisted of a pin-backed badge of an eagle and swastika, with the date 1939 at the base. Generals like Rommel and Bock, who had won the premier award of World War I, the *Pour le Mérite*, wore this neck decoration in addition to their Knight's Cross.

Batons and pennants

The Field-Marshal's baton produced by The Third Reich was a massive, ornate object similar to those awarded to Napoleon's marshals over 100 years earlier. Under-

standably, it was used only at the most formal occasions; for everyday use men like Rundstedt used an *Interimstab,* a lightweight staff similar to a British RSM's stick. Topped in silver and lacquered black, it had a tassel in the German national colours of black, white, and red.

In the early years of the war generals openly displayed their car pennants, rather like a general's stars on American or British vehicles. These pennants were metal flags which denoted a headquarters group or commanding officer. They could also be detached and displayed like a British Army Tactical Sign. The HQ symbol for an army group was a rectangular flag divided into quarters of red and black with a white border; the army HQ symbol was similar, but without the border. A corps HQ had a rectangular flag, with four triangular sections, whilst a division had a triangular pennon with red, white, and black bands. During the days when Germany had air superiority many vehicles, including staff cars, had swastika flags draped over their bonnets. When captured vehicles were used, they were boldly marked with the national

emblem of a black cross with a white border.

The German vehicles used by senior officers ranged from converted half-tracks, tanks or armoured cars, the heavy Horch 4×4 Kfz 21 convertible *Kommandeurwagen* and the medium 4×4 Kfz 15 Horch and Opel, down to the jeep-type Porsche and Volkswagen *leichte Personenkraftwagen.*

Personal transport

Whilst Germany was on the offensive her generals needed large, fast vehicles which could carry the staff and communications equipment, allowing them to keep in touch with the changing battlefield. Photographs show Guderian in a half-track packed with radio equipment and signallers, whilst Rommel used a Fieseler *Storch* liaison aircraft in North Africa.

As Germany's fortunes turned, however, partisans and ground-attack aircraft made it essential that her generals become more anonymous. In Italy in 1944 General von Senger und Etterlin recalled: 'Every time I drove to the front now, I had to pass through a guerrilla-infested district. Nor-

A lieutenant-general of the *Deutsches Afrikakorps* in typical dress for this rather informal theatre. He is wearing the DAK field cap, with the other ranks' silver braiding. The uniform is the standard tropical field service one, and the boots are the canvas and leather lace-up tropical ones.

mally I drove in the little Volkswagen and displayed no general's insignia of rank – no peaked cap, no gold or red flags . . .'

Many generals had a more informal attitude to their transport than their opposite numbers from Britain or the United States. *Oberstgruppenfuehrer* Paul Hausser hitched a lift on a half-track during the fighting around Khar'kov, whilst Rommel did forward reconnaissance in an unarmoured soft-top vehicle and used a captured British armoured command vehicle, called *'Mamut'*, to provide him with a mobile communications base.

Above: **Officers of several nations gathered for some German military manoeuvres present an interesting and varied display of military styles. Some of the German officers are wearing cloth greatcoats, and others leather ones.**

The Conspiracy against Hitler- Military Resistance to Nazism

Why did the German generals of World War II choose to be led to destruction by Adolf Hitler, instead of pulling him down and putting him on trial for his crimes? This obvious question does not have a single answer; but certainly a major reason why the generals shunned such a decision was that it would have been a clear act of treason against the man who had raised Germany (and, in the process, themselves) to unprecedented heights of power and military glory.

This was the most popular excuse put up by the generals when they were interrogated and tried after Germany's defeat. Another obvious – and fair – claim was that a coup against Hitler would certainly have been against the wish of the German people, whose morale did not crack even when the Allied mass air-raids began in 1942. After all, down to November 1942 Germany was winning victory after victory, and those victories (like the *Fuehrer*'s bloodless triumphs in the prewar years) were all very much to the credit – and interest – of the army.

But it was all very well for the German generals to plead conscience as a bar to acting against Hitler: they also knew quite enough about the atrocities and repression which kept Hitler's 'New Order' in being. Instead of agreeing that those atrocities disgraced both Germany and the German army, and that no oath of allegiance to the man on whose authority they were committed could be considered binding, they looked the other way. The most the Army High Command (OKH) ever did by way of protest was to ask that 'house-cleaning' by the *Gestapo* and SS murder squads should not begin until the army had pulled out. The generals, in fact, did not want to get their hands dirty; and they always preferred to fall back on the comforting claim that the army must stay out of politics.

Initially, however, there were indeed no reasons for the generals to conspire against Hitler: the promises he had made to the army were more than adequately kept. They thought they were using him; but in fact they never got the chance.

On 2 August 1934, when Hitler's new combined rôle as *Fuehrer* and Reich Chancellor was announced, every officer and ranker in Germany took the fateful oath of allegiance to their new overlord quoted in the first chapter.

The wording was perfectly clear – unambiguous in every respect. It was meant to be. For every German soldier who took that oath – and it was done by means of mass, repeat-after-me parades all over Germany – any future criticism of Hitler, let alone any attempt to tamper with his authority, was treason pure and simple in the legal meaning of the word. And the oath of loyalty of 1934 overshadowed the story of the military resistance to Hitler from beginning to end.

Moral ascendancy

But the generals were not unwilling to oust Hitler merely because they were afraid of committing treason. One of the *Fuehrer*'s first acts was the carefully stage-managed proclamation that the restrictions imposed on Germany's armed forces by the victors of World War I no longer existed. On 16 March 1935 conscription was announced together with the open secret of the new German air force, the *Luftwaffe*, and the expansion of the German army to 36 divisions – 15 more than the general staff had considered reasonable. This public 'breaking the shackles of Versailles' also had an immense effect on the morale of the generals. Hitler had made soldiering an honourable calling once more in Germany, and had kept his word to foster the develop-

ment of the German armed forces.

Then came a third factor: the repeated successes of Hitler in strengthening the *Reich*, expanding its territories to unprecedented extents while making its frontiers progressively easier to defend: the Rhineland was reoccupied by German troops – March 1936; Austria was annexed by the Reich – March 1938; the Czech Sudetenland, peopled largely by racial Germans, was ripped away from Czechoslovakia (together with that country's most powerful defences) by the international agreement at Munich – September 1938; and what was left of the Czech heartland was occupied as a 'Protectorate' – March 1939. On every one of these occasions the generals forecast armed intervention by Germany's neighbours and total defeat, while Hitler's assurances that the German troops would march in unmolested were proved triumphantly correct. Never in her history had Germany achieved so much without going to war – another potent reason for the generals to back Hitler with enthusiasm. But there was another side to the coin. Every stage of this territorial aggrandisement had indeed been a nerve-racking gamble before it became apparent that Germany would get away with it again; and it was during this three-year period – March 1936 to March 1939 – that the generals' resistance to Hitler made its first tentative and completely unsuccessful stirrings.

On 5 November 1937, in a long and rambling monologue, Hitler told Blomberg, Fritsch and Raeder that his expansionist plans for Germany must make another European war inevitable in time. Blomberg, Fritsch and Foreign Secretary Neurath protested, and Hitler reacted by the early sacking of all three. The excuse for the dismissal of Blomberg was comparatively easy to find, for the general made the mistake

Top: The last Stauffenberg family photograph, taken at the home of Graf von Stauffenberg's mother in Lautlingen. A niece and a nephew are posed with two of the Stauffenberg sons and the daughter. Note the patch over Stauffenberg's left eye, and the strapped-up right hand, the results of an injury incurred in the fighting in North Africa.

Above: Claus Schenk Graf von Stauffenberg, the man who brought new hope to the German conspiracy against Hitler, and in the process almost became a man of destiny.

Left: Colonel-General Ludwig Beck, who resigned as Army Chief-of-Staff in 1938 as a protest against the policies of Hitler, and later became head of the conspiracy to oust the *Fuehrer*. Beck was shot on the day of the disastrous 20 July plot.

of marrying a former prostitute. But a monstrous frame-up was engineered for Fritsch, the charge being that he had disgraced the officer corps by indulging in homosexual relations – an utter lie that incensed the officer corps, which had the highest respect for Fritsch. The generals demanded a court of enquiry to exonerate Fritsch. But before they got their verdict of 'Not Guilty' the triumph of the Austrian *Anschluss* reduced the trial to secondary importance. Fritsch was completely cleared of the charge but the army never got its commander back. After getting rid of Blomberg and Fritsch, Hitler strengthened his own hand by setting up the OKW, the *Oberkommando der Wehrmacht* (Armed Forces High Command) with himself as C-in-C and the pliant General Wilhelm Keitel as chief-of-staff. The new commander for the army was General Walther von Brauchitsch, newly married to a fanatical Nazi.

General Ludwig Beck, army chief-of-staff, was retained in his post, however; and it was Beck who decided that the army must act against Hitler if the risks the *Fuehrer* was courting should lead to war.

Convinced that Hitler's obsession with the reduction of Czechoslovakia had in fact made war inevitable, Beck resigned in August 1938. He had hoped that this act would trigger off a wave of protest in the army high command, but was utterly mistaken. Nevertheless, Beck had succeeded in engineering an embryonic conspiracy of army generals. Beck's successor, Franz Halder, was also prepared to act against Hitler in the last resort. So were the following: Erwin von Witzleben, C-in-C Berlin Military District; Erich Hoepner, Panzer commander; and Erwin von Stulpnaegel, Army Quartermaster-General. But the plan they considered to arrest and try Hitler rather than go to war over Czechoslovakia came to nothing when Hitler won his greatest-ever bloodless conquest at Munich. The conspirators did not have to act – and they had the nerve to blame this on Nevile Chamberlain!

Constant delays

Within six months the renewed danger of war – this time over Poland – caused further heart-searchings among the generals. These were again largely dispelled by Hitler's astonishing diplomatic coup in concluding a non-aggression pact with Stalin's Russia. This totally isolated Poland and gave the *Wehrmacht* the best possible chance of smashing the Polish army in a knock-out campaign. It was never the fear of war which caused the generals to think of dealing with Hitler: it was the thought of war coming before Germany was strong enough to win. As it was, fuel and ammunition stocks were dangerously low for Germany at the outbreak of World War II and the *Wehrmacht* could certainly not have fought an all-out war on two fronts. Germany was spared this, however, by the total inability and strategic unwillingness of Britain and

Far left: **The wrecked conference room at the *Wolfsschanze* after the bomb explosion on 20 July 1944.**

France to attack on the Western Front in September 1939. By the end of the first three weeks of the war the Polish army had been shattered and the campaign was over in all but name. Even before Warsaw finally capitulated on 28 September units were being pulled back for the redeployment for the decisive battle in the West.

Hitler's initial determination to attack in in the West in November 1939 – which the army high command considered a military impossibility – sparked off the so-called 'Zossen Conspiracy', named after the headquarters of the army. Here everything turned on Halder's efforts to get Brauchitsch to stand up to Hitler, and Brauchitsch was a broken reed. His nerves were not up to the strain of confronting Hitler, and he also suffered from heart trouble. When he finally screwed up the courage to try and persuade Hitler to call off the offensive, on 5 November, he limited himself to warning of bad weather and shaky troop morale. This sent Hitler off into an explosion of rage, after which Brauchitsch returned to his HQ on the verge of total nervous collapse. Within 48 hours, however, Hitler postponed the offensive and the immediate crisis was over.

After the early wilting of the 'Zossen Conspiracy', the only part played by Brauchitsch and Halder in inhibiting Hitler's plans was an indirect one inspired by professional stuffiness. The chief-of-staff of General von Rundstedt, commanding Army

Group 'Centre' in the West, was General Erich von Manstein, who was convinced that the existing plan could only result in undecisive deadlock along the line of the Somme. He came up with a revolutionary plan to smash the centre of the Allied front, drive to the Channel, and isolate the Belgian, British and French armies in Flanders; and forwarded repeated memoranda on the subject to Halder and Brauchitsch at OKH. The latter, however, sat on Manstein's idea and refused to send it on to Hitler via OKW. Only at the end of January 1940 did a chance visit to Rundstedt's HQ by the *Fuehrer*'s aide, Colonel Schmundt, reveal Manstein's ideas to Hitler, who adopted them with enthusiasm.

For his part, Hitler showed the greatest astuteness in turning Brauchitsch's feeble excuses against the generals and shortening their leash still further. On 23 November 1939 he harangued all general staff officers and many senior commanding officers in the Reich Chancellery in Berlin. Harping on how he had always confounded his critics by proving to have been right, he accused the generals of being lacking in fighting spirit. By thus impugning their loyalty and professional competence, Hitler played very cleverly on the generals' consciences. The basic oath of allegiance, the accusation of not being up to the job – these were potent weapons. And the result was that the generals flung themselves into the tasks which faced them in 1940 without a flicker

Above: **Hitler, who by all accounts was still visibly shaken by the almost successful attempt on his life on 20 July 1944, greets his old ally Benito Mussolini on the latter's arrival at the *Wolfsschanze***

of further opposition – not even when the invasion of Britain was called off and the conquest of Soviet Russia was mooted as the master-stroke which would win the war. Moreover, with each campaign another factor began to inhibit the generals who still had doubts: the belief that it would surely be treasonable to turn against the head of the German state, not so much because of the oath of allegiance but because enemies of the Reich still remained in the field. Halder in particular found this a decisive stumbling-block. And so the Russian campaign began on 22 June 1941 – the gamble by which the German army – and only the army – could win the war for Germany. In both the planning and execution of the initial attack, the dedication of the generals was unanimous.

Cracks appeared in this unanimity before the Russian war reached its first great turning-point at Moscow in December 1941. Hitler had laid it down that the niceties of war were to be denied the Russians. Prisoners of war were not to be treated according to the provisions of the Geneva

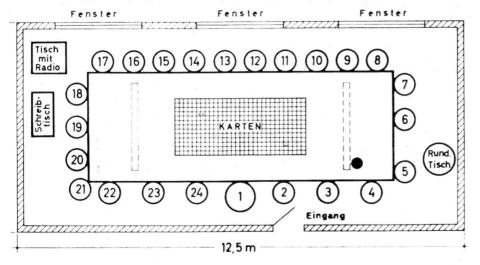

Fenster   Fenster   Fenster

Tisch mit Radio

Schreibtisch

17 16 15 14 13 12 11 10 9 8

18
19
20
21 22 23 24 1   2   3   4

7
6
5

KARTEN

Rund. Tisch

Eingang

12,5 m

Above: Hitler shows Mussolini the debris-scattered room in which, quite remarkably, he had received only very minor injuries.

Left: A diagrammatic representation of the 20 July attempt on Hitler's life. The room measures $12\frac{1}{2}$ metres by 5 metres, and is dominated by the map table around which those present were grouped. Hitler was saved by the fact that the bomb (the black dot) was placed on the other side of one of the table's two heavy supports (the two dashed rectangles), which diverted most of the blast. Among the notables present were Hitler (1), Lieutenant-General Heusinger, Operations Chief of the Army General Staff (2), General Korten, Chief of the *Luftwaffe* General Staff (3), Colonel Brandt, Heusinger's deputy (4), General Bodenschatz, *Luftwaffe* liaison officer at HQ (5), Lieutenant-General Schmundt, *Wehrmacht* adjutant at HQ (6),

Convention. And the notorious 'Commissar Order' made it the duty of the advancing army to shoot all officials of the Communist Party on capture. (Brauchitsch and Halder eased their consciences by passing this order down the chain of command with the rider that it was only to be carried out 'provided the morale and discipline of the troops are not endangered thereby'.) The generals had taken this barbarous brief without a murmur of protest. But once in Russia, despite the smashing initial victories – it was the most successful campaign the *Wehrmacht* had ever fought – they were soon forced to accept that they were faced by an enemy who did not know that he was beaten, and had space and numbers – not to mention superior tanks – on his side. And in Russia, during summer 1941, the conspiracy against Hitler stirred anew.

Chief-of-staff to Field-Marshal von Bock, C-in-C Army Group 'Centre' on the Mos-

cow axis of the Eastern Front, was Major-General Henning von Tresckow, who began to approach junior officers and brother generals he suspected of favouring Hitler's removal. He met with uneasy non-co-operation from the men who mattered: the army group and field army commanders. Bock's reaction: 'I do not allow the *Fuehrer* to be attacked!' Brauchitsch himself was approached. His reaction: 'If you persist in seeing me I shall have to place you under arrest.' Yet the key field-marshals and generals approached by the conspirators, while refusing point-blank to commit themselves, made no move at all to denounce their 'treasonable' subordinates. With no absolute guarantee of decisive backing by their chiefs, the conspirators were reduced to temporary impotence.

Meanwhile, the civilian conspirators in the Reich – foremost among them ex-ambassador Ulrich von Hassell – had hopes of

winning over the army commanders in the West: Field-Marshal von Witzleben (C-in-C West) and General von Falkenhausen (C-in-C Belgium). Witzleben had promised to support the 'Halder Conspiracy' at the time of Munich and he still favoured Hitler's removal. But early in 1942 he took a brief sick leave to have his piles operated on, and while he was away Hitler replaced him with Field-Marshal von Rundstedt, who had been removed from the command of Army Group 'South' in Russia in December 1941. Witzleben's embarrassing complaint was speedily put to rights – but he was not much use to the conspirators, with no troops at his

command and placed on the retired list. It was on this grotesque note that 1942 opened for the conspirators, who had by now adopted ex-army chief-of-staff Beck as their figurehead and provisional head of a German state should the army ever act and purge the Reich government of Nazi domination.

The slump in conspiratorial activity within the army ended dramatically with the disasters of the winter of 1942–43 and the equally disastrous spring of 1943. Stalingrad, El Alamein, the loss of all Libya and the retreat into Tunisia, the Anglo-American landings in French North Africa, and the apparent collapse of the Eastern Front shored up by brilliant improvisation (but for how long?); and the surrender of 91,000 soldiers at Stalingrad in February and of another 250,000 in Tunisia – here with a vengeance was the writing on the wall, rammed home by the announcement of the Allied policy of 'unconditional surrender' to be demanded from the Axis. And by the approach of the summer of 1943 two invaluable German officers had been rendered ripe for conspiracy by the course of events: a brilliant staff officer, Colonel von Stauffenberg, badly wounded in Tunisia and painfully recovering in hospital; and the incomparable Rommel himself, sickened and disillusioned by Hitler's callous abandonment of his *Panzerarmee Afrika*.

New blood needed

Tresckow took up the running again in Russia. For months he had been goading the conscience of another key general, Field-Marshal von Kluge, who had received substantial sums of money from the *Fuehrer;*

Above: The shredded and tattered remnants of Hitler's trousers after the explosion of Stauffenberg's bomb on 20 July 1944.

Right: The inevitable results of the plot's failure – the accused hear their indictment read. Even by the strange standards of Nazi Germany the trial was a mockery, the defendants being humiliated and inveighed against rather than being prosecuted with adequate evidence and then given a chance to plead their defence. The results were condemnation, inevitably.

but Kluge remained uneasily on the fence. And there was a new focus of resistance in Berlin: the HQ of the *Ersatzheer*, the Reserve Army, where General Olbricht was Chief of Supplies – and a close colleague of Tresckow's. And in Hitler's own HQ at Rastenburg in East Prussia there was General Stieff, an administrative officer who acted as explosives-keeper for the conspirators' bombs.

The Tresckow/Stieff partnership got off the mark with an abortive assassination attempt (which they code-named 'Flash') on 13 March 1943. Tresckow's aide Schlabrendorff asked a junior officer in Hitler's entourage to carry a present of 'brandy' back on Hitler's plane and hand it to Stieff. The idea was to blow up Hitler in the air, making it look like an accident. The bomb was duly taken aboard Hitler's plane, which took off

on schedule – but nothing happened. The *Fuehrer* arrived back at Rastenburg safely. With incredible courage Schlabrendorff telephoned the bearer that a mistake had been made and that he would be arriving with the right package. He retrieved the bomb and investigated: the time-fuse had worked but a faulty detonator had saved Hitler's life.

After the failure of 'Flash' came the equally abortive suicide attempts, made by brave young officers who volunteered to get near Hitler with bombs in their pockets. This came to nothing because of the total unpredictability of Hitler's day-to-day time-table, which made it impossible for the volunteers to put any accurate setting on the time-fuses of their bombs.

By January 1944 the state of the army conspiracy was roughly as follows. The Reserve Army members possessed a plan to take over Berlin and the other key cities of Germany, placing all Nazi officers under arrest – a plan, ironically enough, approved by Hitler himself! 'Valkyrie' was its code-name, and the pretext was the supposed danger posed by the millions of foreign workers in Germany staging a revolt. At their posts on the Eastern Front, Tresckow, Schlabrendorff and their colleagues continued their activities unmolested, as did Stieff at OKW. A vital recruit to the conspiracy was General Fellgiebel, a communications officer, whose rôle would be to see to it that OKW was cut off from the rest of Germany when the right moment came. Rommel was being sounded out as to whether or not he was prepared to join the conspiracy and by the end of February he had made up his mind to do so. Most important of all was the sense of optimism and determination generated by Stauffenberg, who was back in harness after convalescing from his wounds, as chief-of-staff first to Olbricht and then to General Fromm, C-in-C Reserve Army. In the latter job Stauffenberg had regular access to the presence of Hitler himself.

The spring and early summer of 1944 were wasted by the conspirators' deluded belief that they could negotiate a separate peace with the British and Americans, give up their conquests in the West, and concentrate their energies against Russia alone. Undercover negotiations via Allen Dulles, head of the Central Intelligence Agency, in Switzerland disillusioned them. And the invasion of Normandy on 6 June 1944 made them realise that the hour had finally come. In Stauffenberg, they had the man to meet the hour.

Within a week it was obvious that Rommel and Rundstedt, the German commanders in the West, were not going to push the Allies back into the sea: the Western Front was a reality. On 20 June the great Russian summer offensive broke upon Army Group 'Centre' in the East. Then, on 4 and 5 July, two key civilian conspirators, Adolf Reichwein and Julius Leber, were arrested by the *Gestapo*. It was vital to act before the full extent of the conspiracy was revealed by their torture; and Stauffenberg was the only man for the job. But the obsession with eliminating Himmler and Goering along with Hitler forced Stauffenberg on two occasions – 11 and 15 July – to abandon his plan of leaving a fused briefcase

bomb in Hitler's presence, simply because conditions were not right for the killing of all three. On Stauffenberg's own insistence it was agreed that he should make another attempt to blow up Hitler on his next summons to OKW; and on 19 July he was summoned to report at Rastenburg for a conference on the 20th.

The results of the 'Twentieth of July' are well known. Stauffenberg's bomb exploded within six feet of Hitler but did not kill him. Stauffenberg himself bluffed himself out of the Rastenburg complex and set off for Berlin. Fellgiebel passed word to Olbricht that the bomb had gone off and then set about sabotaging Rastenburg's communications – but the plotters in Berlin decided to wait for Stauffenberg's return and personal confirmation of Hitler's death. Three vital hours were wasted before Stauffenberg desperately began to make up for lost time – too late. Prompt and effective countermeasures rounded up the Berlin plotters and the coup was over.

It was only the last of a long line of plots, but it failed for the same reason that wrecked them all: the refusal of the key generals to commit themselves until they knew for sure that Hitler was dead. Muddled concepts of duty and a refusal to hazard all that had been gained under Hitler – both for themselves and, to be fair, for Germany – blurred their reasoning. At the time of the 'July Plot' German armies stood everywhere on foreign soil (as at the time of the 1918 armistice) and the frontiers of the Reich were not menaced until the autumn.

This narrow-minded selfishness, this uneasiness at anything that threatened the traditional apolitical mystique of the German officer corps, lay at the root of the German generals' failure to their country between 1933 and 1945. Originally they thought they could use Hitler; the fact that he could reduce the vast majority of them to putty in his hands was a traumatic shock from which they never recovered. As with the entire population of Germany under the Nazis, it was so much easier to don mental blinkers and plunge oneself in one's job.

Thus some of the most shaming documents of World War II are those German army memoranda and communications requesting that the army should not get its hands dirty with the by-products of genocide which their conquests, as they knew perfectly well, unleashed. But it is only marginally more shaming than the story of their conspiracies. Success in the latter could only have been achieved by detailed planning and cool, decisive action, and their combined talents in that direction made them the best-trained and organised band of potential conspirators in Nazi Germany. For in the last analysis, detailed planning and decisive action are a general's daily bread.

The infamous prosecutor at the trial of those accused after the bomb plot's failure, Roland Freisler, presents some of his 'evidence' against Field-Marshal von Witzleben, seen standing at the left of the photograph. The accused were deprived of their belts and braces, and therefore had to hold up their trousers. Witzleben was found guilty and later hanged.

The Campaigns in France and the Low Countries

The fog of war: German infantry move up through the lingering smoke of an artillery barrage. Time and time again in the early campaigns of the war, the Allies were overwhelmed by the superiority of forces and speed of advance the Germans were able to launch on small sectors of the front, controlled by dynamic front-line leadership.

Although Hitler had been of the opinion that Great Britain and France would not come to the aid of Poland by declaring war in September 1939, he reacted with typical swiftness to their declaration by demanding plans for an invasion of France from his high command. An invasion was originally planned for the end of 1939, but the weather intervened to prevent this taking place. Other plans, all based on a modification of the World War I Schlieffen Plan, were then devised for 1940. Various delays ensued, giving General Erich von Manstein the opportunity to go over the heads of his immediate superiors to recommend another plan to Hitler. The revised Schlieffen plan, so Manstein thought, was too obvious a move, and the Allies would have prepared a means of countering it. Rather than use this simple right-hook through Belgium, along the French north coast and then down past the west of Paris, Manstein urged a far more daring plan, based on the mass use of the Panzer forces available.

In Manstein's plan, which Hitler adopted with enthusiasm over the lingering doubts of his high command, powerful armoured forces would strike right through the weakly defended Allied centre in the Ardennes and launch a short left-hook up to the French coast near Calais. This would cut the Allied armies in half, allowing the pocket trapped on the coast to be mopped up by Army Groups 'A' and 'B' before the rest of France was overrun by the combined forces of Army Groups 'A', 'B' and 'C'. It was a courageous plan, making full use of surprise and the advantages of speed and firepower that the massed armoured formations would enjoy.

The Allies, on the other hand, had as Manstein feared considered the overwhelming possibility of another Schlieffen Plan, and had deployed their forces accordingly. As Belgium and Holland were still neutral, the bulk of the British and French forces were based in northern France, to which the Maginot defence line did not extend. This costly, and in the event entirely useless, static line defended France from Longuyon, just west of southern Luxembourg, down to the Swiss frontier. Once Germany moved west into Belgium, as was almost certain, the Allied forces in the north were to move forward into positions along the River Dyle to check a 'Schlieffen' move.

Three army groups

The German armies were deployed in three major concentrations. In the north, opposite Holland and northern Belgium, was General Fedor von Bock's Army Group 'B', of 26½ infantry and three Panzer divisions, in two armies. In the centre, from Aachen to the south of Luxembourg, was General Gerd von

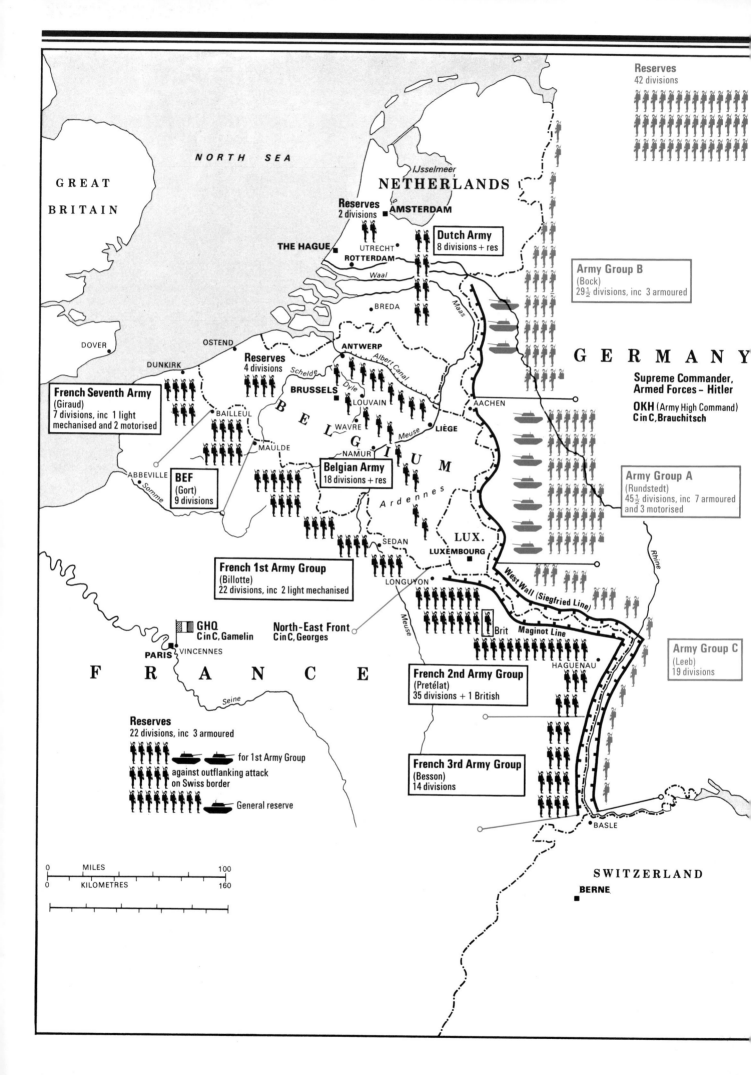

Reserves
42 divisions

NORTH SEA

GREAT
BRITAIN

IJsselmeer

NETHERLANDS

Reserves
2 divisions

AMSTERDAM

THE HAGUE

UTRECHT

ROTTERDAM

Waal

Dutch Army
8 divisions + res

Army Group B
(Bock)
29½ divisions, inc 3 armoured

DOVER

OSTEND

BREDA

Maas

GERMANY

DUNKIRK

ANTWERP

Reserves
4 divisions

Schelde

Albert Canal

Supreme Commander,
Armed Forces – Hitler

French Seventh Army
(Giraud)
7 divisions, inc 1 light
mechanised and 2 motorised

BRUSSELS

Dyle

LOUVAIN

BELGIUM

AACHEN

OKH (Army High Command)
C in C, Brauchitsch

BAILLEUL

MAULDE

WAVRE

Meuse

LIÈGE

ABBEVILLE

BEF
(Gort)
9 divisions

Somme

NAMUR

Belgian Army
18 divisions + res

Ardennes

Army Group A
(Rundstedt)
45½ divisions, inc 7 armoured
and 3 motorised

SEDAN

French 1st Army Group
(Billotte)
22 divisions, inc 2 light mechanised

LUX.

LUXEMBOURG

Rhine

GHQ
C in C, Gamelin

North-East Front
C in C, Georges

LONGUYON

West Wall (Siegfried Line)

PARIS

VINCENNES

Meuse

Brit

Maginot Line

Army Group C
(Leeb)
19 divisions

FRANCE

Seine

French 2nd Army Group
(Pretélat)
35 divisions + 1 British

HAGUENAU

Reserves
22 divisions, inc 3 armoured

for 1st Army Group

against outflanking attack
on Swiss border

French 3rd Army Group
(Besson)
14 divisions

General reserve

BASLE

MILES   100

KILOMETRES   160

SWITZERLAND

BERNE

42

Rundstedt's Army Group 'A', of 35½ infantry, three motorised and seven Panzer divisions, in three armies together with *Panzergruppe* 'von Kleist'. In the south, between southern Luxembourg and Switzerland, was General Ritter von Leeb's Army Group 'C', of 19 infantry divisions, in two armies. Reserves totalled 42 infantry divisions. Overall command was exercised by Hitler himself through Brauchitsch, the commander-in-chief of the army, and Keitel, the chief-of-staff. The centre-piece of the German offensive was to be the armoured punch of Hoepner's XVI Panzer Corps (6th Army of Army Group 'B'), Hoth's XV Panzer Corps (4th Army of Army Group 'A'), and Reinhardt's XLI and Guderian's XIX Panzer Corps (*Panzergruppe* 'von Kleist' of 12th Army of Army Group 'A').

The Allied armies were also poised in three major concentrations. In the north, as far south as central Luxembourg, was General Gaston Billotte's 1st Army Group, of 36 infantry, two motorised, and three light mechanised divisions, in five armies including the nine-division British Expeditionary Force. In the centre, between central Luxembourg and Strasbourg, was General Gaston Pretélat's 2nd Army Group, of 36 infantry (including one British) infantry divisions, in three armies. In the south, from Strasbourg to the Swiss frontier, was General Henri Besson's 3rd Army Group, of 14 infantry divisions in one army. Allied reserves in France consisted of 19 infantry and three armoured divisions.

In addition to the Allied forces were those of neutral Belgium and Holland, who both threw in their lots with the Allies once they were invaded. Belgium could field 18 infantry divisions, with another four infantry divisions in reserve; Holland could supply eight infantry divisions, with two infantry divisions in reserve.

Fewer men

Germany's forces totalled some 2½ million men, with 2,574 tanks and nearly 2,750 aircraft. France and Great Britain had forces totalling some 2 million men, 3,609 tanks, and some 1,700 aircraft. The slight disparity in numbers of men was of little importance, but that in aircraft was.

Left: The line-up for Germany's onslaught against the West in May 1940. Note the German superiority in armoured divisions, and the main weight of the German offensive with Army Group 'A' and the southern part of Army Group 'B'. With the exception of the sector between Longuyon and Haguenau, the Allied forces are deployed fairly evenly along the whole front. German reserves also exceed Allied ones.

Right: The culmination of Germany's attack on France – German troops march past the Arc de Triomphe before marching down the Champs Elysées. Rather than have their capital city devastated by fighting, the French declared Paris an open city.

It enabled the *Luftwaffe* to dominate the skies above the German advance and provide the ground forces with excellent tactical support. The difference in tank numbers, however, was of crucial importance. Although the Germans had fewer vehicles, these were grouped into homogeneous formations, and had been carefully rehearsed in the doctrines and tactics of deep-penetration tank warfare.

The Allies on the other hand, had only three homogeneous armoured formations, and for these no adequate tactical theories had been evolved. The rest of the Allied tank strength was scattered amongst the field units to provide local infantry support. This was all the more tragic for the Allies as many of their tanks were qualitatively superior to the German vehicles, with better armour and heavier

armament. The Dutch and Belgian armies fielded 400,000 and 600,000 men respectively under General H. G. Winkelman and King Léopold III.

The German offensive broke on 10 May with major efforts by Army Groups 'A' and 'B' into Belgium and Holland. The infantry advances into both countries were preceded by special attacks: parachute drops around Rotterdam and The Hague in Holland, to create havoc in the country and seize vital airfields; and a glider-borne attack on Fort Eben-Emael, the linch-pin of the Belgian defence line along the Albert Canal and River Meuse. With Eben-Emael neutralised, the German forces swept through the Belgian defences, which would otherwise have hampered them considerably. Isolated Belgian and Dutch pockets fought on bravely, but the very speed and strength of the German advance, coupled with the panic-striken streams of civilian refugees fleeing from the German bombing, so confused matters that little co-ordinated defence could be offered to the Germans. Although the British and French had implemented their Dyle plan and moved forward into Belgium and western Holland, there was little that could be done. Holland was effectively beaten by the 14th, and Belgium by the day after.

Ardennes triumph

The real drama of the German offensive was taking place further south, however, in the Ardennes. Here the German Panzer forces swept through the wooded hills, which had been considered impassable to armour, and poured into the Meuse valley, where only inferior-grade French troops were stationed. XV and XIX Panzer Corps secured bridgeheads across the Meuse at Dinant and Sedan respectively, followed the next day by XLI Panzer Corps at Monthermé. The move had to come as a complete surprise to the Allies, but what followed surprised them even more. Leaving their infantry units to follow as quickly as they could, the Panzer divisions set off in a mad rush to the English Channel coast, supported by the *Luftwaffe*. The Panzer columns' surest defence was the complete surprise of the Allies. The German armour raced through Cambrai and Arras on the 18th, and by the 20th had reached Abbeville and the coast at Noyelles. By the 25th Boulogne had fallen, and with the arrival of the German infantry, the Allied armies in the north were completely cut off by the 'Panzer corridor'. By the 21st, the corridor's southern flank had been established along the line of the Rivers Somme and Aisne.

The Allied armies in the north had realised quickly the import of the German armoured advance – not only were they cut

German troops march in empty triumph down the deserted Champs Elysées after passing the Arc de Triomphe. While this propaganda exercise was taking place, the German army was continuing to drive the shattered remnants of the French army south.

A German military band, its bandmaster at the head, leads the march down the Champs Elysees.

off, but also completely outflanked on their right. Immediately they fell back, but it was already too late. A small armoured force under Colonel C. de Gaulle had attempted to cut the Panzer corridor without anything but some good tactical successes between 17 and 19 May, but now a more ambitious scheme was evolved by General Maxime Weygand, who had taken over supreme command from General Maurice Gamelin on 19 May. French armour was to strike north across the River Somme past Albert to link up with a British thrust coming south from Arras. Scheduled for 21 May, only the British half of the pincer materialised, and although it made good progress in its attempt to cut the corridor, it was doomed without its French counterpart.

In the north the Germans were now gradually squeezing the Allied pocket back towards the Channel ports in a series of concerted armoured and infantry assaults. By the 25th the position was very difficult, and despite Hitler's order that the Panzers were to advance no further, the surrender of Belgium on the 28th meant that the position in the Dunkirk beach-head was no longer tenable. Plans to evacuate the troops trapped in the beach-head to England were immediately implemented, and carried out with great courage and ability. By the time the evacuation was

completed on 4 June, leaving the Germans in control of the Low Countries and France as far south as the River Somme, the navies of France and Great Britain, helped by some hundreds of small craft, had lifted some 338,000 men off the beaches around Dunkirk.

The Germans could now turn their attention to the rest of France. Despite a determined and very able defence of the River Somme line, the Germans broke through to the line formed by the Rivers Seine and Oise by the 12th, after starting their renewed offensive on the 5th. The French decided not to fight for Paris, which the Germans entered on the 14th. By now the French were beginning to break, and on 13 June the Germans poured over the Seine-Oise line, driving the French before them. On 10 June Italy had entered the war and invaded southern France, with risible results. The French armies were now in full retreat, and the Germans pressed on in a relentless pursuit south of Paris. Army Group 'B' passed through Rouen and then branched out to the west to take Brest on the 19th, and to the south-west to take Nantes and Saumur on the same date, reaching Royan on the 25th. By the 27th German troops had reached St Jean-de-Luz near the Spanish frontier. The troops of Army Group 'A' fanned out through Paris and Reims to take Tours, Orléans, Vichy on the 20th and Lyons by the same day. Other elements of Army Group 'A' swept the remnants of the French armies back against the Maginot Line, where they were trapped by Army Group 'C' and surrendered on the 22nd.

Pétain takes over

Paul Reynaud was succeeded as prime minister by Marshal Henri Pétain on 17 June, and the latter immediately sued for armistice terms, which were granted on the 21st. Hostilities between France on the one hand, and Germany and Italy on the other, ceased on the 25th, and France was partitioned into the Occupied and Unoccupied, or Vichy, Zones. French losses had been enormous, but they had inflicted very heavy casualties on the Germans as well. Nevertheless, the Germans had fought an excellent campaign, and further ironed out the lingering problems of their armoured theories. It is worth noting, however, that the Germans still had, and continued to have until the end of the war, problems with the different speeds attainable by the armour and their supporting infantry, a large proportion of which was still dependent on horse transport.

In 1944 the Allies were at long last ready to invade France and fight Germany into defeat on mainland northern Europe. A variety of plans had been devised for landings in northern France between 1942 and 1944, but finally it had been decided to land in Normandy rather than in the Pas-de-Calais. Careful security planning kept the Germans in ignorance of the landing area, although both Rommel and Hitler suspected that it was to be Normandy. The Allied plan finally adopted called for assault landings by Lieutenant-General Omar Bradley's US 1st Army and Lieutenant-General Sir Miles Dempsey's British 2nd Army, both elements of General Sir Bernard Montgomery's 21st Army Group, on beaches between the Caen area and the Cotentin peninsula. The naval forces escorting the landing forces were to be commanded by Admiral Sir Bertram Ramsay, and the air forces by Air-Marshal Sir Trafford Leigh Mallory. Overall Allied commander was General Dwight D. Eisenhower, with Air Chief-Marshal Sir Arthur Tedder as his deputy. The Allied armies totalled some one million men, in 45 divisions.

The German defence, under the theatre command of Rundstedt, was entrusted to Field-Marshal Erwin Rommel's Army Group 'B', with 30 infantry, two parachute and seven armoured divisions. Further south Blaskowitz's Army Group 'G' in southern France had 13 infantry and three armoured divisions to halt any invasion of the area. The Germans, although fairly strong numerically, were inferior troops compared with those who

had conquered France in 1940, and their lack of air support meant that movement was restricted to nights. The Allies were able completely to dominate the skies over France during the reconquest of north-western Europe, and destroy German transport and armour whenever it appeared in daylight. Two final items put nails into the Germans' coffin. The armoured reserve that might have thrown back the Allies on the first day of the invasion was held too far back, against Rommel's wishes, and could only be used with Hitler's express authority; and the 'Atlantic Wall', so beloved of German propaganda, was a mere fiction in the Normandy area.

The Allied invasion began on 6 June, and after some desperate moments in the American sector, a good lodgement had been secured by the 10th. By the 30th the Cotentin peninsula had been cleared, and Cherbourg was about to become the Allied main port. The British had run into determined opposition in and around Caen, however, and it was not until 20 July, after extremely heavy fighting, that the area was cleared. German defence was still strong, and the Allies were penned into their bridgehead. On 25 July, however, the US 1st Army broke out past St Lô after an exceptional heavy bombing attack had pulverised the German defences. By the 30th the Americans were in Avranches, and the German containment of the Normandy beach-head was unseamed.

Falaise gap

The Allied forces were now reorganised into the 12th Army Group under Bradley, with the US 1st and 3rd Armies, commanded by Lieutenant-Generals Courtney Hodges and George Patton respectively; and the 21st Army Group under Montgomery, with the British 2nd and Canadian 1st Armies under Dempsey and Lieutenant-General Henry Crerar respectively. After the break-out to Avranches, Patton's forces fanned out to the west, into Brittany, and south and east towards Orléans and Paris. The British also broke out, past Falaise, closing the German pocket there just too late to trap considerable German armoured forces. Rundstedt had been replaced early in July as supreme commander in the west by Kluge, and when Rommel was injured on 17 July, Kluge also took over command of Army Group 'B'. But there was nothing Kluge could do to halt the Allied forces now sweeping, with overwhelming air support, towards Paris. Despite Hitler's orders that the French capital should be destroyed, it was not, and when the Allied forces arrived in the city on 25 August they found it in the hands of the French resistance. Kluge was now sacked, shortly afterwards committing suicide, his place as head of Army Group 'B' being taken by Model.

Meanwhile in the south the US/French forces of Lieutenant-General Alexander Patch's 7th Army had landed between Cannes and Toulon on 15 August, and in a remarkably swift advance swept up the Rhône valley to make contact with French forces of the 12th Army Group north of

Dijon on 12 September. Most of the forces of Blaskowitz's 1st and 19th Armies managed to slip through to the east before the Allied armies joined up, however. Patch's forces, which later became part of the 6th Army Group under Lieutenant-General Jacob Devers, continued to press north into the Vosges area.

Further north the 12th and 21st Army Groups had advanced over the River Seine and had reached the *Westwall* or Siegfried Line between Aachen and Trier by 15 September, British forces having liberated Brussels on the 3rd of the month and Antwerp on the 4th. There now occurred the bold venture to seize the bridges over the River Rhine at Arnhem. The ground forces that were to have moved up to the positions seized by the British and Polish paratroops on 17 September could not advance fast enough, and the unexpectedly strong German forces in the area crushed the paratroops' positions by the 25 September. It was, however, a bold Allied operation, and

perhaps deserved better success.

The Allies continued to press their advantages, and by 15 December had cleared the Germans from the Metz-Strasbourg corner of France with the exception of the Colmar pocket, had advanced into Holland as far north as the River Maas, and had broken through the Siegfried Line around Aachen.

Hitler's last throw in the West came as a complete surprise to the Allies. In this final major offensive Model's Army Group 'B' launched an attack through the Ardennes, with the aim of cutting through the Allies to Antwerp. But the scope of the offensive, which started on 16 December, was too great for the Germans. Fuel for the tanks began to run out, and the Allies failed to crumble away, as Hitler had expected. The Germans had shot their bolt by 24 December, and nothing was left to stop the Allies when they counter-attacked. The Germans had been driven back beyond their start lines by 7 February 1945.

On this date the Allies launched their major offensive towards the River Rhine, which they reached in a month of very heavy fighting. The Americans managed to secure a bridge across the river at Remagen, and quickly built up a formidable bridgehead against desperate German resistance. Another bridgehead was secured by the British east of Wesel. By the 27th the Allies had cleared the east bank of the River Rhine between Nijmegen to Mannheim, and were poised for the final advance into Germany to link up with the Russians from the east.

Ruhr pocket

At the end of March the Allies fanned out into Germany, a huge pocket being formed in the Ruhr industrial region. The British and Canadians advanced into northern Germany, reaching Hamburg on 3 May. The Americans moved east and south-east, reaching the River Elbe on 24 April and České Budejovice in

A French destroyer blown in two just forward of the bridge during the desperate Allied evacuation of the troops trapped in the vast pocket around Dunkirk by the German drive to the channel coast. The French XVI Corps fought an heroic rear-guard action at Lille, greatly facilitating the seaborne evacuation to Great Britain.

Czechoslovakia by 7 May. The French and Americans moved south-east into Austria, reaching Linz on 5 May. By agreement amongst the political leaders, Berlin was the Russian prize, and the Allies halted along the line of the Elbe.

In 1944 and 1945 the Germans had stood less chance against the Allies than had been the case (the other way round) in 1940. Yet they fought with their normal tenacity and courage against overwhelming odds to check the Allied advance. That they managed to hold out for so long was a considerable feat.

Field-Marshal Ewald von Kleist

invasion of France in May 1940.

In the invasion of Russia, Kleist had the 1st *Panzergruppe*, of five armoured divisions, as the spearhead of Rundstedt's Army Group 'South'. In 1942 he led the German advance into the Caucasus, but failed to take the all-important oilfields, principally as a result of Hitler's constant interference with the Panzer forces of his Army Group 'A'.

Kleist was shelved by Hitler in 1944, but continued to plot against the *Fuehrer*, an activity he had been involved with since before the war. Kleist was later taken into custody by the Gestapo

Kleist was a soldier of the old German school. He was a good, if uninspired, general, and a patriot rather than a Nazi.

Ewald von Kleist was born at Braunfels in August 1881, and served as a cavalry officer with a hussar regiment during World War I.

Retained in the *Reichswehr* after the Treaty of Versailles, Kleist rose in rank and held a variety of staff and training appointments during the 1920s and early 1930s.

By April 1934 Kleist had reached the rank of lieutenant-general, and was commanding the 2nd Cavalry Division in Breslau. Eighteen months later, although still only a lieutenant-general, Kleist found himself commander of VIII Corps, based in Breslau, with two infantry divisions and two frontier zone commands under him. Kleist kept

the corps up to 1938, when it had grown to three infantry divisions and two frontier commands. The commander, however, had been advanced in rank to general.

In February 1938, in the Nazi purge of the army after the fall of General Fritsch, its commander-in-chief, Kleist lost his corps. But by the time of the Polish campaign the worth of Kleist had been recognised once again, and he received command of a Panzer corps in Army Group 'North' for this first campaign of World War II.

Kleist's performance in Poland was notable enough for him to be given a *Panzergruppe* of Reinhardt's and Guderian's Panzer corps for the

Field-Marshal Ewald von Kleist

'If this Panzer Group had advanced on a single road its tail would have stretched right back to Koenigsberg in East Prussia, when its head was at Trier.' So said General Kleist in a conversation with Liddell Hart after the war. The magnitude of the German operation on the Belgian right flank can be gauged by the fact that by 10 May 1940 the Germans had massed 45½ divisions, including seven Panzer and three motorised along the 100-mile frontier. Whilst the men of Army Group 'B' were fighting in Belgium and Holland, the three armies of Army Group 'A' were filtering through the Ardennes and Luxembourg. They were deployed into three waves, armoured divisions in the first two and motorised infantry in the third. Behind them, in columns stretching back to the Rhine, came the infantry, marching through the dust of the Panzers singing the songs of the wars their fathers and grandfathers had fought against the French.

Drive to the Meuse

The country chosen for what was at the time the greatest concentration of tanks in the war had been described by some military experts as impassable for armour. The Ardennes region had few good roads,

was heavily wooded with dense conifers, was intersected by steep valleys with streams and narrow bridges and had patches of marshland. Ideal defensive country – providing it was defended. General Blumentritt recalled afterwards that 'we met no resistance in Luxembourg, and only slight resistance in Belgian Luxembourg – from the *Chasseurs Ardennais* and French cavalry divisions. It was weak opposition, and easily brushed aside.'

Had the French or Belgians been able to fly over the area they would have seen an awesome traffic jam grinding along every track and road that was practicable – with infantry using forest footpaths and lanes. However, the *Luftwaffe* provided air cover against reconnaissance and would later give bomber support at the critical Meuse crossings.

Two days after they had crossed the Belgian border the advanced guards of *Panzergruppe* 'Kleist' reached the Meuse and occupied the town of Sedan. The river in this area is about 60 yards wide, unfordable, and fairly fast flowing. The banks consist of a series of gentle wooded hills, sloping down to the river and affording good fields of fire on either side. To the north, between Mézières and Givet, the valley becomes steeper, with entrenched meanders.

The Meuse sector was defended by two French armies, the 2nd and the 9th. They held a mixture of field fortifications and fixed concrete emplacements. The latter, however, were far from finished, lacking doors and armoured shutters over the embrasures.

The French 2nd Army, which held the Sedan–Mézières sector, was under the command of General Huntziger. It included two 'Series B' divisions, the 55th and the 71st, which consisted of men who were overaged, undertrained and inadequately armed.

The 9th Army, commanded by General Corap and covering the Mézières–Namur sector, contained similarly discouraging material. Of its seven infantry divisions, four were reservist and two of these, the 53rd and 61st Infantry Divisions, were

The advance guard of a German Panzer division, in the form of two PzKpfw II light tanks, ford a French river in the course of reconnoitring for their main forces. The river is the Semois, which flows through Belgium and Luxembourg to join the Meuse at Montherme in France. German river-crossing capabilities caused the Allies some surprise.

'Series B', while the 102nd Infantry was a 'Fortress' regular division.

Kleist, whose Panzer group consisted of XLI Panzer Corps under Reinhardt and XIX Panzer Corps under Guderian, decided that he would force the Meuse crossings on 13 May. On that morning the men of the 1st Rifle Regiment of the 1st Panzer Division, who were to spearhead Guderian's central thrust at Sedan, were worried. 'The French artillery was alert and the slightest movement attracted fire. The German artillery was held up on congested roads, and could not get into position in time, and neither the engineers nor the bulk of their equipment had reached the river.'

However, by ill fortune or bad planning Corap and Huntziger had positioned in a line from Monthermé to Sedan their three poorest divisions, the 61st, 51st and 71st Infantry Divisions. Against these men, with their inadequate training and poor equipment, Kleist would send Reinhardt's 6th and 8th Panzer Divisions and Guderian's 2nd, 1st and 10th Panzer Divisions.

On the left flank Guderian planned to put his troops over the Meuse at 1500 hours in three separate attacks. The 2nd Panzer Division on the right would cross at Doncherry. In the centre the 1st Panzer Division would assault Glaire, at the foot of a meander of the Meuse. The 1st would receive the greatest support from artillery and assault pioneers, and would be the chief recipient of potent assistance from the *Luftwaffe*. The 10th Panzer Division would cross south of Sedan and secure the high ground on the west bank of the Meuse above Pont Maugis.

Reinhardt had a tougher objective than Guderian. The river at Monthermé was more of a natural barrier, and the men of the French 102nd Infantry had been in position since the beginning of the war. Moreover, Reinhardt could not count on receiving the same volume of air support as

Above: **German artillery crosses the Marne river over a pontoon bridge. Contrary to popular belief, the German army was not a completely mechanised force, but relied to a very great extent on horses for heavy towing duties, a problem that was to get worse as the war progressed.**

Right: **A German light anti-tank gun. Although the Allies had more, and better, tanks than the Germans, their tactics were inferior, and German anti-tank units could usually deal with Allied armour.**

Guderian.

Guderian had told his men that they would have 'the whole of the Luftwaffe' supporting their crossing – it was an exaggeration, but not far from the truth. They had the whole of *Fliegerkorps* I under Lieutenant-General Bruno Loerzer and

Fliegerkorps VIII under Major-General Wolfram von Richthofen, a total of nearly 1,500 aircraft.

The effect of these attacks on the French troops covering the Meuse was terrifying. They pulverised the bunkers, overturned exposed gun positions and kept the men blinded by smoke and dust. Besides this, few men wanted to look over the parapets of their positions, preferring to keep under cover. Meanwhile light and heavy flak guns were being moved down to the river to engage the French bunkers with direct fire.

River crossing

At 1500 hours the assault went in. During the afternoon's fighting the men of the 2nd Panzer Division exceeded the expectations of Kleist and Guderian, for their division had been slowed down on its approach march through the Ardennes. The French held the south bank in a line of heavily reinforced bunkers about 500 yards apart and 300 yards from the river. Covered by direct fire from tanks which had driven down to the river, however, German assault pioneers managed to get a foothold on the far bank by the evening, and throughout the night more men were ferried across.

In the centre the men of the élite *Grossdeutschland* Regiment and the 1st Rifle Regiment made rapid progress. Lieutenant-Colonel Balck of the 1st Rifle Regiment realised that it was essential that they capture a firm bridgehead, and by sunset on the 13th he had thrust three miles over the river to a ridge designated his objective. Without tank or artillery support he pushed a further three miles in the dark to a position south-west of the village of Chéhéry. In the middle of the crossings Guderian landed on the south bank of the Meuse and met Balck, who welcomed this front-line conference, but could not resist greeting his superior with 'Joy riding in canoes on the Meuse is forbidden!' – words used by Guderian during an exercise on the Moselle. Guderian had felt that the attitude of the younger officers had been too light-hearted at that time. 'I now realised that they had judged the situation correctly,' he commented.

To the south the 10th Panzer Division suffered many casualties in the first wave of its crossings, for it was under fire from flanking guns undamaged by the Stuka attack. Some units were pinned down on the north bank and withdrawn at nightfall, but individual detachments, notably the men of the assault pioneers, made a lodgement on

the far bank and hung on, destroying French bunkers with their demolition charges.

Success – just

Down the river at Monthermé the men of Reinhardt's XLI Panzer Corps had one of the least successful crossings. They had scrambled down the steep rocks on the right bank to find the river shrouded in smoke. It was silent. The first pneumatic assault boat was launched, but as soon as it was exposed a machine gun opened up killing and woundings its crew. Tanks destroyed the bunker, but the stream carried the assault boats away from their launching point and wedged them in the spans of the demolished bridge at Monthermé. Here the engineers discovered that they were under cover and began to build an extemporised foot-bridge. By night fall the remainder of a rifle battalion had crossed the river and dug a defensive position.

Panzergruppe 'Kleist' had achieved its first objective – the culmination of staff wargames, air-ground liaison, numerous night marches in the wooded borders of Germany and infantry assault crossings of the Lahn and Moselle. They were over the Meuse – just.

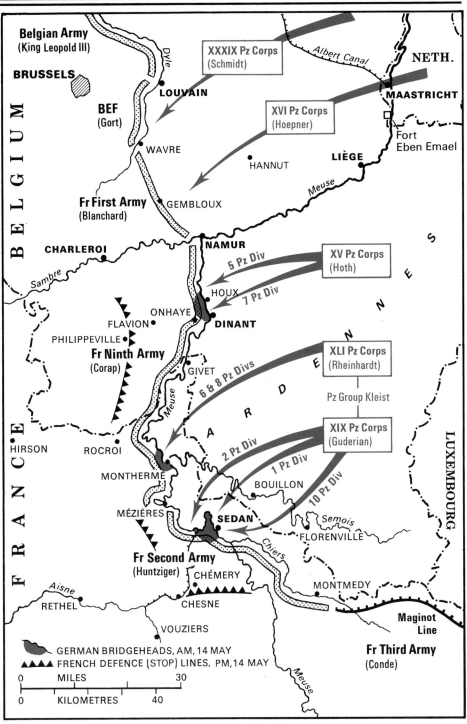

Belgian Army
(King Leopold III)

XXXIX Pz Corps
(Schmidt)

Albert Canal

NETH.

BRUSSELS

LOUVAIN

BEF
(Gort)

XVI Pz Corps
(Hoepner)

MAASTRICHT

Fort
Eben Emael

WAVRE

HANNUT

LIÈGE

Fr First Army
(Blanchard)

GEMBLOUX

Meuse

CHARLEROI

NAMUR

XV Pz Corps
(Hoth)

Sambre

5 Pz Div

HOUX

7 Pz Div

ONHAYE

FLAVION

DINANT

PHILIPPEVILLE

Fr Ninth Army
(Corap)

GIVET

XLI Pz Corps
(Rheinhardt)

6 & 8 Pz Divs

Meuse

Pz Group Kleist

HIRSON

ROCROI

XIX Pz Corps
(Guderian)

MONTHERMÉ

2 Pz Div

BOUILLON

1 Pz Div

10 Pz Div

MÉZIÈRES

SEDAN

Semois

FLORENVILLE

LUXEMBOURG

Fr Second Army
(Huntziger)

CHÉMERY

Chiers

MONTMEDY

Aisne

RETHEL

CHESNE

Maginot
Line

VOUZIERS

Meuse

Fr Third Army
(Conde)

GERMAN BRIDGEHEADS, AM, 14 MAY
FRENCH DEFENCE (STOP) LINES, PM, 14 MAY

| 0 | MILES | 30 |
| 0 | KILOMETRES | 40 |

Above: The drive to the Meuse, the key element of Germany's attack on France and the Low Countries.

Above left: A PzKpfw III medium tank, the mainstay of the German *Panzerwaffe,* in a French town severely damaged in the course of the thrust into central France.

Far left: Three of the five-man crew of a PzKpfw IV rest in the open air while they wait for the advance to resume. Note the all-black battledress and beret worn by tank crews of this period.

Left: Field-Marshal von Brauchitsch, C-in-C of the Army, greets Colonel-General von Kleist (right). Although taken on the Eastern Front in 1941, this photograph illustrates the two men's warmth of feeling.

Colonel-General Heinz Guderian

in June 1934 Guderian became Chief-of-Staff of *Kommando der Panzertruppen*. The first German tank manoeuvres were held in July 1935 at Muensterlager, and in October of the same year Guderian, although only a colonel, was given command of the 2nd Panzer Division; he relinquished this post for command of XVI Corps on 4 February 1938, and this latter to become *Inspekteur der Panzertruppen* in November of the same year.

Guderian came to the fore as a front-line commander when the Panzer division he led took Brest Litovsk in the Polish campaign of September 1939, and continued to enhance his reputation as an armour commander in France and Russia.

Disagreement with Hitler, however, led to his dismissal on 25 December 1941. He was recalled as *Inspekteur* in February 1943 and Chief of Army General Staff in July 1944. Sacked on 28 March 1945, he was captured on 10 May 1945.

Heinz Guderian was born on 17 June 1888 in the small town of Kulm, and commissioned at the age of 19, in 1907, into the 10th Hanoverian *Jaeger* Regiment of the Imperial German Army. October 1913 saw the young Guderian posted to the War Academy in Berlin for the higher training befitting an up-and-coming young officer.

During World War I Guderian held a number of posts, for the most part staff and signals appointments, before being allocated to the Great German General Staff during the course of 1918.

After the Treaty of Versailles had been signed, Guderian was kept on in the 100,000-man *Reichswehr*. In 1922 he was posted to the *Inspektion der Kraftfahrtruppen* or Inspectorate of Motorised Troops, and with increased German interest in armoured forces in the late 1920s, Guderian became a lecturer in tank tactics in 1928 before becoming commander of the 3rd *Kraftfahr-Abteilung* (Motorised Battalion). In October 1931 Guderian became Chief-of-Staff of the Inspectorate of Motorised Troops.

After his rise to power in 1933, Hitler took a keen interest in the new armoured forces and pressed for their early development. Thus

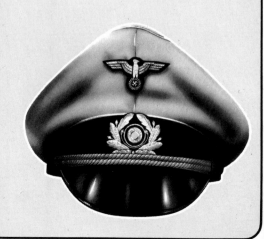

Colonel-General Heinz Guderian

'Soldiers of the XIX Army Corps!
'For 17 days we have been fighting in Belgium and France. We have covered a good 400 miles since crossing the German border : we have reached the Channel Coast and the Atlantic Ocean. On the way here you have thrust through the Belgian fortifications, forced a passage of the Meuse, broken the Maginot Line extension in the memorable Battle of Sedan, captured the important heights of Stonne and then without a halt, fought your way through St Quentin and Péronne to the lower Somme at Amiens and Abbeville. You have set the crown on your achievements by the capture of the Channel Coast and of the fortresses at Boulogne and Calais.

'I asked you to go without sleep for 48 hours. You have gone for 17 days. I compelled you to accept risks to your flanks and rear. You never faltered.

'With masterly self-confidence and believing in the fulfilment of your mission, you carried out every order with devotion.

'Germany is proud of her Panzer divisions and I am happy to be your commander.

'We remember our fallen comrades with honour and respect, sure in the knowledge that their sacrifice was not in vain.

'Now we shall arm ourselves for new deeds.

'For Germany and for our leader, Adolf Hitler!

signed, GUDERIAN'

Thus on 26 May 1940 General Heinz Guderian summed up the achievements of his men in an order of the day. There were greater victories to come (the corps was to thrust to the outskirts of Dunkirk), and by the end of World War II its commander was to rise to be Chief of the General Staff. However, as the climax of imaginative planning, good staff work and the application of the new doctrines of armoured penetration, the breakthrough at Sedan, and the drive to the Channel stand unrivalled.

The seven armoured and three motorised

The smoke clouds of destruction. Often impatient with orders from the rear, which he felt often did not reflect the true front-line position, Guderian was up with the leading elements of his formations as frequently as he could manage, to the exasperation of his superiors. In the photograph on the left he is seen in such a situation, in his command vehicle.

divisions (and their 35½ supporting infantry divisions) in Army Group 'A' had worked through the Ardennes and crossed the Meuse at Sedan and Monthermé. The men of Guderian's XIX Panzer Corps were installed in a bridgehead about five miles deep. While the infantry paused, awaiting the counterattack they felt must come, the engineers worked quickly to construct pontoon bridges to allow tanks and heavy weapons to cross the river.

The French had planned a two-pronged counterattack, but only one was ready on time. The 213th Infantry Regiment and the 7th Tank Battalion attacked the 1st Panzer Division near Chéhéry. It gained a temporary advantage, was held by a mixed defence of flak and anti-tank guns, and then for the loss of nearly half its tanks (light F.C.M. marks with 37-mm guns) it was crushed by the German armour.

There were to be other attacks by French armour, but each time they ran into Guderian's tanks and guns. In failing to attack the German infantry on the afternoon and night of the 13th–14th, when they were exposed on the south bank of the Meuse, the French were now to pay very heavily.

Feeling free to start the drive to the sea Guderian gave General Kirchner of 1st Panzer Division the dramatic order: 'For the right wheel, road map Rethel!' His forces were now to cross the Ardennes canal and break through what remained of the French defences.

Counterattack

During the 14th the Allies had attempted to destroy the German bridges at Sedan with air attacks. Their light bombers (Fairey Battles, Bréguets, Amiots and LeOs) braved the German flak and fighter screens. When they penetrated this defence their light bombs caused little damage, and even this was easily repaired. By the end of the day the Allies had lost nearly 90 aircraft. The RAF official history states that 'no higher rate of loss in an operation of comparable size had ever been experienced by the Royal Air Force'.

Despite these attacks, the lead elements of Guderian's forces pressed westwards. Colonel Balck had captured a crossing over the River Bar and the Ardennes canal near Omicourt. From this point to the River Somme at St Quentin it was rolling open farmland – perfect tank country. The 1st and 2nd Panzer Divisions began to move up.

On the south flank, the critical area of the whole breakout, Guderian had placed the élite *Grossdeutschland* Regiment. It was against them that the French deployed a company of heavy Char B tanks of the 3rd Armoured Division and a battalion of light H-39 tanks. Throughout 15 May the tanks of the 10th Panzer Division and the anti-tank guns of the *Grossdeutschland* Regiment fought the 3rd Armoured and 3rd Motorised Divisions. While other Frenchmen were scattering or surrendering these tank crews showed a courage and *élan* of an earlier generation. By the end of the day the regimental commander of *Grossdeutschland* reported that his men had been forced out of Stonne and were 'in a state of complete physical exhaustion and hardly fit for

combat'.

At 1730 the French launched their last and strongest counterattack towards the village of Chéhéry. Like so many of their attacks it had been delayed, and when it went in it was in insufficient strength. The tank crews fought bravely, but the attack was called off before it had achieved anything. The French had missed their last opportunity. On the following day fresh German units arrived and Stonne was recaptured. The south flank was secure.

Now nothing but new orders could stop Guderian. On 15 May Kleist had a 'fit of nerves' and ordered Guderian to halt so that infantry could catch up with him and so cover his south and south-east flanks. By the values of World War I these were sound tactics. But Guderian was fighting a new war and winning it because his adversaries were still thinking in World War I terms and time-scales. Guderian contacted the chief-of-staff of the *Panzergruppe*, Colonel Zeitzler, and then Kleist himself. After a

heated exchange he received permission to advance for a further 24 hours.

Having regained his freedom Guderian drove to the front on 16 May to see the 1st Panzer Division. Here he met Colonel Balck, standing dust-covered and red-eyed in the blazing main street of the village of Bouvellemont. Earlier one of Balck's officers had said that the men were overtired and an attack on the village would not succeed. Balck picked up his walking stick and strode off with the reply: 'In that case I'll take the place on my own.'

Morale was soaring as the troops moved deeper into France. Guderian encountered tank crews of the 1st Panzer Division who shouted: 'Well done, old boy' and 'Did you see him? That was Heinz *der Rascher* (hurrying Heinz)'. 'All this was indicative,' comments Guderian.

At Montcornet he met General Kempf. Their two staffs worked out routes for the three Panzer divisions which were now roaring through the town. The two generals

Guderian – the 'Panzer Corridor'

Above: **French vehicles abandoned and destroyed in the chaotic retreat before the advancing German columns. Quite apart from the speed with which the German columns pushed forward, the Allies were also hampered to a great extent by the streaming columns of refugees fleeing the advent of the Germans.**

Left: **The pattern of German tank warfare – while the crews of Rommel's 7th Panzer Division, equipped with PzKpfw 38(t) tanks developed from the Czech LTH, rest under the summer sun of northern France, a Fieseler Fi-156 *Storch* liaison aircraft makes a low pass, probably to drop a message. The use of such aircraft for front-line reconnaissance was greatly valued by more enterprising German generals, such as Rommel, Guderian and Manstein. Mussolini was rescued by such an aircraft.**

fixed the routes for their units (Guderian's 2nd and 1st Panzer, and Kempf's 6th Panzer, XLI Corps) and ordered that the advance go on 'until the last drop of petrol was used up'. By now the point sections had reached Marle and Dercy, 40 miles from their morning's start line and 22 miles from Sedan.

But now on the 17th, just as the battle was developing as Manstein had planned, Guderian, who was making it possible, received a message from *Panzergruppe*. He was to halt the advance and report to Kleist. The meeting was stormy, Kleist claiming that Guderian had disobeyed orders. Shocked and surprised, Guderian asked to be relieved of his command. Happily for the Germans they were not to lose their tank expert. Kleist accepted the resignation, but on behalf of Colonel-General von Rundstedt, head of Army Group 'A', Colonel-General List explained that the halt order came from OKW. List, commander of the 12th Army, understood the reasons for pressing on and authorised Guderian to carry out a 'reconnaissance in force'. The corps headquarters, however, must remain where it was so that OKW could keep in contact.

Enter de Gaulle

Welcoming the freedom implicit in these new orders Guderian left his corps headquarters at Soize and moved on with the tanks. His advanced headquarters were linked by telephone so that OKW and OKH monitoring units could not intercept any radio traffic between his two headquarters.

The delay had been frustrating for Guderian, but for his tank crews the 17th was a welcome break. There was time to get some sleep, service the tanks and allow supplies to catch up. It was also the day on which the French proposed mounting two counterattacks from the north and south on Guderian's 'Panzer corridor'. Only the attack from the south materialised on time, however.

The man chosen to lead the French 4th Armoured Division in this attack was Colonel Charles de Gaulle. His forces consisted of two battalions of obsolete light R-35 tanks and one battalion of Char B tanks. Despite this his tanks fought their way to Montcornet 'destroying everything which had had no time to flee'.

It was a nasty moment, but again the Germans demonstrated that they could react quickly and extemporise a defence before collecting tanks for a counterattack. Using light flak units and some tanks which were returning from workshops, junior officers halted the French. One wrote afterwards: 'Here the lack of fighting spirit of the enemy became abundantly clear to us; German tanks against so weak a defence would certainly not have turned round.'

Whilst the drama of armoured attack and counterattack was being fought on the flanks and point, and whilst the generals argued and planned, the German infantry debouched from the Ardennes and marched over the pontoon bridges at Sedan. The Panzer corridor was now getting its infantry lining, and the fears of the more conventionally minded officers at the OKW were

put to rest.

Guderian remained as far ahead as his telephone link would allow him. On the 19th his corps began to cross the World War I battlefield of the Somme. Rivers like the Somme, Aisne and Serre were an asset for the Germans – for covered by a screen of reconnaissance troops, anti-tank units and combat engineers they protected the south flank of the corridor.

Amiens falls

On the 19th de Gaulle attempted another attack. There was one disturbing moment when tanks from the 4th Armoured Division came within a few miles of Guderian's headquarters. It was protected only by some 2-cm flak guns, but Guderian dismissed the danger as 'a few uncomfortable hours until at last the threatening visitors moved off'.

A day earlier the German 2nd Panzer Division had captured St Quentin, whilst the 1st, after covering 30 miles in a morning, captured some bridges over the Somme. This was no longer war but a 'live firing exercise'. Guderian could have used the words of General George Patton in 1944, that he was 'touring on the continent with an army'.

By the evening of 19 May Guderian's XIX Panzer Corps had reached a line Cambrai-Péronne-Ham. The corps headquarters

were moved forward to Marle and received full freedom of movement, with authorisation to move on to Amiens as from the 20th.

The following morning Guderian visited the 10th Panzer Division at Péronne, where they had taken over from the 1st Panzer Division. Here he heard that the impetuous Colonel Balck, who had taken command of the 1st Panzer Brigade when its commander, Colonel Nedtwig, had collapsed from exhaustion, had offended his successor, Colonel Landgraf. When taken to task for leaving Péronne so that he could be in on the assault on Amiens, Balck had cheerfully replied: 'If we lose it you can always take it again. I had to capture it in the first place, didn't I?'

Amiens was German by noon on the 20th and with it they held a bridgehead over the Somme four miles deep. Returning to Albert, Guderian encountered the 2nd Panzer Division, which 'was almost out of fuel and therefore proposed to stop where it was, but was soon disillusioned'. By adjusting available fuel stocks he gave them enough to reach Abbeville by 1900 hours. Tough with himself, Guderian was equally demanding of his men. He writes: 'One must always distrust the report of troop commanders: "We have no fuel". Generally they have. But if they become tired they lack fuel.'

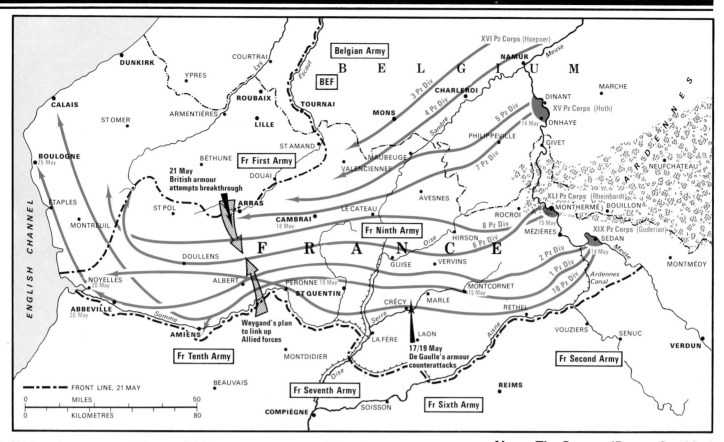

Above: The German 'Panzer Corridor' from the Ardennes to the coast of the English Channel near Abbeville. With the taking and holding of this corridor, the Germans had sealed the fate of France. The British Expeditionary Force, the Belgian army and major elements of the French army were cut off to the north, and the rest of the French army was desperately attempting to form a defence line along the Aisne and Somme rivers.

Left: The dejection of defeat mirrored in the faces of these French prisoners-of-war. Poorly trained and equipped, and often thrown into a type of warfare for which they had no preparation, they stood little chance against the Germans. It should be noted, however, that many of the regular French units put up an able and, to the Germans, unexpected resistance. The defence of Lille is a good example of this.

During the night of the 19th/20th a reconnaissance unit of the 2nd Panzer Division passed through Noyelles. These tired, sweaty, dust-covered young men were the first Germans to reach the Channel. They were the men who had turned Hitler's dreams and Manstein's plans into reality.

XIX Panzer Corps had achieved its prime objective of cutting off the Allied armies in northern France and Belgium. Now it awaited orders. It waited for a day on the Somme. Visiting his units Guderian asked the tank crews how they had enjoyed the operations. An Austrian serving in the 2nd Panzer Division gave him a tough professional reply: 'Not bad, but we wasted two whole days.' 'Unfortunately,' comments Guderian, 'he was right.'

Field-Marshal Gerd von Rundstedt

Gerd von Rundstedt was born on 12 December 1875 in Aschersleben, near Halle, the son of a military family. He joined the army in 1892, at the age of 17. By the outbreak of World War I, Rundstedt had reached the rank of captain, had been a pupil at the War Academy in Berlin, and served as a regimental officer and in several staff positions, the latter including a two-year period on the Great German General Staff. Rundstedt was promoted major on 28 November 1914, and served in his rank throughout World War I.

Serving with the *Reichswehr* after the war, Rundstedt held a variety of posts as a staff officer and commander. He reached general rank on 1 November 1927, and became a full general on 1 October 1932, the same day that he was appointed commander of the 1st Army Group.

Rundstedt was deeply involved in the improvement of infantry equipment and tactics, so that casualties in any future war might be minimised. On 1 March 1938 he was again promoted, to colonel-general, and on 1 November of the same year he retired from active service.

On 1 June 1939, however, Rundstedt was recalled, and given command of Army Group 'South' for the Polish campaign. It was this army group which captured Warsaw.

After the successful conclusion of this first campaign of World War II, Rundstedt was appointed on 20 October to the command of Army Group 'A' for the Western campaign. After the fall of France, Rundstedt was promoted field-marshal on 19 July 1940.

The post next taken up by Rundstedt was as commander of Army Group 'South' for the Russian campaign, with the job of driving into the Caucasus. Rundstedt resigned and was put on the reserve on 3 December 1941 when he was not allowed to make a tactical withdrawal to the Mius line.

On 1 March 1942 Rundstedt was again called forth, this time as acting Commander-in-Chief West, a posting that was confirmed on 1 May. Rundstedt held this position until nearly the end of the war, with the exception of the period 7 July–5 September 1944. He was finally replaced by Kesselring on 11 March 1945.

Field-Marshal Gerd von Rundstedt

Dignified and aristocratic in outlook with a tall, spare frame, Field-Marshal Gerd von Rundstedt was already an old man at the outbreak of World War II. He had always been wary of the British, and with America's entry into the war, the risk of an Allied invasion of the European continent increased.

Hitler persuaded Rundstedt to come out of retirement and take up the position of Commander-in-Chief West to meet this threat. Once again, Rundstedt obeyed the call to duty and took up command at St Germaine, France, in March 1942.

The task of defending Western Europe was a formidable one. The years 1942–43 were spent by the Western staff trying to forecast where the Allies might launch their attack. The possibilities for an invasion zone seemed endless – the Western theatre of operations stretched from Norway along the coast of Europe to Spain and along the Mediterranean to Greece.

During 1942, the German losses in the East were so devastating that from early

German medium artillery, part of the much-vaunted, but still largely imaginary 'Atlantic wall' beloved of the German Propaganda Ministry.

1943, no offensive policy could be envisaged for the West, and the planners concentrated on strategic defence. Great reliance was placed on the Atlantic Wall, a line of static fortifications on or near the coast, to halt the invasion. In parts of Normandy, the Pas de Calais and Holland, the fortifications were quite strong, but elsewhere the Wall was practically non-existent. The technicalities of the Wall were entrusted to the Todt Organisation, and Rundstedt was not consulted. A fortress system was organised, a strongly defended fortress being constructed every so many miles along the defence line, whilst the lines linking these fortresses were extremely weak. Crack divisions were stationed in the fortresses, but these came under Hitler's direct command. Rundstedt was very unhappy about the defence system, and considered it would probably hold an invasion for 24 hours at the most. Moreover, once the Allies had breached the main defence line, what good were the fortresses facing the sea?

Not enough men

Rundstedt also complained about the manpower allotted to him. On his arrival in 1942, only 30 divisions were stationed in France and the Low Countries, but with the increasing threat of invasion, the number was increased by D-Day to 60 divisions, shared between four army commands. Field-Marshal Rommel, commander of Army Group 'B', controlled the 7th and the 15th Armies, whilst Colonel-General Blaskowitz, commander of Army Group 'G' had the 1st and 19th Armies under orders. Rommel's army group was responsible for the defence of the Channel coast, the 15th Army being deployed along the coast from Holland to the River Seine, and the 7th stationed between the Seine and the Loire rivers. The southern front, from the Loire to the Alps, was entrusted to Blaskowitz. Rundstedt was supreme commander.

By the end of March 1944, it was thought that the landings would probably take place on the beaches of northern France. German agents in Britain confirmed that the invasion was to be launched from southern England. But to where in northern France? And how should the threat be met? Rommel, new to the West in November 1943 as commander of Army Group 'B', and Rundstedt were to argue over these questions. The overall situation demanded that the Allies be beaten swiftly in the West so that Hitler could send much needed reinforcements to the Eastern Front. Defences were therefore stepped up in the West, but unfortunately without a unified command structure. Rundstedt could not give orders to the German naval forces, or to the anti-aircraft corps. Naval and army gunners could not reach agreement over the coastal batteries, the setting up of obstacles and anti-aircraft defences.

In June 1944, Rundstedt supposedly commanded two army groups ('B' and 'G' with between them 15 corps totalling 42 infantry, three parachute, three Luftwaffe field, 10 Panzer and one *Panzergrenadier* divisions. But he had only tactical control over the Luftwaffe units, the *Waffen* SS divisions and I SS Panzer Corps. He had no authority over appointments or discipline.

Such a command structure was to lead to inevitable delays when the Allies landed.

The wrong target

Rundstedt considered that the Allies would cross the Channel via the shortest sea-route and land in the Pas de Calais, which was also the quickest way to the Ruhr and industrial Germany. The V1 and V2 sites were in this area, too. The staff officers in Berlin thought the attack would be launched further west than this – between the Somme and Seine rivers. Coastal defences here and in the Pas de Calais were accordingly built up. Rommel and Hitler, however, decided that the landings were most likely to take place on the beaches of Normandy, as the Pas de Calais would appear to the enemy to be very strongly defended. Rommel immediately set to work to set up effective coastal defences in this region but, unfortunately for the Germans, his efforts were curtailed by a shortage of resources and labour. Most of the workers of the Todt Organisation had been drawn off to Germany by this time to repair air-raid damage. The scope of the planned defences was too extensive for the German

troops to achieve much on their own, and both they and the movement of supplies were hampered by the raids of the Allied air forces. Thus, on D-Day, both the underwater obstructions and the coastal fortifications were incomplete. Rommel complained that this state of affairs need not have happened, and blamed Rundstedt for placing too much reliance on mobile defence.

With regard to the strategy to be adopted in the event of an enemy landing, while they agreed that they must defeat the invaders in the shortest possible time, Rundstedt and Rommel held differing opinions concerning the deployment of *Panzergruppe* 'West', Rundstedt's armoured reserve. These forces – 2nd Panzer, 21st Panzer, 103rd Panzer *Lehr*, 116th Panzer, 1st SS '*Leibstandarte Adolf Hitler*' Panzer, 12th SS '*Hitlerjugend*' Panzer and 17th SS '*Goetz von Berlichingen*' *Panzergrenadier* Divisions – came under the command of General Geyr von Schweppenburg, who naturally wanted to keep the force concentrated. Rundstedt agreed with this, as did Guderian, but he was wary of committing all his reserves without first being quite sure of the Allies' intentions. He did not want to commit them to what might be a diversionary feint.

Rundstedt – the Defence of France

Rundstedt's plan was therefore to hold back his strong armoured force approximately 30 miles from the coast and, when he was certain about what was happening, release the reserve in a powerful counter-offensive against the Allied bridgehead. Rundstedt was also doubtful of Germany's ability to prevent a landing, as there were so many miles of coastline to cover.

Rommel's experiences in Africa had led him to hold a different opinion on the best way of blocking an invasion by an enemy with superior air power. He saw a seaborne attack as being weak at the moment of landing, but increasing in momentum and strength afterwards. He therefore thought it best to hurl the armour against the Allies as they were landing and so exploit their initial weakness. The invasion would thus collapse on the very first day. Rommel had assessed correctly the danger of the Allies' superior air power, which would be able to harass any large-scale movement of German troops after the invasion. The armour must be immediately available to aid the coastal defenders as the Allies landed. But only three Panzer divisions were under Rommel's direct control.

Rundstedt's ideas should have prevailed

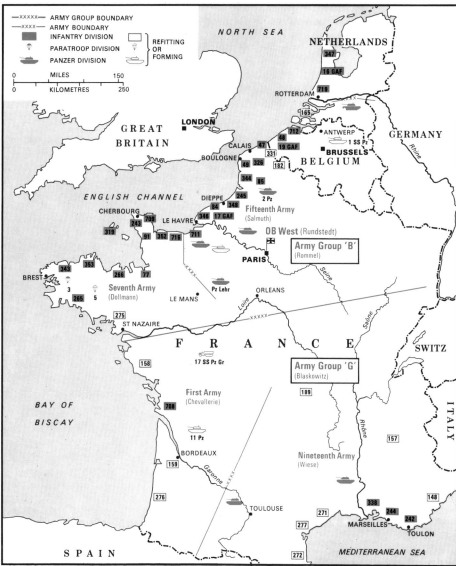

Above: The German forces in France to meet the expected Allied invasion. Naturally enough, Army Group 'B' had the lion's share of the divisions, with the heaviest concentration of these deployed between Le Havre and Brussels. Note the location of the armoured formations in northern France – well behind the coast. Although this meant that these powerful forces should be able to concentrate quickly at any point on the north coast, it also meant that the forces available to meet the invasion at its two most likely landing points (Normandy and the Pas de Calais), would be without immediate armoured support.

Far left: A German machine gunner scans the sea for signs of the impending invasion. His weapon is an MG 34, fitted on a tripod for the sustained fire role.

Above left: A heavy gun emplacement on the French channel coast. Although such guns were adequate pieces, they lacked the fire-control system to hit moving ships.

Left: An unhappy Rommel watches anti-invasion preparations being carried out along the coast.

as he was the senior commander. Rommel, however, had influence with Hitler and was therefore able to 'dilute' Rundstedt's orders. On 20 March Hitler gave Rommel permission to take over Panzergruppe 'West', but no orders followed from OKW and von Geyr absolutely refused to deploy his force as Rommel wished. He thought Rommel was trying to cover everything and would in all probability defend nothing when the time came. He complained of Rundstedt's hesitation in overruling Rommel. It may be that Rundstedt was coming round to Rommel's plan, but at this time, also, Rundstedt was an old man and suffering severe mental and physical fatigue. Von Geyr went himself to see Hitler to protest about Rommel's forward plan, and Hitler consequently ordered that four Panzer divisions, including 'Hitlerjugend' and Panzer Lehr, were to form the OKW reserve and were not to be moved without his permission. This meant that Rommel's plan was considerably weakened and Rundstedt had fewer reserves to call on.

On D-Day, then, the armour was neither deployed near the beaches nor concentrated ready for a decisive counterattack. The infantry divisions were stretched thinly along the coast from Holland to Marseilles and only in the Pas de Calais did Rundstedt succeed in producing a second layer of infantry. Hitler would not create enough reserves from other theatres, and vetoed

63

Rommel's suggestion that the troops from the southern front be brought up so that they would be in a position to counterattack.

Seven of the 11 Panzer divisions were placed north of the Loire, with the remaining four acting as a reserve for the south and south-west coasts. Rommel stationed his armour as near to the coast as possible, while Rundstedt kept his further back. On 23 April, Rommel vainly requested Hitler to allow him to move the Panzer *Lehr* Division to between the Orne and the Vire rivers and to deploy the '*Hitlerjugend*' Division near St Lô, and to reinforce this sector with more anti-aircraft batteries.

On 5 June, Rommel left France to attend his wife's birthday celebrations in Germany. Everything looked quiet, but just before midnight, it was discovered that the BBC was broadcasting a large number of messages to the French Resistance. The 15th Army east of the Seine was alerted, but Lieutenant-General Speidel, deputising for Rommel, did not alert the 7th Army in Normandy. As Allied paratroops landed in Normandy after midnight, feverish activity at Rundstedt's headquarters tried to determine whether this signalled the start of the invasion, or whether it was merely a diversion. British and American secret agents had employed many tricks to mislead the German generals and signals experts as to the landing site. An entire 'ghost' army had been assembled which led many to believe the main attack would be launched elsewhere.

At 0400 hours Rundstedt decided the landings must be dealt with. Off the five selected landing points, six battleships had appeared, together with 23 cruisers, 105 destroyers, 495 coastal craft and numerous frigates. Under the cover of this great armada, a force of 6,480 transports, landing craft and special-purpose vehicles landed the invasion forces with their amphibious tanks. As Rundstedt decided his forces must counterattack, the infantry divisions in the bunkers along the coast were unable to resist the naval, air and land assault and surrendered in their thousands. The underwater obstacles were swept away by the first wave of attacking infantry. The Allied air forces flew over 10,500 sorties on 6 June, and dropped nearly 12,000 tons of bombs on the German defences, which was as much as was dropped on Hamburg in the whole of 1943.

Early in the day, Rundstedt urgently requested that OKW release the armour reserve, but he received the answer from Jodl that they were not yet convinced that this was the main invasion and that a second landing east of the Seine river was imminent. Rundstedt finally obtained the release of I SS Panzer Corps at 1600 hours, but the armour took two days to reach the invasion zone as a result of air attack and broken bridges. By that time the Allies were firmly established in their bridgeheads. Had Rommel not been absent, perhaps the tanks would have been available earlier, as he had more influence at OKW than Rundstedt.

However, the 21st Panzer, 1st '*Leib-standarte*' SS Panzer and Panzer *Lehr* Divisions constituted a striking force of approximately 600 tanks, together with the best troops in France. They should have been able to deliver at least a counter-blow

to be reckoned with, but they never achieved the co-ordination for a counter-offensive. None of the armour reached the coast before the afternoon of 6 June, when it was already too late to push the Allies back into the sea. After the Panzers arrived, they were frittered away in desperate attempts to plug the gaping holes in the Atlantic Wall, where the infantry had been smashed. In the first days after the landing, the Germans lost 10,000 prisoners and 150 tanks. Reinforcements did not get through. By 8 June, the Anglo-Americans had a continuous front between the Dives and St Marcouf. The German forces were dazed and weary and could only wait for help.

In the second week, Rundstedt no longer feared a second landing east of the Seine. Hitler's headquarters still expected such a landing and Hitler was reluctant to move troops from Calais to Normandy to be re-deployed as Rundstedt wished. In desperation, Rommel and Rundstedt tried to make Hitler see reason. They wanted to withdraw from Caen, leave the infantry to hold the line of the Orne river and pull out the armoured divisions to reorganise for a powerful counter-offensive against the Americans in the Cherbourg peninsula. Hitler ordered that all troops must remain where they stood. He was still hoping it was possible to drive the Allies back. Hitler brushed aside Rundstedt's objections and said that the new V weapons would soon take effect, but he would not hear of using them against the Allies on the beaches.

At the end of June, Rommel and Rundstedt again appealed to Hitler who reiterated his order for no withdrawal. Rundstedt said he could not carry on without a free hand and was then dismissed, to be replaced by Field-Marshal von Kluge.

Above: Members of the gun crew cover their ears against the shock waves as a German heavy gun is fired in a practice shoot on the Channel coast.

Right: German infantry in training. Unfortunately for the Germans, however, such forces had neither the firepower nor the mobility to check the Allied mechanised units.

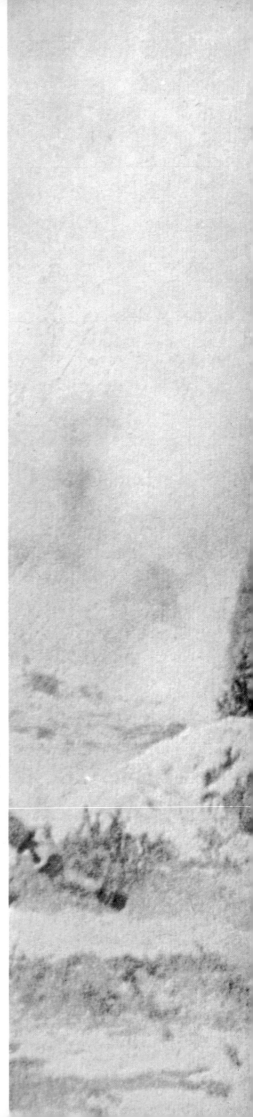

The Western Front

Colonel-General Sepp Dietrich

In the 1950s, Dietrich was given a prison sentence by a Federal German court for his part in the occasion.

With the growing importance of the military aspect of the SS organisation, later the *Waffen-SS*, Dietrich found himself turned into a field commander, first of the 1st SS Panzer Division, then of I SS Panzer Corps and finally of 6th SS *Panzerarmee*. This last formation played the central parts in the Battles of the 'Bulge' and of Lake Balaton.

After the war this most senior of SS men, who ended with the rank of *Oberstgruppenfuehrer und Generaloberst der Waffen-SS*, was sentenced to 25 years' imprisonment for his responsibility for the massacre of unarmed US prisoners at Malmédy during the Battle of the 'Bulge'. The best that can be said of Dietrich was that he was 'decent, but stupid', as Rundstedt claimed.

Joseph 'Sepp' Dietrich was born in 1892 in upper Bavaria, and held several jobs in the years before World War I. These included farm labourer, waiter, policeman, foreman in a tobacco factory, customs official and petrol pump attendant.

During World War I Dietrich reached the status of a senior non-commissioned officer in one of Germany's few tank units.

Dietrich was an early adherent of the Nazi doctrine, and joined the party in 1928, whilst working for the Nazi publisher Franz Eher of Munich.

In 1930 Dietrich was made organiser of the SS in southern Bavaria, a sure sign of his growing importance in the party hierarchy. During 1931 he became head of the major SS organisation in north Germany, *Oberabschnitt Nord*, with headquarters in Hamburg.

Dietrich's close relationship with the central figures of the Nazi party was further enhanced by his elevation to commander of Hitler's personal bodyguard. On 17 March 1933 he formed the SS Headquarters Guard, Berlin, which was renamed '*Leibstandarte Adolf Hitler*' in September.

A loyal SS man, Dietrich was called upon to play a major part in the purge of the SA, the 'Night of the Long Knives' on 30 June 1934.

Colonel-General Sepp Dietrich

Physically 'Sepp' Dietrich did not look the part of a German general. Squat, thick-necked and with the battered face of a bouncer, he also lacked the mental attributes of the rank to which he had been elevated. Rundstedt had called him 'decent but stupid'. *Obergruppenfuehrer* Bittrich had been less generous: 'I once spent an hour and a half trying to explain a situation to Sepp Dietrich with the aid of a map. It was quite useless. He understood nothing at all.'

It was on the broad shoulders of this man, however, that Hitler had laid the responsibility of commanding the 6th SS *Panzer-armee* in the surprise attack in December 1944 that was to be known as 'The Battle of the Bulge' by the Allies and Operation *'Herbstnebel'* (Autumn Fog) by the Germans. Of the units involved his was to launch the *Schwerpunkt*, the main weight, of the offensive. With him would go the 5th *Panzer-armee* under General Hasso von Manteuffel in the centre and to the south the 7th Army under General Brandenberger would cover their flank.

The 6th SS *Panzerarmee* consisted of LXVII Corps under General Hitzfeld, with the 272nd and 326th *Volksgrenadier* Divisions; I SS Panzer Corps under General Priess with the 277th and 12th *Volks-grenadier*, 3rd Parachute, 3rd *Panzer-grenadier*, and 1st and 12th SS Panzer Divisions; and II SS Panzer Corps under General Bittrich with the 2nd and 9th SS Panzer Divisions. Dietrich's *Waffen*-SS Panzer divisions had been brought up to

strength for the offensive with 640 Panther and Pzkw IV tanks. In addition he had some powerful Tiger II tanks with their potent L/71 8·8-cm gun.

The choice of the *Waffen*-SS to bear the main weight of the attack did not mean that the men of the army were no longer effective soldiers, but rather that after the July Bomb Plot of 1944, the army had fallen out of favour. It was ironic, therefore, that two army generals proposed a *'kleine Loesung'*, a 'small solution' which would have had a far greater chance of success than Hitler's grandiose scheme.

While the *Fuehrer* envisaged a punch

which would reach as far as Antwerp and cut off the Allied armies allowing them no Dunkirk evacuation, Model and Hasso von Manteuffel proposed a more modest and more practical operation. They suggested that 'the 15th Army, with a strong right flank, would deliver an attack north of Aachen, towards Maastricht. The 6th *Panzerarmee* would attack south of Aachen, and cut in behind that place with the eventual objective of establishing a bridgehead over the Meuse in the Liège area. The main aim here was to fix the Allies' attention. The 5th *Panzerarmee* would strike from the Eifel through the Ardennes towards Namur, with

Above: German assault troops move up past a burning Allied vehicle on the successful first day of the 'Battle of the Bulge', 16 December 1945.

Left: Allied transport (Willys Jeeps and White M3 halftracks) caught in the open and destroyed by the advancing Germans in the early hours of the Battle of the Ardennes. The Germans had no comparable transport.

the aim of gaining a bridgehead there. The armies would then turn and roll up the Allied position along the Meuse. If opposition seemed to be collapsing, they could exploit their success by an advance towards Antwerp, but otherwise they could limit their risks.' This plan, as explained after the war to Liddell Hart by Manteuffel, was within the capabilities of the forces available and had it succeeded would have destroyed

20 Allied divisions.

Surprisingly, Hitler listened to the proposals without interrupting, but at the end rejected them. He did not want a sortie to gain time and stave off defeat for a few extra weeks or months, he wanted a major victory. Of all the generals involved Dietrich was probably the one who could be trusted to obey his orders with unquestioning loyalty – however ambitious those orders might be.

Hitler's plan envisaged reaching the Meuse in 48 hours. Here Dietrich would cross the river north of Liège and drive for Antwerp via St Truiden and Aarschot. Manteuffel would go for Brussels. Their south flank would be covered by the 7th Army pivoting on Echternach, while paratroops under Lieutenant-Colonel von der Heydte would be dropped to block the northern roads. In addition teams of German soldiers dressed as Americans in captured vehicles, under the command of *Sturmbannfuehrer* Otto Skorzeny, were to infiltrate the American lines, sow confusion and capture bridges over the Meuse.

On the Allied side there was an optimism which was heightened by the lack of intelligence available about the German forces facing them. The Germans were now on their home ground and so there were no friendly civilians to bear information to the Allies about troop concentrations. In fact General

Bradley's intelligence summary for 12 December said 'It is now certain that attrition is steadily sapping the strength of the German forces on the Western Front.'

Snow had been falling in the Ardennes for a week and the men of the 6th SS *Panzerarmee* were kitted out in a mixture of waterproof cold-weather clothing, camouflaged smocks and jackets. They carried belts of ammunition, entrenching tools and stick grenades, and some were equipped with the modern StG 44 assault rifle. In their ears rang the words of Field-Marshal von Rundstedt, Commander-in-Chief West: 'Soldiers of the Western Front, your great hour has struck. At this moment the veil which has been hiding so many preparations has been lifted at last.'

Early success

Even before dawn had broken on that heavily overcast 16 December, men of the 6th SS *Panzerarmee* were beginning to advance. At 0530 hours a soldier of the 1st SS Panzer Division had turned to his officer, grinned, and said: '*Auf wiedersehen, Herr Leutnant, seh dich in Amerika!*' or 'Cheerio, Lieutenant, see you in America!' Morale was very high. Dietrich had decided to commit his infantry first, and to hold back his armour to exploit the first successes.

A *Sturmgeschuetz* III (a 7.5-cm gun mounted with limited traverse in a converted PzKpfw III as an assault gun) leads the way for a German column. Behind the *Sturmgeschuetz* is an SdKfz 251 halftrack carrier.

On his right he came up against the American 2nd and 99th Divisions of V Corps under Major-General Leonard Gerow. The 2nd Division was a veteran unit which overcame its surprise quite quickly, but the 99th, which had never been in action before and, moreover, been on the receiving end, took longer to recover. However, despite attacks by the I SS Panzer Corps the Americans hung onto the Elsenborn ridge. To the south elements of I SS and II SS Panzer Corps brushed aside a screen of the 14th Armoured Division and streamed through the Losheim gap. This opened up the Stavelot road and turned the flank of the 106th Division.

While these attacks were in progress, von der Heydte was giving a condensed briefing to his officers whose paratroops were to cover the Eupen-Malmedy road. Although these 1,200 men were a scratch force, of whom only about 300 were experienced paratroops, they managed to sow confusion and concern among the Americans. The drop on the night of the 16th/17th was hope-

Above: A cheerful group of Germans tug a camouflaged searchlight, part of an anti-aircraft gun battery, towards the front. The manpower indicates the German shortage of fuel at this stage of the war. Because of very poor weather conditions, the Allies were not able to put up any aircraft during the first days of the offensive, much to the cost of the ground troops.

Left: Dejected American prisoners-of-war await transport to Germany.

lessly scattered, and some of the lumbering Ju 52s came under fire from their own men, who automatically assumed that any aircraft was Allied. Von der Heydte later recalled that Dietrich was 'obviously drunk' when he briefed him.

German newsreels of the period show SS men and paratroops advancing along roads blocked with abandoned and burning American Jeeps and half-tracks, and indeed there was an exhilaration in the opening days which had not been felt since the 'glorious days' of May 1940. Suddenly the enemy was on the run, and the sky, covered with low cloud, was no longer filled with enemy aircraft.

However, in isolated positions the

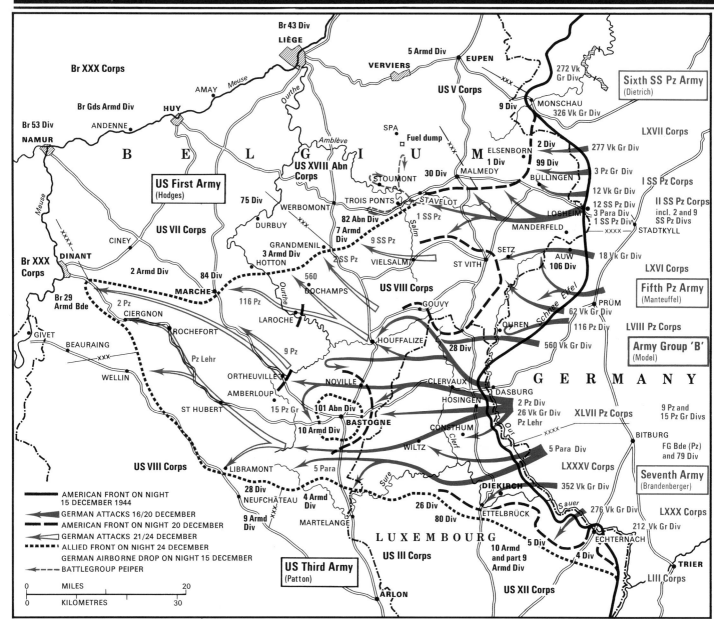

MILES
0 ——————— 20
0 ——————— 30
KILOMETRES

AMERICAN FRONT ON NIGHT
15 DECEMBER 1944
GERMAN ATTACKS 16/20 DECEMBER
AMERICAN FRONT ON NIGHT 20 DECEMBER
GERMAN ATTACKS 21/24 DECEMBER
ALLIED FRONT ON NIGHT 24 DECEMBER
GERMAN AIRBORNE DROP ON NIGHT 15 DECEMBER
BATTLEGROUP PEIPER

Americans showed a resource and courage that saved themselves and their units. At Buetgenbach an artillery unit hung on and prevented the outflanking of the 2nd and 99th Divisions. A company of the 51st Engineer Combat Battalion halted the advance of *Kampfgruppe* 'Peiper' when it demolished the bridge at Trois-Ponts across the Salm. Peiper was forced to return via Amblève to find another bridge at Werbomont. Here he was again confronted by determined engineers, men of the 291st Battalion who blew up the bridge. Like Hitler, the man who launched the attack, the Ardennes offensive was bogging down into 'a corporal's war'.

Dietrich, with the tactical sense of a battering ram, continued to attack the Elsenborn ridge. Gerow, however, had been able to reinforce the position with a first class unit, the 1st Division, and the young men and boys of the 12th 'Hitlerjugend' SS Panzer Division were halted around Buetgenbach.

The aggressive *Obersturmbannfuehrer* Jochen Peiper of the 'Leibstandarte Adolf Hitler' Division lead his *Kampfgruppe* to the little town of Stavelot, which he captured on the 17th. Two days later it was recaptured, and Peiper, isolated, fought for five days in the wooded valley of the Amblève.

Then, out of fuel, he was forced to withdraw after destroying all his equipment, including his Tiger II tanks.

Meanwhile Manteuffel was making better progress because it was more difficult for the Americans to reinforce their units in the south. Seeking to exploit this success both Model and Rundstedt urged Hitler to transfer II SS Panzer Corps from the 6th to the 5th *Panzerarmee*. They were refused categorically since this would have been an admission that the Nazi Party soldiers and officers of the *Waffen*-SS were inferior to their *Wehrmacht* counterparts.

The Allies recover

By now, however, the Allies were beginning to adjust their dispositions: to the north Montgomery, who had taken temporary command, moved XXX Corps down to the Meuse to cover the American 1st Army. To the south Patton's 3rd Army swung north and on 22 December launched a strong attack up the road from Arlon to Bastogne. As Patton gleefully described it, 'this time the Kraut's stuck his head in a meatgrinder. And this time I've got hold of the handle.'

'About 25 December I saw that it would now be impossible for us to attempt a crossing of the Meuse,' said von Manteuffel.

The 'Battle of the Bulge' or, more properly, the Battle of the Ardennes. Here the Germans achieved total strategic and tactical surprise in their gamble to reach Antwerp. The 101st Airborne Division's defence of Bastogne, and determined Allied fighting, soon halted the Germans.

He fought for another week, but now his men were trapped in their own salient. On the 23rd the weather had improved and the Allies had been able to enjoy air dropped supplies, while the Germans were subject to strikes by ground-attack fighters.

As they pulled back from their salient the Germans left behind them the last of their pool of tanks and half-tracks. Some had been destroyed by resolute GIs armed with infantry anti-tank weapons, some had been split apart by aircraft rockets and cannon fire, but many had been abandoned when they ran out of fuel. For Dietrich's 6th SS *Panzerarmee* it was a tragic irony that on the 19th they had come within about a quarter of a mile at Andrimont near Stavelot of a fuel dump containing 2,500,000 gallons.

With the failure of his forces to make any progress in the north and the squeezing out of Manteuffel in the south, Dietrich was forced to withdraw. He had never been

Dietrich — the Battle of the Bulge

happy with the plan, and after the war told Milton Shulman: 'All I had to do was cross a river, capture Brussels and then go on and take the port of Antwerp. And all this in December, January and February, the worst three months of the year, through the Ardennes where snow was waist deep and there wasn't room to deploy four tanks abreast, let alone six armoured divisions; when it didn't get light until eight in the morning and was dark again at four in the afternoon and my tanks can't fight at night; with divisions that had just been reformed and were composed chiefly of raw untrained recruits; and at Christmas time.' 'The crack in Dietrich's voice when he reached this last obstacle,' recalls Shulman, 'made it sound like the most heart-breaking one of all.'

The Ardennes operation left behind 76,890 American casualties and 81,834 German, and though American losses in tanks and aircraft were greater, 733 to 324 and 592 to 320, the German losses were now almost irreplaceable. The Battle of the Bulge also left an atmosphere of bitterness between the Allies and also within the German camp. After the war Rundstedt asserted that Dietrich sent few reports during the operation, 'and what I did receive was generally a pack of lies. If the SS had any problems they reported them directly to the *Fuehrer*, who would then make them known to Model.'

Despite this Dietrich was not a bad officer; he simply lacked the training and experience to command an army. Goering said of him: 'He had at the most the ability to command a division.'

Left: A PzKpfw IV tank, armed with a long-barrelled 7.5-cm gun, in typical Ardennes winter conditions.

Below: US bombs burst in the snow. As the weather cleared, Allied fighter-bombers were able to take a decisive part in the battle.

Analysis-
German Generalship in the West

In 1940 the Germans had 2,600 tanks whilst the Anglo-French allies had 3,600; moreover, many of the German marks had thinner armour and lighter guns than those of their adversaries. Despite this, their 136 divisions defeated the 137 divisions of four nations and sent the British Expeditionary Force back across the Channel from the beaches of Dunkirk. In the months that followed May 1940 the Western world tried to understand what had enabled the Germans to score such a decisive victory.

The reasons for the German successes were simply, good training, air superiority (1,490 bombers and 1,260 fighters against 1,690 first-line combat aircraft) and the concentrated use of armour into fast moving spearheads.

An Italian journalist called it 'Lightning War', and 'Blitzkrieg' became the name for these deep-penetration tactics. The Germans launched their marching infantry on the Low Countries to draw off the Allied mobile units. These spoiling attacks diverted Anglo-French attention from the discreet approach march by the armoured units through Luxembourg and the Ardennes. French reservist units in positions on the Meuse became the target of concentrated aerial attack, and their inadequate positions were pounded to destruction. Through the gap that had been punched the Germans poured their tanks and armoured infantry in a wild drive across northern France to the sea – cutting off the Anglo-French forces in France and Belgium.

Ground-air liaison

Since they could not bring up heavy artillery at the speed of their tanks, the Germans used dive-bombers as flying artillery. The Stukas and marching infantry could finish off pockets of resistance that had been bypassed by the Panzer columns. The French, who had fought stubbornly during the bulk of World War I, were ill-prepared for a war of movement. Their communications systems were grossly inadequate for assessing a situation which was changing

hourly; their tanks, though good, were spread along the front in small formations; and they had obsolescent aircraft and few anti-tank guns. There was also the important factor of morale – the men of 1940 were not the hardened peasant classes of 1914 burning with a desire to revenge the defeats of the Franco-Prussian War. The long cold winter of the 'Phoney War' (another journalist's creation) of 1939 had sapped the will of many soldiers. The government, unwilling to incur anything like the awesome casualties of World War

I, had embarked on no real offensive actions when the bulk of German forces were in action in Poland. Though the British Expeditionary Force kept itself busy with many of the mindless chores that only the services can invent, they were at least busy; the French troops, however, sat in the Maginot Line and its pill-box extensions along the Belgian border. Their officers went on long weekends in Paris and the soldiers failed to practise the skills they had learned as conscripts.

In 1940 the French had been

immobilised by ruptured communications and supply lines, and by orders which arrived too late to affect a constantly changing situation. In 1944, despite five years experience of war, the Germans found themselves in much the same situation. It was only the training and discipline of their soldiers, and the fact that they could trade space for time which prevented their collapse. In 1940 a Panzer column had only to drive 200 or 300 miles and it had captured enough towns and territory to make further resistance pointless in countries as small as Holland or Belgium, whilst France was cut off from her industries in the north-east.

Air power was again a major factor in the fighting in 1944, but the Germans had one disadvantage which never beset the Allies even at the nadir of their fortunes. The overall commander of the *Wehrmacht* was Adolf Hitler, a man who in 1940 had demonstrated a surprising grasp of the tactical possibilities of paratroops and glider-borne infantry, and who had supported Manstein's novel reverse Schlieffen plan. However, by 1944 the *Fuehrer* was a prematurely old man, with a brain addled by the crude medication of his personal physician, Dr Morell. Hitler insisted that no ground was to be given up, and also that he direct operations, even those of a very local nature involving quite small forces.

After the war Rundstedt said that the Ardennes offensive 'was planned in all its details, including formations involved, time schedules, objectives and so on, by the *Fuehrer* and his staff. All counter-proposals were rejected. Under such circumstances, there could be little faith in its success. Even during the attack the Supreme Command conducted the operations by means of liaison officers and direct wireless orders to the armies involved.'

Over-control

Earlier, in the counter-attack on the American break-out at St Lô in July 1944 Hitler had taken personal control. Blumentritt recalls: 'OKW settled the precise divisions which were to be used and which were therefore to be taken out of the line as soon as possible. The exact limits of the sector in which the attack was to take place were laid down, as well as the routes to be taken and even the villages the troops were to pass through. These plans were all made in Berlin on large-scale maps and the opinions of the

Above left: An MG 34 machine gunner. The Germans made excellent use of their automatic weapons, and were especially skilled in the location of machine guns for defensive work.
Left: German infantry rush across a road in the Ardennes to the cover on the far side. The man nearest to the camera appears to be armed with a captured American M1 carbine. Although German infantry had been good at the beginning of the war, the later conscription of old men and boys had reduced the standard.

commanding generals in France were neither asked for nor encouraged.'

Problems of tactical doctrine were not confined to the misty heights of the Eagle's Nest in Obersalzburg. Rommel and Rundstedt disagreed about the way the defence of the French coastline should be conducted in the event of the Allied invasion. Rundstedt, with a wealth of experience of mobile war in the East, proposed the conventional tactic of letting the Allies get a lodgement, and then moving in with his tanks to crush them against their beach-head. There were precedents for this concept: Anzio had been a near disaster for the Allies. Rommel, however, had been able to appreciate the enemy's growing air power and knew that movement by day would be impossible – even for single vehicles, as he himself discovered when he narrowly escaped death when his car was shot up by fighters soon after the invasion. Rommel maintained that the invasion must be stopped on the beaches – he had the precedent of the abortive Anglo-Canadian raid on Dieppe. Inevitably the two commanders temporised and resources were split, the armour (which could only be used after it had received clearance from Hitler) was held in reserve inland and lost heavily in its approach march to the beach-heads. The Allies were able to get ashore in reasonable order and the only place where Rommel's theory was vindicated was at Omaha beach where due to a series of disastrous coincidences the German defences were largely undamaged and manned by a fresh unit.

No new *matériel*

In 1944 and 1945 the Germans were also low in vital raw materials, fuel and men. In 1940 their tank crews were highly trained: some had seen action in Spain, and most were blooded in Poland. They were cross-trained so that a driver could serve as a gunner, or a radio-operator as a driver, if one of the crew became a casualty. In 1944 their Panzer divisions had been worn down in the East, and while there were still some exceptional crews like that of *Hauptsturmfuehrer* Wittman's Tiger, the average age and training of many crews had now decreased. Part of the problem was that the Allied air attacks on Germany's petrochemical industry had reduced her stocks of fuel so that little could be used for training. Indeed one of the main local objectives of the troops engaged in the Ardennes offensive was the capture of American fuel stocks. It was this lack of fuel that crippled many of the heavily armoured and armed tanks that were produced in the latter part of the war. But it was not only the tank crews that suffered in quality. The change in Germany's fortunes was more noticeable in her infantry. The Atlantic Wall, which propaganda films showed as a massive concrete barrier garrisoned by alert young soldiers and tough veterans, was a fraud. While in the Pas de Calais a wide range of emplacements had been built, elsewhere the bulk of the defences were still incomplete.

Above: The Germans placed great faith in the fixed defences known as the 'Atlantic Wall'. They lacked the men and *matériel*, however, to build these in sufficient depth along the likely landing-beaches, and lacked the mobile reserves necessary to push back the Allies once they had broken inland from the beaches. Moreover, without air cover the German army could not move the reserves it did possess without prohibitive losses in daylight.

Left: An American M4 Sherman medium tank, victim of a forest gully. Although qualitatively inferior to the best German tanks, Allied armour was available in large quantities, and later in the war was handled with some imagination. The Allies also did not have the fuel problem that so bedevilled the Germans.

Some of the soldiers were elderly members of 'Stomach and Ear' or 'White Bread' Battalions, units formed largely of men with disorders which required special diets or medication. Divisions which had been exhausted and used up on the Eastern Front were rotated back to France and the West for rest and refitting. Until the summer of 1944 the West, with the exception of Italy, remained a soft posting, while the East became increasingly a one-way journey.

The Germans won in the West in 1940 because they were able to assemble their tanks under a friendly sky. Their opposition could not afford to lose ground, but was inadequately equipped both in tactical doctrine and *matériel* to defend it. The Germans lost in 1944 for almost the same reasons: they no longer controlled the skies, their men were physically unfit and insufficiently trained, but their chief disadvantage was that they were tied by inflexible orders from Hitler.

The Campaign in Russia, from Minsk to Stalingrad

A column of prisoners wends way back towards the rear, an from which very few of these unfortunate men was ever to return.

The Eastern Front, June 1941 – February 1943

At the time of its inception in June 1941, Germany's invasion of Soviet Russia was the largest military undertaking ever attempted, and was exceeded in scope later in the war only by the Russian riposte from the middle of 1943. Operation 'Barbarossa', as the German invasion was code-named, was the logical conclusion of a major portion of Hitler's racial, political and economic thinking. Russia must be dismembered so that the 'Slavic sub-humans' might be put in their correct place as underlings of the master-race, so that communism might be stamped out as a threat to national-socialism, and so that the German race might possess the necessary *Lebensraum* or living space in the east, together with its enormous potential in foodstuffs and industrial raw materials, not to mention oil. As always, this last item was well to the front of all Hitler's thinking.

The need to invade Russia had always been with Hitler, and although he had declared that a two-front war was anathema to him, planning for 'Barbarossa' began in December 1940, before Great Britain had been driven into defeat. The idea of an invasion filled the German general staff with foreboding, but detailed planning progressed through a series of basic plans until the definitive version, for implementation in May 1941, emerged. As a result of Hitler's last-minute insistence on the conquest of Yugoslavia and Greece, the launch-date of the offensive had to be put back from 25 May to 22 June; the month's delay was to have disastrous consequences for the German invaders late in 1941.

The final plan called for a major drive into western Russia in three prongs, eached formed by a complete army group. In the north, starting from East Prussia, Field-Marshal Ritter von Leeb's Army Group 'North' of two armies and Hoepner's 4th *Panzergruppe* was to advance through the Baltic states and take Leningrad, the spiritual capital of communism. (On Leeb's northern flank, Mannerheim's Finnish forces would drive south towards Leningrad through Karelia, and Falkenhorst's Army of Norway, with some Finnish troops, would seize the Murmansk–Leningrad railway.) In the centre, starting from northern Poland, Field-Marshal Fedor von Bock's Army Group 'Centre' of two armies with Guderian's 2nd and Hoth's 3rd *Panzer-gruppen* was to advance on Moscow, the administrative hub of the communist world. In the south, starting from southern Poland and from Rumania, Field-Marshal Gerd von Rundstedt's Army Group 'South' of four armies and Kleist's 1st *Panzergruppe* was to advance on Kiev and the River Dniepr to destroy all Russian forces between the Pripet marshes and the Black Sea. Thus the main strategic moves

were decided. So were the tactics – similar to those employed against the West in 1940, with the armoured forces encircling the Russian armies in vast, fast-moving pincers, and the following infantry mopping up, leaving the armour to press on again. What had not been fixed, however, was the grand strategic objective of the campaign. This mattered little to the fighting troops, as they had their objectives, but it reflected on the lack of thought by Hitler and his staff generals. All that was envisaged was that once Moscow had fallen, the Russians would capitulate, and the Germans could consolidate on a line running basically from Astrakhan on the Caspian Sea to Archangel in the Arctic. No thought was given to the fact that Russia might not capitulate, but fight on from the enormous tracts of land that lay beyond Hitler's immediate objectives. This lack of concrete, objective planning was to bedevil the 162 German and satellite divisions involved in the invasion.

Too far forward

To meet any invasion from the west, the Russian armies defending the German, Polish, Hungarian and Rumanian frontiers were divided into three major groupings, designated by the Russians as Fronts. In Western terminology these would be called army groups. In the north was Colonel-General F. I. Kuznetsov's North-West Front of 24 divisions defending the Baltic states and the approaches to Leningrad. In the centre was Marshal Semyon Timoshenko's Western Front of 38 divisions defending the area between the southern border of Lithuania and the Pripet marshes. In the south was Marshal Semyon Budenny's South-West Front of 72 divisions defending the area between the Pripet marshes and the Black Sea. These forces were well supplied with *matériel*, although much of it except the artillery was obsolescent. Although the Russians deployed about the same number of men in the forward areas as the Germans were to use, the tactical

The map shows the disposition of the belligerents in Operation 'Barbarossa', 22 June 1941. Hitler's master plan was to prove a failure largely through its own weaknesses and not so much through the unexpected strength of the Russians. The main striking force was positioned in the centre, opposite Moscow, but it was to be dissipated during the campaign when the two Panzer groups were sent to aid Army Groups 'North' and 'South' before resuming their advance on the Russian capital. This delay proved fatal to the German chances of success. Initial victories turned to defeat as the German armies came to a standstill against the Soviet determination. What had seemed certain victory, as German troops made their way with astonishing speed across Russian territory, was turned sour by mistakes and painful by the cold.

disposition of the forces was poor, being too far forward, with insufficient reserves echeloned in depth to check German breakthroughs. Russian leadership was also poor, many formations having lost their leaders in the purges of the late 1930s. The new leaders had been pushed up the ladder of command very quickly, and many lacked the skills and abilities to command large formations in the type of mobile warfare that was to take place between June and November 1941. Russia's great strengths, however, lay in the size of the nation, and the enormity of the manpower resources she could call upon. And although the major portions of the Red Army were deployed in western Russia to meet the invasion, there were still powerful forces in reserve behind Moscow and in Siberia. The nature of the state, with its all-powerful communist control, also meant that the national effort could be devoted to the war to the exclusion of all else. This last, combined with the stubborn defence of the ordinary soldiers, was to prove Russia's salvation.

The German offensive opened on 22 June, and immediately achieved enormous success. The Russians had been taken completely by surprise and were driven back in disarray. Although some units fought with great determination, the general collapse of the Russian forces left such units to be surrounded and annihilated. Russian losses in *matériel* were extremely heavy, especially in aircraft, guns and tanks. It is perhaps worth nothing here that the Russians had known of the obsolescence of much of their *matériel*, and several new types of aircraft and tank were being rushed into production. The destruction of the obsolete *matériel* was therefore something of an advantage to the Russians, forcing them to accelerate further the introduction of new weapons. One of these, the T-34 medium tank, was to prove a superlative weapon, and a considerable shock to the Germans.

In the first weeks of the campaign, the German pushed on victoriously along the whole length of the 2,000-mile front. But

Above left: **The German armed forces stream into Soviet Russia after 22 June 1941. As with the German overrunning of France and the Low Countries, popular opinion has it that the Germans could only have defeated the numerically stronger Soviet forces by the use of vast mechanised forces. And while there is indeed an element of truth in this assertion, in that the main striking forces, the *Panzergruppen,* were mechanised, this photograph of a mixed horse and motor logistic convoy puts the lie to the popular impression. Moreover, it was often a bone of contention between the different commanders that the foot infantry, supplied often by horse convoys, could not keep up with the tank forces and their motorised supply columns.**

Left: **A German regimental command post outside a knocked-out Russian bunker in the Ukraine.**

the nature of Russia gradually led to the slowing down of the advance: as they pushed on the troops became increasingly exhausted by the sheer length of their marches, vehicles and tanks began to wear out in the heat and poor conditions under which they had to operate, and the shape of Russia, widening towards the east, diluted the concentration of troops along the front. Nevertheless, the Germans scored some remarkable victories: by mid-July Army Group 'Centre' had trapped a Russian pocket around Minsk, capturing nearly 330,000 men, 2,500 tanks and 1,500 guns; driving on from Minsk, the two *Panzergruppen* of Army Group 'Centre' then trapped in Smolensk another 310,000 men, 3,200 tanks and 3,000 guns by 5 August. Although the German supply services at this time were under the utmost strain to keep up with the front-line forces, they were just managing to do so, and the strategic objectives of the campaign looked attainable before the onset of winter. But now Hitler made a major blunder.

Different speeds

Army Group 'Centre', principally by virtue of its two *Panzergruppen,* was advancing faster than either Army Group 'North' or Army Group 'South'. Hitler became increasingly worried about this, as these latter groups were to seize the all-important Ukraine and open up the way to the oil-producing Caucasus, and to take Leningrad respectively. He therefore removed the two *Panzergruppen* and one army from Army Group 'Centre' despite Bock's objections, to strengthen the two flank army groups. At first the changes in strategic direction proved useful. Army Group 'South', with the aid of Guderian's armour, trapped some 665,000 Russians in the Kiev pocket. Kiev itself fell on 20 September. In the north Leeb's army group moved on towards Leningrad, investing the city in October, whilst Rundstedt's forces reached the River Don on 15 October, threatening the major cities of Kharkov and Rostov. By this time the autumn rains had started, and the German advance lost further momentum. At this point Hitler once again changed his mind about the campaign's strategic objectives, reinstating Moscow as the primary target. The forces taken from Army Group 'Centre' were now given back, and Bock was ordered to take Moscow at all costs. The army group pressed on, and trapped another vast horde of Russians, 650,000-strong, in a pocket at Vyazma between 30 September and 7 October. By 20 October Army Group 'Centre' had reached Mozhaisk, only 40 miles from Moscow.

But by now the German armies had all but shot their bolt. They had advanced deep into Russia against strong opposition, and most units, both infantry and armour, were down to below half strength in men and equipment. The autumn rains, which were to turn into the winter snows of one of the coldest winters in living memory, also hampered the German advance. No provision had been made for winter clothing, it having been anticipated that the campaign would be over by this time,

and the men were beginning to suffer the torments of the cold. Russian resistance, moreover, was strengthening as reserves from the east were called in and the lessons of the early days of the campaign were absorbed. Finally, in General Georgi Zhukov, newly appointed to command the defence of Moscow, the Russians had placed in high command one of the greatest generals to serve any nation during World War II. All along the front Russian defences were beginning to hold, and in the south the Russians had even launched a major counter-offensive, driving the Germans back from Rostov on 15 November. Hitler began to lose patience with his commanders, and Rundstedt was replaced by General W. von Reichenau on 1 December. In the north Leeb was

Above: Germany's amazingly successful drive into the western parts of Soviet Russia. On paper this appears, and in fact was, a remarkable feat by the German and satellite armies. But a map such as this cannot reveal the failings in the planning and execution of the German plan: the time wasted in the conquests of Yugoslavia and Greece, thereby delaying the start of Operation 'Barbarossa' by three vital weeks, and the lack of strategic planning, best exemplified by the failure to fix definite strategic objectives, by Hitler and his military advisers.
Right: A PzKpfw III medium tank for which all did not go well.

making no further progress against Leningrad, and in the centre Bock, later replaced by Kluge as commander of Army Group 'Centre', pushed slowly on towards Moscow, getting within 25 miles of the city by 5 December. Hitler now decided on a wholesale reshuffle of his high command. Leeb was replaced by General von Kuechler; General von Brauchitsch was sacked as commander-in-chief of the army, Hitler himself taking over this position and controlling operations in the East by radio; and the OKH under Halder was restricted to Eastern Front operations, responsibility for other theatres being allocated to an enlarged OKW under Keitel.

But now it was the turn of the Russians. Despite the appalling difficulties of the Russian situation before Moscow, Zhukov had managed to prepare a counter-offensive, which broke upon the Germans on 6 December. The main strength of the counter-offensive lay with the fresh divisions called in from Siberia after reports from the spy Richard Sorge in Tokyo that the Japanese had no plans to invade Russia from the east. The Russian offensive broke upon the stunned Germans at Kalinin, north of Moscow; at Tula, south of Moscow; and at Izyum, in the Ukraine. The German generals, shaken by the very fact and scope of the Russian stroke, were all for falling back to defence lines that could be improvised in their rear. Hitler, however, would hear no suggestion of retreat. He feared that in such climatic conditions a retreat might become a rout, and ordered the armies to hold on where they were at any cost. Although they were pushed back slowly, the Germans did manage to hold on near their furthest advances until the Russians called off the offensive. Never was one of Hitler's decisions more justified. He had saved the German armies in the East from almost certain rout in this instance. But the unfortunate consequence was that Hitler acquired an unshakable belief in the need to hold ground at any cost. This was to prove disastrous to the Germans in later years, when orderly retreat might have saved vast numbers of men.

Balance of losses

Thus finished the first stage of the German campaign in Russia. Russia herself had lost some three million men, and the Germans 800,000. But whereas the Russians could replace their losses, the Germans could not. And although the Russians had lost vast amounts of *matériel*, they were able to replace it with more modern equipment, produced by the factories that had been moved back from western Russia to behind the Urals in the weeks that their troops had gained by their huge losses. At the same time the Russian commanders had learned how to fight the right type of warfare. Poor commanders had been weeded out, and the new generation of able officers had moved in to teach the new lessons to their men.

The Russian counter-offensive continued against determined German defence until the end of February, making some progress

everywhere except around Leningrad and in Finland. The spring thaw, with its attendant mud, halted operations in March, by which time both sides were exhausted. The Germans were the first to recover. On 8 May 1942 their reinforced armies went over to the offensive, in an effort to recover the losses to the Russin winter offensive. Considerable advances were made, the Russians suffering heavy casualties, and once again revealing themselves to be tactically inferior to the Germans. In the far south of the German front, the 11th Army (Manstein), swept through that part of the Crimea it had not cleared the previous year and laid siege to Sevastopol. The clearing of the Crimea cost the Russians 150,000 men, and the loss of Sevastopol on 2 July another 100,000.

These offensives had only been preliminaries to the main summer offensive, which started on 28 June. Under the command of Bock, who had taken over from Reichenau in January, Army Group 'South' drove eastwards from Kursk to take Voronezh on the River Don on 6 July. In the command reshuffle that followed this victory, Army Group 'South' was divided into Army Group 'A' in the south of the sector, under General W. von List,

and Army Group 'B' in the north of the sector, under General M. F. von Weichs. These two army groups were to co-operate in clearing the River Don and River Donets valleys, take Rostov and then Stalingrad, and finally swing south to take the oil-producing areas of the Caucasus. But on 13 July Hitler once again changed his mind, again for the worse. Instead of the concerted drive by the two army groups, which stood a good chance of success, the *Fuehrer* decided that each of the groups should undertake half the offensive independently: Army Group 'B' would head for Stalingrad, and Army Group 'A' for the Caucasus. In fact neither of the two groups was strong enough for the task entrusted to it. Apart from the logistic difficulties raised by the new plan, there was also the strategic disadvantage that the further each group advanced, the greater would be the gap between the two forces, inviting the Russians to take either one or both in flank.

The new two-prong offensive started immediately, with some success. Army Group 'B' moved south-east on Stalingrad, but its lack of resources allowed most of the Russian forces which would otherwise had been destroyed to escape to the east and fight again. The advance was

still making good progress when Hitler decided to reallocate Hoth's 4th *Panzerarmee* to Army Group 'A', which was making only limited advances in the Caucasus. Despite the loss of most of its armoured forces Army Group 'B', in the form of General F. Paulus' 6th Army, reached the River Volga above Stalingrad on 23 August.

Stalingrad

In the south Army Group 'A' had at first also made good progress, taking Rostov on 23 July and pressing on towards the Caspian Sea. Reinforced by the 4th *Panzerarmee*, Army Group 'A' at one time got to within 75 miles of the Caspian. But then the 4th *Panzerarmee* was once again moved, back to help in the struggle for Stalingrad, and the understrength army group was left to struggle on hopelessly. At the same time the theatre reserve, Manstein's 11th Army, was shipped off to Leningrad in the far north. Halder and List, who had dared voice objections to the moves, were both sacked. Hitler himself took over command of Army Group 'A' by radio.

The 4th *Panzerarmee* had been given back to Army Group 'B' as its the latter's progress towards Stalingrad had slowed to

a halt. With the help of the armoured force, the attack once again got under way, and the Germans reached Stalingrad. The Russians were determined to hold the city, and perhaps the fiercest house-to-house battle of the war swiftly developed, the Germans gradually inching forward with great casualties against fanatical resistance. The Russians, meanwhile, were preparing their own counterstroke. This broke on 19 November, once the temperature had fallen far enough to make tankable ice out of the autumn mud that had made movement so difficult for the last month. Under the command of Zhukov, the Russians launched a massive pincer movement, making full use of the gap between Army Groups 'A' and 'B'. The Germans were completely overwhelmed by the size and ferocity of the Russian attack, and Army Group 'B' fell back, leaving the 6th Army cut off in Stalingrad. Weichs urged Paulus to fight his way out, but Hitler insisted that the 6th Army hold on to Stalingrad whilst a relief force fought its way through. Meanwhile, Goering assured Hitler, his *Luftwaffe* could keep the beleaguered garrison supplied. This proved a completely idle boast. The counterstroke was organised by Manstein, who managed to get within 35 miles of

Above left: A mass grave, dug by impressed Russian labour. The war on the Eastern Front was notably costly in casualties for both sides, especially the Russian. But whereas the Russians could call up more and more men to replace these losses, often throwing new conscripts into battle with little or no training, the Germans and their allies soon reached the point where their losses were constantly outstripping their replacements. From this point final Russian success was almost inevitable.

Above: German PzKpfw III medium tanks rumble through the deserted outskirts of Rostov, a major Russian city on the Don river. The loss of this town, with its numerous industrial plants, was a serious blow to the Russians.

Stalingrad on 19 December. Manstein urged Paulus to fight his way out to the relief force, but again Paulus listened to Hitler and refused to do so. It was now only a matter of time before the city fell to the Russians. Paulus and his men fought on with extraordinary courage and determination, but their lack of fuel and food, combined with another hard winter, gradually took their toll. On 2 February 1943, Paulus surrendered with 93,000 men. In all, Hitler's ill-advised bifurcated summer offensive had cost the Germans 300,000 men and 1,000 tanks, all of which Germany could not adequately replace.

In the Caucasus Army Group 'A', now under the command of Kleist, had not been able to progress, and the Russians had finally been able to drive it back. With the end in Stalingrad Army Group 'B' ceased to exist, being replaced by Manstein's Army Group 'Don', formed in November 1942. Army Group 'A' had fallen back at the end of 1942, the 1st *Panzerarmee* joining Army Group 'Don' and the rest of the group forming a defensive line between the Black Sea and the Sea of Azov. All along the southern part of the Russo-German front the Soviet forces were putting great pressure on the Germans and their satellites whilst preparing their own major offensive.

The advance into the Caucasus and the taking of Stalingrad marked the high-water point of the German war against Russia, and the defeat of the 6th Army in Stalingrad the beginning of the ebb. Although the Germans tried to wrest the strategic offensive away from the Russians at the Battle of Kursk in July 1943, from the moment of Paulus' capitulation in Stalingrad it can fairly be said that the Germans could not prevail over the Russians in the East.

Above: A German machine gunner uses the frozen body of a Russian soldier near Stalingrad to rest the bipod of his gun on. The fighting for the city of Stalingrad reached heights of bitterness seldom if ever again reached in World War II.

Above right: A scene of devastation typical of the war on the Eastern Front.

Right: A good example of the *matériel* problems affecting the German army: an artillery unit, with some of its guns drawn by horses, and others by the excellent *Schwerer Zugkraftwagen* 12t prime-mover.

Field-Marshal Günther Hans von Kluge

In 1942 Kluge was made head of Army Group 'Centre', and the lines he developed proved good defences against all the Russian drives until 1944.

On 7 July 1944 the *Fuehrer* gave Kluge the thankless task, up till then faced by Rundstedt, of Commander-in-Chief West. Hitler ordered that there be no more retreats. So under the thumb of Hitler was Kluge that he tried to obey this stupid ordinance, only to be removed from his post on 17 August in favour of Model.

On the day after this, Kluge committed suicide by taking poison: he had been implicated in, but had not been party to, the July Plot.

Known as 'clever Hans', Kluge was a brilliant staff officer and energetic, though traditional, field commander. He was non-Nazi rather than anti-Nazi, but politically naive.

Guenther von Kluge was born in Posen (Poznan) on 30 October 1882, and joined the army as an artillery officer. During World War I Kluge served in this capacity, but also learned to fly. As a result he always realised the full implications of air power on modern war.

Kluge remained in the army after the defeat of Germany in World War I. By October 1935 he had risen to the rank of lieutenant-general, and commanded VI Corps in Muenster. His command was made up of two infantry divisions and one frontier zone command. A year later, his corps had received an extra infantry division and Kluge himself had been promoted general.

Kluge remained with VI Corps until he lost his command in the purges after the fall of General Fritsch, the commander-in-chief of the army. Later, however, Kluge was recalled, and in January 1939 commanded the 6th Army Group in Hanover, with three corps under him.

In the invasions of Poland and France, Kluge led the 4th Army, and was promoted field-marshal for his services on 19 July 1940.

Kluge again led the 4th Army in the attack on Russia in June 1941, and was deeply involved in the great struggle for Moscow in November and December of the same year.

Field-Marshal Günther Hans von Kluge

Operation 'Barbarossa' was the code-name for the German invasion of Russia, which was to be a three-pronged advance, aiming at Leningrad in the north, Moscow in the middle and the Caucasus in the south. The ultimate objective was to occupy within the shortest possible time practically the whole of eastern Europe from Archangel to Astrakhan. The Germans would ultimately fail in this objective, but the first weeks of the invasion were to prove absolutely disastrous for the Russians – they lost thousands of tanks, many planes and hundreds of thousands of troops taken prisoner.

The Russians were not psychologically or technically prepared for the German attack launched on 22 June 1941. Some formations were hardly at paper strength and many units were away from their positions on summer training exercises. Stationed near the Russo-German border were the forces of the Western District under the command of General D. G. Pavlov and comprising the 3rd, 4th and 10th Armies. After the outbreak of hostilities, this became known as the West Front. Pavlov's forces were deployed almost wholly in the Białystok salient in a line running south from the Latvian frontier to Voldava on the fringe of the Pripet marshes.

On 22 June Pavlov's forces are thought to have consisted of six mechanised corps, one cavalry corps and 24 rifle divisions divided between the three armies, with further mechanised and a cavalry corps in reserve. It is difficult to be certain of the exact forces, as secrecy still covers some aspects of Russia's participation in the war. The Red Army had a large number of tanks, but most of these were obsolete and a shortage of spare parts meant that a great many of them were not operational. The new tanks, KV and T-34, were not yet available, although they would prove a match for the Germans later. The production rate of guns, mortars and automatic weapons was very slow, with the production of ammunition lagging even further behind. Radio equipment was also in short supply and functioned poorly. The vast majority of army planes were obsolete.

Another serious deficiency was the absence of motorised transport. A very large number of guns were therefore drawn by horses or tractors.

Many objectives

Very few Russian officers had had direct experience of warfare and many had only lately been drafted to replace the thousands of officers purged during 1937–38. The training of tank and air crews had been badly neglected.

The German army on the Soviet frontier was divided up into three main army groups – 'North', 'Centre' and 'South'. We are concerned with Army Group 'Centre' under the command of Field-Marshal von Bock, which was stationed in northern and central Poland between Lublin and Suwalki and comprising the 4th and 9th Armies and 2nd and 3rd *Panzergruppen*. Altogether, Army Group 'Centre' totalled 49 divisions including six motorised, nine Panzer and one cavalry divisions. In addition, Field-Marshal Kesselring's *Luftlotte* 2 was assigned to Bock, a powerful force with approximately 1,000 planes. The mission entrusted to Army Group 'Centre' was to encircle and then to destroy the enemy in Belorussia by way of two deep thrusts, one in the north from the area of Suwalki and one further south along the northern edge of the Pripet marshes from Brest-Litovsk. The 9th Army, under Colonel-General Strauss with General Hoth's 3rd *Panzergruppe* was to make the northern thrust, while Field-Marshal

Men of the leading elements of the first German forces to reach the key town of Vitebsk pause for refreshment. Apart from the speed at which they had to move in an effort to keep up with the armoured forces, the infantry also found that the distances they had to cover, combined with the intense summer heat of 1941, forced them to the point of exhaustion. Moreover, an extreme winter followed, exacerbating the troubles of the men on the ground.

Guenther von Kluge's 4th Army of 21 infantry divisions with General Guderian's 2nd *Panzergruppe* comprising five Panzer, one cavalry and three motorised infantry divisions would execute the southern pincer movement. Both the *Panzergruppen* were under control of the infantry commanders.

The two Panzer groups were to drive eastwards and join at Minsk, the Belorussian capital, lying some 250 miles from the Russo-German frontier. Part of the infantry was to follow the Panzers to Minsk, whilst the rest was to make two shorter enveloping thrusts to the north and south of Białystok, meeting at a point on the Białystok-Minsk road about 100 miles from the frontier. The enemy would therefore be trapped inside two pockets, one inside the other, and was to be destroyed before the advance resumed to Smolensk.

A good start

Bock, however, disagreed with the order that the pincers should be closed at Minsk. He thought the primary objective should be Smolensk. He requested Brauchitsch and Halder at OKH to change the plan, but he had heard nothing definite when the offensive started, and so Guderian and Hoth set off on their armoured advances to the east uncertain of their first objective.

On the night of 19/20 June, the German armoured forces began arriving in the forests about three miles from the River Bug (which formed the frontier) in preparation for the invasion. Surprise was to be a very important factor and so the Germans were careful to hide themselves before battle commenced. Hitler's HQ was sited in the thick forest near Rastenburg in East Prussia.

Because he thought the Germans would not break the Nazi–Soviet Non-Aggression Pact, Stalin refused to believe there was anything sinister about the German troop movements. Stalin was in a difficult position here – if he took any preparatory measures, for example moving his troops on the border to defensive combat positions, this might give Hitler the 'evidence' for a German invasion, on the grounds that Russia had broken the non-aggression pact. Stalin stuck to this even though information concerning the invasion was received in Moscow, and, in the event, never was an army so ill-prepared to meet an invasion as was the Red Army on the eve of Operation '*Barbarossa*'.

On 22 June, Kesselring's *Luftflotte* 2 started a sustained and intensive bombing campaign of all Russian ground movements and cleared the skies of Russian planes. On this day alone, the Soviet Union lost 2,000 planes. The German planes attacked roads, grounded planes, tanks and fuel stores as well. German assault parties crossed land frontiers, achieving surprise almost everywhere, making a special effort to destroy Soviet communications and to isolate units from their staffs.

General Hermann Hoth and his 3rd *Panzergruppe* got off to a good start on their northern pincer movement. They travelled quickly through the forests of Augustow on the frontier. The left wing of the *Panzergruppe* cut the Russian 11th Army in two, captured Kaunas, the bridges of the Niemen intact and the city of Vilnyus on 24 June. A

counterattack by Soviet 11th Army's XII Mechanised Corps broke down, thus freeing the tanks to swing south and on towards Minsk. The right wing of the 3rd *Panzergruppe* drove back the Russian 3rd Army (General Kuznetsov) which had evacuated Grodno, and cut through its XI Mechanised Corps on its way to Lida and Volkovisk.

Further west, the Russian 10th Army was already threatened with encirclement. The *Luftwaffe* caught its VI Mechanised Corps in the open trying to counterattack. Its lines of retreat were being steadily narrowed and on 25 June, the 10th Army received permission to withdraw, but by this time Guderian had reached the outskirts of Minsk.

On 22 June the infantry of the German 4th Army attacked into Brest Litovsk while Guderian's Panzers bypassed the fortress, with XXIV Panzer Corps crossing the River Bug to the south of the town and XLVII Panzer Corps to the north. Some of the armour forded the 13-foot river by underwater wading – a technique developed for the proposed invasion of England. Brest Litovsk was the scene of much bloody fighting and the town held out until 29 June, causing heavy casualties to the German 45th Division. Meanwhile, Guderian's Panzer thrust went as planned, his rate of advance proving quite spectacular. He was troubled only by XIV Mechanised Corps of the Soviet 4th Army, which engaged the 18th Panzer Division of the left-flanking XLVII Panzer Corps in battle near Pruzhany. The

Kluge—the Minsk Pocket

Above: A PzKpfw III medium tank of the 18th Panzer Division makes light of a river ford deep in Russia. As with the campaign in the West in 1940, the Germans found that the opposition had numerical and at times qualitative superiority in armour, but that the carefully considered and forcefully implemented German tank tactics were more than sufficient to turn the tide in favour of the Nazi offensive.

Left: A scene typical of the first days of Operation *'Barbarossa'* as German armour (PzKpfw II and III tanks, SdKfz 250 and 251 halftracks) stream across open country.

country here was well suited to armoured warfare. By 26 June, Slutsk, 60 miles due south of Minsk, had been taken by XXIV Panzer Corps, although the Russians trying to break out of Białystok fired heavily on its left flank.

The Russians apparently did not see the threat of the pincers closing at Minsk. They were in a state of utter confusion and shock. Pavlov's West Front, deployed close to the frontier in the Białystok salient, seemed to be just waiting to be trapped. When Pavlov did see the danger to the forward elements of his 3rd and 10th Armies from the shorter pincer movement by the German infantry, he ordered all the army and front reserves forward, thus leaving the Minsk area practically undefended and making the task of the German armour that much easier.

The Russians stood and fought bravely where they were, encountering the Germans head-on. There was no co-ordinated defence, partly because of the breakdown in communications. Defence arrangements were left to the initiative of the local commanders and the tenacity of the forward troops, who held on grimly in the undermanned and incomplete fortifications. In the early days of the invasion, there were no orders or directions except the standing order to attack the enemy whenever and wherever he was encountered.

Russian failure

A two-day armoured and cavalry counter-offensive by VI and XI Mechanised Corps started on 24 June, under General Boldin, the Deputy Commander of the Western Front. The Russians attacked from the area of Grodno to north-east of Białystok, against the infantry of the German 9th Army, which was moving south-east in the shorter pincer movement. This was beaten off easily, however, by German infantry and anti-tank gunners, and Soviet losses were heavy. On 26 June, Hoth's 3rd *Panzergruppe* arrived 18 miles north of Minsk, and Guderian received orders to turn north with the majority of his force and join Hoth and so close the pocket. Guderian's right-flanking XXIV Corps was permitted to continue its drive to the east towards Bobruysk on the River Berezina and on to the Dniepr.

Whether the Panzers should wait at Minsk for the infantry or continue their fantastic easterly thrust was a cause of great friction. Guderian, a tank expert, had absorbed the teaching of Liddell Hart on the importance of speed, mobility and firepower. He saw the tank as a separate arm, not part of the infantry. His commander, Kluge, held the opposite view. He disliked seeing the tanks so far ahead and would rather use them to contain the Russian pockets, waiting to advance further until the encirclement battle was completed. Guderian considered containing the enemy pockets to be the infantry's task, and that the armour must be mobile. For tanks to be stationary was to be vulnerable.

Kluge, therefore, was happy that the pincers were to close on Minsk, whereas Guderian felt frustrated that his advance was slowed down. He and Kluge argued over the formations Guderian filtered off from the pocket and sent on to the Dniepr. Kluge's

counter-order conveniently got lost. Hitler agreed with Kluge and was worried whether the pincers should close before Minsk, at Novogrodek, so that the thousands of Russians already trapped at Białystok should not escape, but he was persuaded that Minsk as the objective would result in even more Russians trapped. And so the pocket was sealed on 28 June after Guderian's tanks had been involved in a sharp clash with the Russian 13th (Reinforcement) Army.

Guderian's drive to Minsk has been called one of the most spectacular marches in history.

Inside this trap 20 Soviet divisions were encircled. By nightfall on 28 June, the marching infantry of the German 9th and 4th Armies had joined up and closed the smaller pocket. Thus the Białystok pocket was completely cut off from the larger Novogrodek pocket to the east. As a result of this catastrophe, Pavlov was recalled and shot.

By 3 July, the enemy in the Białystok pocket had surrendered, and by 9 July,

Top: Part of the huge German bag of Russian prisoners shuffles back towards the rear.

Above: Two-way traffic during the German advance towards the great Russian city of Smolensk.

Right: A German 3.7-cm anti-tank gun in action against Russian tanks outside Smolensk.

328,000 Russian prisoners were 'in the bag' and at least 2,500 Soviet tanks had been knocked out or captured, together with 1,500 guns.

Kluge was probably right in maintaining that the pocket should be closed at Minsk. Had the Panzers raced on to Smolensk, the infantry would have been way behind and would have been hard-pressed to seal off such a gigantic pocket. Kluge and Guderian did not get on at all, and the fact that no explicit written orders for the conduct of the operation were provided only made relations between them worse.

Field-Marshal Fedor von Bock

invasion of Russia, Bock received the command of Army Group 'Centre' on 1 April 1941. He held this command until 18 December 1941, when he and several other commanders who had incurred Hitler's disapproval as a result of the check before Moscow were dismissed.

Bock's final command was Army Group 'South' in Russia from 18 January to 15 July 1942, when he was put on the retired list.

For almost the next three years Bock, who had been promoted field-marshal on 19 July 1940 after the successful conclusion of the French campaign, lived quietly in retirement. The 64-year old field-marshal was killed in an Allied air raid on Schleswig-Holstein on 4 May 1945, only a few days before the end of the war.

Although not an inspired military leader, Bock was in every way typical of the competent generals inherited by Hitler.

Fedor von Bock was born on 3 December 1880 in Kuestrin, and joined the crack 5th Regiment of Prussian Foot Guards. Bock served as a line officer during World War I and had a distinguished career culminating in the award, rare for junior officers, of Germany's highest decoration, the *Pour le Mérite*.

Bock was retained in the *Reichswehr* after World War I, involved principally with the intensive training of the few troops allowed that army by the Treaty of Versailles. In 1934 he was appointed to the command of the 2nd Infantry Division, and a year later to that of 3rd *Gruppenkommando*,

with its headquarters in Dresden. By the outbreak of war in 1939 Bock had risen further, to the command of the 1st *Heeresgruppe* (Army Group), with its headquarters located in Berlin.

In the war against Poland, Bock commanded Army Group 'North' up to 3 October 1939, when he was transferred to the West to take over Army Group 'B' in the proposed winter campaign against the Low Countries and France. Bock led his army group with great distinction when the campaign was launched in May 1940, and remained with this formation until 12 September 1940.

For Operation 'Barbarossa', the

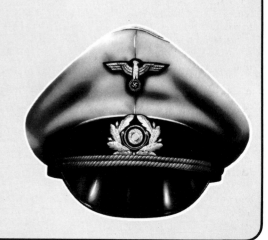

Field-Marshal Fedor von Bock

'Moscow is merely a geographical concept,' Hitler had said at the beginning of Operation 'Barbarossa'. He ordered that the main thrusts should be on Leningrad, 'the cradle of the Revolution', and on Kiev. Only after they had been isolated or destroyed would the men of Army Group 'Centre' drive for the Soviet capital. Yet before Kiev had been taken on 15 September, or Leningrad completely encircled on 8 September, Hitler ordered that units be switched to Army Group 'Centre' for its final drive. It seemed a logical move since Moscow was not only the capital of Russia, but also its communications hub and an emotional focus for the Soviet armies. By attacking Moscow Army Group 'Centre' would also be able to destroy the bulk of Russian forces which were sure to be concentrated in front of the capital.

Double pincer

The attack on Moscow, which bore the code-name 'Typhoon', could not be launched until 2 October for the Germans had to collect their forces. Bock's Army Group 'Centre' was reinforced to a strength of 78 divisions, with 7 Panzer and 4 motorised divisions in addition to the 7 and 5 of these divisions already in the group. On paper it looked a very powerful force, but by now these units were hardly up to strength. The tanks had been operating across the dusty tracks of European Russia, and not only had they been moving from west to east, but units like Guderian's 2nd *Panzerarmee* had had to travel north by road from the Ukraine and Hoepner's 3rd *Panzergruppe* had to drive down from the Leningrad front. The dust and heat, and the very poor condition of the roads had worn out the engines of many of the German tanks, and the inadequate communications with the west, based largely on a few overstretched railway lines, meant that insufficient spares had reached the front. The marching infantry, though footsore and dusty, were still reasonably up to strength.

Using a by now well-tried tactic, Bock was going to envelop the Russian forces opposite him in a double pincer movement. The

Russian forces, according to German intelligence, were the Bryansk Front under General Eremenko and the West Front under General Konev which between them contained 14 armies of 77 divisions, including six armoured and six cavalry.

Guderian opened the offensive in the south with his *Panzerarmee* and the men of the 2nd Army, on 30 September. In two days he drove 90 miles and captured Orel. XLVII Panzer Corps, following in his dust, swung north and captured Bryansk, linking up with units of the 2nd Army. The Ger-

mans surrounded two pockets to the north and south of the city, and though these surrendered on 25 October, strong elements of the northern pocket, composed of the Soviet 50th Army, managed to slip eastwards through the woodland and marshes.

On 20 October the 4th Army and 4th *Panzergruppe*, concentrated near Roslavl, struck the left wing of Konev's West Front. A day later Hoepner's tanks swung northeast and punched through the 'Vyazma Defence Line'. While this thrust was in progress the 9th Army and 3rd *Panzergruppe*

A mixed armour-infantry team moves up towards an objective outside Moscow. Note the swastika flag draped over the turret of the tank from which the photograph was taken, placed there as an identification marking for ground-support aircraft. It was outside Moscow that the onset of the severe winter of 1941–42 caught the unprepared and tired German forces.

had started a drive to the east and south. On 18 October XL Panzer Corps of the 4th *Panzergruppe,* under General Stumme, linked up with advanced units of LVI Panzer Corps of the 3rd *Panzergruppe,* under General Schaal. They had captured the important rail link of Vyazma, and cut the Moscow highway, but more than this, they had encircled parts of four Soviet armies. Between them the Germans estimated that the Vyazma and Bryansk pockets had yielded 663,000 prisoners from 67 infantry divisions, six cavalry divisions and various armoured units, as well as 1,242 tanks and 5,412 guns. With the able support of his energetic subordinates Bock had scored a resounding victory – and moreover with their static defence plan the Russians had done much to contribute to their own defeat. On 7 October Russia's Marshal Zhukov was to recall that 'all roads to Moscow were in essence open'. However, a day earlier Guderian had noted in his war diary that the Germans had experienced the first snowfall of winter. The dusty roads had turned to a deep soft mud and the Panzers had churned to a temporary halt – it was an ominous foretaste of the rigours of a Russian winter.

Two days later the Chief of the Russian General Staff, Marshal Shaposhnikov, appointed a new commander of the West Front. General Zhukov, a tough ex-cavalry NCO of the Imperial Russian Army, was to become Russia's greatest general, and second only to Stalin the man who would destroy the German forces in the East.

Renewed attack

When Zhukov arrived Bock had become temporarily bogged down in the reduction of the Vyazma/Bryansk pockets, chiefly because the *rasputitsa* had set in. The *rasputitsa,* or 'season of bad roads', comes twice in Russia: in autumn and spring when the early snows and rain, or the melting snow of winter turn the dirt tracks of central Russia into rivers of mud.

On 14 October, however, the Germans got under way again and Hoth's 3rd *Panzergruppe* broke through the screening forces to the north and reached the 'Sea of Moscow', a reservoir 70 miles to the northwest of Moscow. When the news reached the capital, civilian morale plunged, and between 16 and 20 October, in the words of the official Soviet historian Samsonov, 'there were those who spread panic, abandoned their places of work and fled hastily from the city. There were traitors who took advantage of the situation to pillage Soviet property and to try to sap the strength of the Soviet state.'

Bock and Zhukov were now fighting a race with the winter. Bock did not realise as clearly as his Russian opponent what a Russian winter could mean, but he knew that time was running out. Now generals like Rundstedt and Leeb wanted to call a halt to the operations, but Bock, Brauchitsch and Halder argued that superior will-power would carry their troops to Moscow. Blumentritt recalls a conference of chiefs-of-staff which took place on 12 November at Orsha: the chiefs-of-staff of Army Groups 'North' and 'South' were against continuing

the attacks, but 'the Chief-of-Staff of Army "Centre", von Greiffenberg, took a more indefinite line, pointing out the risks but not expressing opposition to an advance. He was in a difficult position. Field-Marshal von Bock was a very capable soldier, but ambitious, and his eyes were focused on Moscow, which seemed so near.'

Whatever their views, the men of Army Group 'Centre' received their marching orders from Hitler. After protests from Kluge, they were ordered not to attempt to encircle Moscow and cut its railway links to the east, but were to occupy the capital. Blumentritt said that they were ordered to blow up the Kremlin 'to signalise the overthrow of Bolshevism'.

The final advance began on 16 November. The ground was now hard with winter

Top: German infantry advance up a street cleared of Russian defenders, still keeping cautiously to the sides lest any snipers might have been missed by the house-clearing parties.

Above: Tanks and infantry of *Panzergruppe* 'Reinhardt' in Kalinin, the most north-easterly point reached by the Germans in 1941.

Right: The German offensive to take Moscow, Operation *'Taifun'* or 'Typhoon'. At first progress was good, but then the Russian defence, stimulated by the presence of General Zhukov and fresh Siberian troops, forced it to a halt.

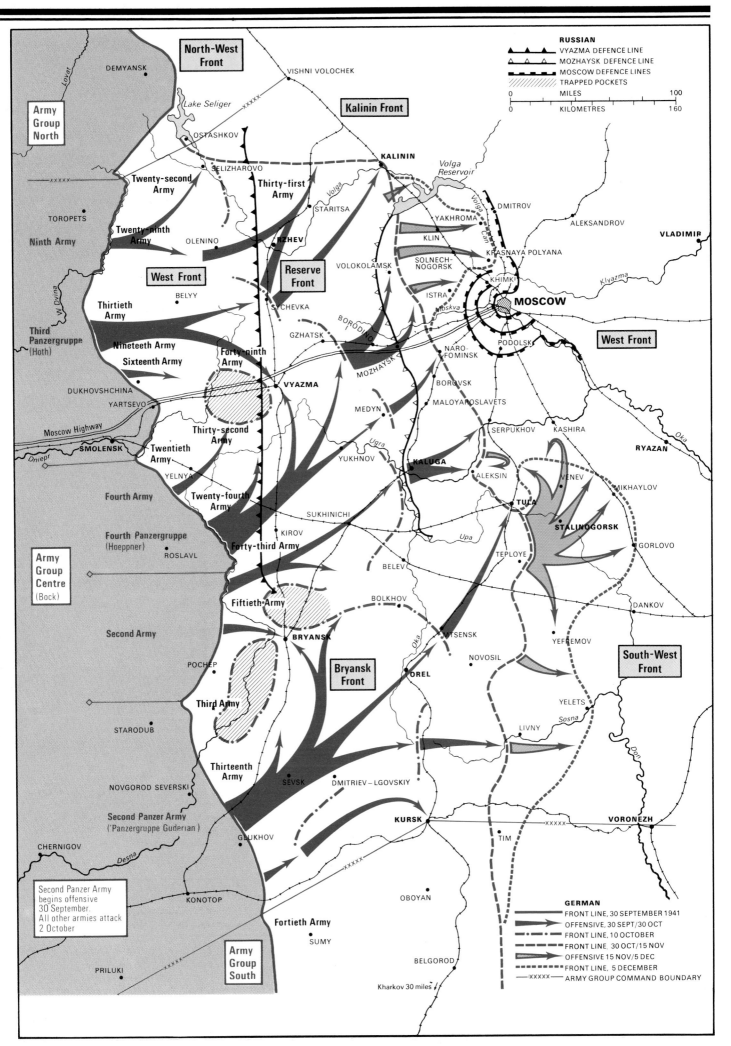

North-West Front

Kalinin Front

RUSSIAN
- VYAZMA DEFENCE LINE
- MOZHAYSK DEFENCE LINE
- MOSCOW DEFENCE LINES
- TRAPPED POCKETS

0   MILES   100
0   KILOMETRES   160

DEMYANSK

Lovat

Army Group North

Lake Seliger

OSTASHKOV

VISHNI VOLOCHEK

SELIZHAROVO

KALININ

Volga Reservoir

Volga Can.

DMITROV

ALEKSANDROV

VLADIMIR

TOROPETS

Twenty-second Army

Thirty-first Army

STARITSA

RZHEV

YAKHROMA

KLIN

KRASNAYA POLYANA

Ninth Army

Twenty-ninth Army

OLENINO

West Front

Reserve Front

VOLOKOLAMSK

SOLNECH-NOGORSK

Klyazma

Third Panzergruppe (Hoth)

W. Dvina

BELYY

Thirtieth Army

SYCHEVKA

BORODINO

ISTRA

KHIMKI

Moskva

MOSCOW

West Front

Nineteeth Army

Sixteenth Army

Forty-ninth Army

GZHATSK

MOZHAYSK

NARO-FOMINSK

PODOLSK

DUKHOVSHCHINA

VYAZMA

MEDYN

BOROVSK

YARTSEVO

Thirty-second Army

MALOYAROSLAVETS

SERPUKHOV

KASHIRA

Oka

RYAZAN

Moscow Highway

Dniepr

SMOLENSK

Twentieth Army

YELNYA

YUKHNOV

Ugra

KALUGA

ALEKSIN

VENEV

MIKHAYLOV

Fourth Army

Twenty-fourth Army

SUKHINICHI

TULA

Upa

STALINOGORSK

GORLOVO

Fourth Panzergruppe (Hoeppner)

ROSLAVL

KIROV

Forty-third Army

BELEV

TEPLOYE

DANKOV

Army Group Centre (Bock)

Fiftieth Army

BOLKHOV

Oka

MTSENSK

YEFREMOV

Second Army

POCHEP

Bryansk Front

NOVOSIL

South-West Front

Third Army

BRYANSK

OREL

YELETS

Sosna

STARODUB

Thirteenth Army

SEVSK

DMITRIEV – LGOVSKIY

LIVNY

Don

NOVGOROD SEVERSKI

Second Panzer Army ('Panzergruppe Guderian')

KURSK

TIM

VORONEZH

CHERNIGOV

Desna

GLUKHOV

Second Panzer Army begins offensive 30 September. All other armies attack 2 October

KONOTOP

OBOYAN

Fortieth Army

SUMY

BELGOROD

GERMAN
- FRONT LINE, 30 SEPTEMBER 1941
- OFFENSIVE, 30 SEPT/30 OCT
- FRONT LINE, 10 OCTOBER
- FRONT LINE, 30 OCT/15 NOV
- OFFENSIVE 15 NOV/5 DEC
- FRONT LINE, 5 DECEMBER
- ARMY GROUP COMMAND BOUNDARY

PRILUKI

Army Group South

Kharkov 30 miles

95

frosts, and some units had difficulty retrieving their vehicles, which were frozen into the mud. To make up for the losses and wastage in his units Bock regrouped them. The 4th *Panzergruppe* was moved towards the 3rd *Panzergruppe*, which was now commanded by Reinhardt. However, this meant that Kluge's 4th Army, now weak in armour, had a broader front than before. To the south Guderian and his 2nd *Panzerarmee* were out on their own.

Whatever their generals might think, the men were determined to reach Moscow. 'They could see the flashes of the AA guns over Moscow at night, and it fired their imagination – the city seemed so near. They also felt that they would find shelter from the bitter weather.' By now the Russian winter was beginning to tell on the men of Army Group 'Centre'. Dressed as they were in the lightweight uniforms that they had been wearing at the beginning of the Russian campaign, many men went down with frostbite. Guderian noted that on 17 November there were 400 cases in each regiment of the 112th Division. Oil was beginning to thicken up, the grease on shells had to be chipped off before each would fit the breach, without anti-freeze tank engines had to be kept running – or fires lit beneath the engine to make them start – and the German artificial rubber called *Buna* became friable or as rigid as wood.

The final check

Despite the resistance of nature and the Russians, Bock displayed, in Keitel's words, 'incredible energy' and his men fought hard. It was to the north that they came within reach of the city. Here the Russians were trying to consolidate their defences on the Volga Canal and the Sea of Moscow. The 9th Army broke through and on 27 November the 3rd *Panzergruppe* linked up with it on a line south of Dmitrov. A day later men of the 7th Panzer Division established a bridgehead across the canal, but were driven back by a Russian counterattack.

Bock's attack was reaching its high water mark: at Krasnaya Polyana the tanks of the 3rd *Panzergruppe* were only 18 miles from Moscow, while the 4th Army was a mere 25 miles from the city. To the south Guderian had actually reached a point east of Moscow. His 2nd *Panzerarmee*, having isolated the industrial town of Tula where resistance had proved too strong, was now at Mikhaylov nearly 40 miles to the east, while his northern units were 69 miles from Moscow. On 30 November motorcycle patrols of the 62nd Panzer Engineer Battalion, part of the 2nd Panzer Division, reached Khimki, a small river port five miles from Moscow. They returned from their reconnaissance, but not before they had added to the alarm in the city. A combat group of the 2nd Panzer Division under Lieutenant-Colonel Decker reached the town of Ozeretskoye and were able to stand at the terminus stop of the Moscow tram system. At Gorki men of the 2nd Battalion, 304th Rifle Regiment, were 19 miles from the Kremlin, or 12 miles from the suburbs of Moscow, while an assault party of the 38th Panzer Engineer Battalion demolished the station at Lobnya

Above: The severe winter conditions, combined with strengthening Russian opposition, finally brought German efforts to take Moscow to an end, and then forced the Germans onto the defensive as the Russians launched a major counter-offensive. After the summer campaign, fought in scorching heat, men were exhausted and vehicles almost worn out, and Germany had not prepared for winter warfare.

Left: A PzKpfw III outside Moscow. Unless the engines of such vehicles were left running overnight, with consequent wear and heavy fuel consumption, the engine froze up.

to prevent it being used for tactical resupply – they were just ten miles from the city.

But now even Bock realised that his men could go on no longer. And writing to Halder on 1 December he said: 'The idea that the enemy facing the Army Group was on the point of collapse was, as the fighting of the last fortnight shows, a pipe dream. To re-remain outside the gates of Moscow, where

the rail and road systems connect with almost the whole of eastern Russia, means heavy defensive fighting for us against an enemy vastly superior in numbers. Further offensive action therefore seems to be senseless and aimless, especially as the time is coming very near when the physical strength of the troops will be completely exhausted.'

Total exhaustion

In fact many of the men of Army Group 'Centre' had already reached their 'limit of strategic consumption'. Frostbite was now a more deadly enemy than the Russians, though Soviet forces were showing a determination which reflected the firm leadership that Stalin was exercising by telephone from his office in the Kremlin, and which Zhukov was transmitting to his subordinates.

On 4 December Kluge ordered his 4th Army to cease any further attacks and to go onto the defensive. Guderian adopted the same tactics a day later. After the war Zhukov explained that Bock overestimated the capabilities of the forces he employed for the final attack on Moscow: 'To gamble

entirely on Panzer formations in the given situation, proved in practice to be erroneous, as they became worn out, suffered heavy casualties, and lost their ability to break through.'

However, it was the well-tried tactics of pincer attacks which rebounded on the Germans: 'The German command failed to arrange for a pinning-down attack in the centre of our front, even though it had adequate forces to do so. This made it possible for us to transfer all reserves, from the central sectors to the flanks of the Front, to fight the enemy assault groups. Their heavy losses, their unpreparedness for fighting in winter conditions, and the fierceness of the Soviet opposition had a sharp effect upon German battle-worthiness.'

The attack on Moscow marks the high point of German operations in World War II. In 1942 they were to drive to Stalingrad and the Caucasus, but though this was spectacular, it would never yield results to compare with the capture of Moscow. By failing to destroy the Soviet capital in the first year of the war in the East they had jeopardised their chances of ever gaining complete victory.

Field-Marshal Wilhelm Ritter von Leeb

received command of the most northerly of the three main groupings involved, Army Group 'North'. Leeb and his forces were entrusted with the task of moving swiftly through the Baltic states to capture Leningrad.

Leeb set about his job in a methodical but uninspired way, and the last chance of a conclusive end to the campaign were lost when Hitler ordered that Leningrad was to be invested, rather than seized by a *coup de main*.

This proved the end of Leeb's career, for Hitler relieved him of his command and placed him on the retired list on 18 January 1942.

Wilhelm, Ritter von Leeb was born at Passau on 5 September 1876, and was commissioned into the 4th Field Artillery Regiment, based in Augsburg, in 1897. During World War I, Leeb served as an artillery officer in the field.

Remaining in the army after World War I, Leeb had risen to the rank of major-general by 1929, and in 1934 he was appointed to the command of 2nd *Gruppen-kommando* (Army Group Headquarters), based in Kassel. Soon after this, however, Leeb retired in protest against the increasing number of Nazi rules and regulations being imposed upon the army.

With the outbreak of war in 1939, Leeb was recalled to the colours and given command of Army Group 'C' in western Germany, with the task of protecting the *Reich* from invasion by France. The army group was given only slightly more aggressive a role in the actual invasion of France in May 1940, but nevertheless Leeb's forces played a main part in the destruction and capture of the remnants of the French army trapped against the Maginot Line in June. For his part in the conquest of the West, Leeb was promoted field-marshal on 19 July 1940.

For the invasion of Russia, Leeb

Field-Marshal Wilhelm Ritter von Leeb

Although Hitler was at fault with his grand strategy for 'Barbarossa', his planning was sound. He stipulated that Leningrad should be captured before German forces united to thrust deeper into Russia to capture Moscow. The capture of Leningrad appealed to him on political as well as strategic grounds. It was the birthplace of the Bolshevik revolution and bore the name of its originator. However, the elimination of Leningrad would also secure Hitler's left flank and commit the Finns deeper into the war. Communications would be quicker through the Baltic rather than by the vulnerable road and rail links of north and central Russia, and the Red Army would lose the support of Leningrad's considerable arms and engineering industry.

Army Group 'North' was alloted the task of taking the city. Leeb, its commander, had two armies, the 18th and the 16th under Kuechler and Busche, and the 4th *Panzergruppe* under Hoepner, in all a force of 23 infantry divisions and three Panzer divisions.

Opposite him was the Russian North-West Front under Kuznetsov, which consisted of the 8th and 11th Armies totalling 20 infantry divisions and two mechanised corps. They had the advantage of defending an area of low-lying coastal plains with rivers, marshes, woodlands and lakes, impassable to the narrow-tracked German tanks, and disturbingly new territory for German infantry.

Realising that this terrain lent little freedom of movement for major encircling actions, Leeb arranged his forces for a concentrated thrust for Leningrad. The 4th *Panzergruppe* was the meat of a sandwich composed of the 18th Army to the north and the 16th to the south. Whilst the infantry secured the flanks and mopped up Russian forces paralysed by the armoured thrust, the *Panzergruppe* would drive in an almost straight line for Leningrad.

The Germans were lucky to have secured a bridgehead over the River Niemen even before they went to war. Hitler's annexation of the city of Memel gave them nearly 100 miles of the right bank, and a handy jumping off point.

Baltic advance

At 0300 hours on 22 June, Army Group 'North' started crossing into Russian-occupied Lithuania. The *Panzergruppe* which came under Leeb's personal control had been assigned the primary objective of securing a bridgehead over the River Dvina, the broadest river on the north-east Baltic coast. Though the German forces encountered few effective fixed defences they were surprised by the numbers of Russian troops who had been moved into Lithuania and Latvia since their annexation in 1940.

On 26 June the Germans captured two bridges over the Dvina at Daugavpils. The 150-mile drive from East Prussia to the

Above left: **A German MG 34 machine gun and its crew outside Leningrad in September 1941, when this rich prize was open to swift capture but lost as a result of Hitler's conflicting strategic ambitions.**
Left: **German infantry cross a bridge over the River Narva under the ancient walls of the city of Narva, on the southern coast of the Gulf of Finland half way between the Estonian capital of Tallinn and Leningrad.**

Dvina had taken the *Panzergruppe* a mere four days. Now that LVI Panzer Corps had secured bridges at Daugavpils, XLI Panzer Corps struck downstream and captured bridges at Jekabpils. On their right the infantry blocked the Russian escape route from Kurland by securing the river around Riga.

On parallel courses the two Panzer corps now drove for the 'Stalin Line' near Ostrov. This was the old Russian/Estonian border and had been fortified before 1940. XLI Panzer Corps punched through the line and swung north to Ostrov. It was counterattacked after it had captured the town, and in heavy fighting against Russian KV-1 and KV-2 tanks was saved only by the intervention of the heavy field howitzers of the 73rd Artillery Regiment.

Five days after the capture of Ostrov, the town of Pskov fell to XLI Panzer Corps on 9 July. A day later LVI Panzer Corps joined in a massed attack along the whole front. It had broken through the Stalin Line on 6 July and thrust through to Opochka on the Velikaya river. Now, south of Lake Ilmen the full *Panzergruppe* met heavy resistance. Leeb was faced with a problem: the main strength of the Soviet forces seemed to be on the right flank – just where he had been instructed to put his main weight. Ignoring the OKW edict he began switching the 1st and 6th Panzer Divisions and the 36th Motorised Infantry Division to a position north of Luga. They moved off on 13 July through difficult swampland and woods.

Despite this 100-mile forced march, an advanced unit of the 6th Panzer Division took the little town of Porechye on 14 July, while to the south the 1st Panzer Division established a bridgehead over the Luga river at Sabsk. The men of Leeb's army group were now a mere 70 miles from Leningrad, just a two days' march.

Then, inexplicably, OKW ordered a halt for three weeks. Hitler and his staff gave up the opportunity to capture Leningrad by a direct coup in favour of encirclement by an outflanking movement on the right. This decision gave the Russians a break similar to that enjoyed by the BEF at Dunkirk when Hitler ordered that his Panzers should not move in to clear the beach-head. Leeb could see that it was tactically unsound to put his main weight on the right, and that with his forces on the left he could not only drive for Leningrad but also seal off the Russian forces retreating up the Baltic coast. He had received his orders, however, and unlike some of his more adventurous colleagues he was unwilling to circumvent them.

While Reinhardt's XLI Panzer Corps paused on the Luga, Manstein's LVI Panzer Corps became entangled in heavy fighting around Shimsk west of Lake Ilmen. On 8 August the whole *Panzergruppe* was able to resume the offensive, but this time they were up against fixed defences which had been built by impressed civilian labourers. It took them nearly a week to break out from the northern Luga defences, while Manstein's Panzer division remained stuck in the well-defended lines around the town of Luga.

Having broken through in the north, Hoepner again pleaded with Leeb to give him some forces to cover his left flank – two

Above: **PzKpfw III medium tanks south of Lake Ilmen ready for an attack. Two crewmen on the leading vehicle are apparently watching for the opening air bombardment.**

Right: **War on the Russian front, as seen from the cockpit of a low-flying Fieseler *Storch* aircraft.**

divisions, perhaps even one, would be enough he said. This time Leeb agreed to detach the 3rd Motorised Infantry Division from LVI Panzer Corps and place it under Reinhardt's command. Once again it seemed that Leningrad was within reach of the men of Army Group 'North'.

Counterattack

Then on 12 August the Russians intervened. On the right flank, south of Lake Ilmen and along the River Lovat, the 126th, 30th and 290th Infantry Divisions had been involved in heavy fighting, breaking into the Russian fixed defences. It was against these forces that Marshal Voroshilov launched a counterattack through the gap between Lake Seliger and Lake Ilmen, which had been formed by the division between Army Group 'North' and 'Centre'. He pushed eight rifle divisions, one cavalry corps and an armoured corps through, hoping that these forces could swing round to cut off the Germans from their communications and lift the pressure on Leningrad.

On 19 August, however, four days after he had received his first order to break off fighting and move south-east, Manstein led the 3rd Motorised Infantry Division and the SS Division '*Totenkopf*' in a counterattack on the Russian incursion. They struck the exposed left flank of the Russian forces, who were pressing against Lake Ilmen. Paralysed by this unforseen German reaction and attacked by the infantry they had trapped against the lake the Russian forces fell apart. They left behind them 246 guns and the first intact multiple rocket-launcher, the 'Stalin Organ'.

Although the Germans had won a victory at Lake Ilmen, the Russians did not give up the pressure, and Manstein's Panzer corps

remained in that area to deal with these attacks.

About the time that Manstein was moving his forces south, German infantry were fighting to capture the ancient city of Novgorod. In their operations they were greatly aided by the capture of a marked map of the Russian units deployed in the area, and also by a Karelian engineer who possessed detailed plans of the fixed defences of the city. Novgorod was captured on the 16th and the German forces pressed on to capture a railway bridge over the River Volkhov near Chudovo.

At Luga the Russians still hung on, though their position had been bypassed to the south by the German thrust to Novgorod. However, in order to reach Leningrad on a practicable road, the Germans had to eliminate the Luga position. They had tried frontal assault and this had proved too expensive, so on 13 August XXVIII Corps began its attacks to the east of the town. It took a week before the corps reached the River Oredezh. The corps crossed the river and became involved in fierce Soviet counterattacks. Indeed, it was not until 3 September that the metalled road beyond Luga was declared secure and the Luga pockets had been destroyed. The Germans captured 600 guns, 316 tanks and 21,000 prisoners.

While this fighting was going on to the

south, Leeb received pleas from Hoepner that the 4th *Panzergruppe* should be given more support in its drive on Leningrad. It had lost Manstein's LVI Panzer Corps and needed men to cover its northern flank against the Russian troops retreating along the coast from the Baltic states. Though he received some units to cover the flank, the 8th Panzer Division was drawn southward into the fighting around Luga. Advancing slowly, Hoepner reached a point 25 miles from Leningrad on 21 August. He could not move faster even though there was only limited opposition to his front, for now he had only the 1st and 6th Panzer Divisions and the 111th Panzer Regiment. On 16 August the 1st Panzer Division had reported that besides two weakened infantry battalions in armoured carriers, it had only 44 serviceable tanks.

Leeb eventually agreed to give Hoepner the infantry support he so badly needed. On 17 August he instructed Colonel-General Kuechler of the 18th Army to destroy the Russian 8th Army in Estonia and then move from the Baltic coast to Narva. At the same time he was also ordered to capture the coastal defences along the southern coast of the Gulf of Finland. This elaborate order meant that the men were tied up in unnecessary assaults on fixed defences when they were desperately needed before Leningrad. The positions they attacked could have been starved out after the capture of the city. It did, however, give Kuechler, Leeb's friend, a chance to collect a little of the glamour that had been the preserve of the fast moving Panzers – but doling out favours does not win battles and every delay meant that the Russians were able to strengthen their city. It was only by September that all the necessary forces were echeloned up to the Leningrad lines.

Assault tactics

The attack began on 8/9 September and ran into belts of fixed fortifications which had been built by women and children from the city. The Russians had taken every opportunity that German delays had given them, and now the city was surrounded by concentric belts of fortifications which reached right into the streets. The first belt was 25 miles from Leningrad and the second a mere 15 miles.

The Russian defenders received a demonstration of thorough German assault tactics. Dive-bombing by the Stukas of Richthofen's *Fliegerkorps* VIII, attacks by pioneers and infantry and breakthroughs by tanks after the tank-traps and defences had been neutralised. Around midday on 11 September a German tank commander reported: 'I can see St Petersburg and the sea.'

Four days later men of the 209th Infantry Regiment were a mere six miles from the city centre. They captured a tram carrying workers to their factory in Leningrad. On the 16th German infantry captured Pushkin, the one-time summer residence of the Tsar.

On the first day of the attack two combat groups under Colonels Count Schwerin and Harry Hoppe, with the reinforced 76th and 424th Infantry Regiments, had attacked the Russian industrial settlements at Schluesselburg without Stuka support after they had

Above: German infantry survey the pathetic remnants of a Russian village outside Leningrad destroyed in the German advance on the birthplace of Soviet Russia.

Far left: A well-camouflaged German 3.7-cm anti-tank gun in action south-west of Leningrad.

Left: The bodies of Russian troops washed up on the coast west of Leningrad receive a casual examination by a German soldier.

cleared the eight industrial settlements outside the town. With its capture the Germans had sealed off Leningrad from the Russian hinterland – the only contact the Russians would have would be via Lake Ladoga. Now the time seemed ripe for the last attack which would be the culmination of all the German efforts; but Hitler had other plans.

On 12 September he had informed the German commanders that Leningrad was not to be attacked but surrounded and starved out. Everyone said that it would capitulate before the winter frosts. It was not Hitler's first mistake, but it was one of his worst for it lost him two cities: Leningrad and Moscow. Leeb's reluctance to go beyond his orders and take risks and the determination of the people of Leningrad not to be starved into submission meant that the city fell neither to a *coup de main* nor to slow starvation.

Colonel-General Erich Hoepner

against France.

For the invasion of Russia, Operation 'Barbarossa', Hoepner was given the 4th *Panzergruppe*, which played an important part in the early German successes, and which early in December 1941 reached a point only 20 miles north of Moscow.

In the crisis that followed the Russian counter-offensive in front of Moscow, Hoepner insisted on a tactical retreat, fell foul of Hitler and was summarily discharged dishonourably from the army.

Even in disgrace Hoepner continued with his anti-Nazi work. His involvement in the July Plot of 1944 was discovered by the Gestapo, and Hoepner was tried before the 'People's Court', sentenced to death and hanged on 8 August 1944.

Erich Hoepner was born at Frankfurt-am-Oder on 14 September 1886, and soon decided that the army offered him the career he desired. During World War I Hoepner served in a number of staff posts, and was retained in the *Reichswehr* after the war.

In these interwar years Hoepner developed an interest in mobile tactics and the tanks needed to implement them. By 1938 he had risen in rank to major-general, and was the commander of the 1st Light Division, based in Thüringia. In this capacity he was drawn into the abortive plans for a coup against Hitler formulated by General Ludwig Beck. Hoepner's forces

were intended to prevent SS reinforcements moving from Munich to Berlin once Hitler had been arrested. Although the plans came to naught, the Nazis so disliked by Hoepner suspected nothing.

Next year Hoepner received promotion to lieutenant-general, and with it the command of XVI Corps, made up of four armoured divisions commanded by such up and coming men as Reinhardt, Geyr von Schweppenburg and Vietinghoff-Scheel. Hoepner led this formation in the invasions of Czechoslovakia and Poland, and also as the transmogrified XVI Panzer Corps in the campaign

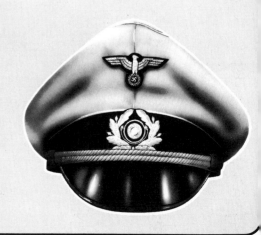

Colonel-General Erich Hoepner

'Victory', goes an Italian proverb, 'has many fathers; but defeat is an orphan.' It was Hitler's attempt to foist the responsibility for the German defeat at Moscow on any one but himself that led to a purge of his generals. Besides retiring Rundstedt, Guderian and Brauchitsch, he had Colonel-General Hoepner dishonourably discharged, deprived of the right to wear uniform, draw his pension, live in the house that had been allocated to him and even to wear the medals he had won.

Hoepner's 4th *Panzergruppe*, along with Hoth's 3rd *Panzergruppe*, had as we have seen made the closest penetration to Moscow, and on 5 December had halted, exhausted, in an arc from the Volga Canal through Krasnaya Polyana to Istra. Totally unequipped for winter war, their vehicles and weapons seized up in the severe cold, and men were forced either to pack out their uniforms with paper for insulation, or wear layers of clothes like old tramps. Many took to wearing the clothes of dead or captured Russians so that only their national insignia distinguished them from their enemies.

A day after the Germans had been forced to a halt, the Russians under General Zhukov launched a counter-offensive which caught their enemies badly off balance. Stalin had received information from a spy in Tokyo, Richard Sorge, that though the Japanese had plans for major operations in the Far East, these were not to be directed against the Soviet Union. Trusting his security services, and working on the assumption that if Russia lost the war on her western borders, she would be unlikely to retain her Far Eastern provinces, Stalin ordered that his Siberian troops be sent west. These men were fresh, well-equipped and inured to severe weather. They came from an army which had a reputation and experience similar to the British Indian Army, in that they were independent and battle-wise after border clashes and fights with the Japanese Manchurian Army.

The Germans had been meeting units from this army as they approached Moscow, but it was not until 5/6 December that they began to realise the full quality of their opposition. The clashes on the front line, however, were almost as fierce as the arguments between the generals of Army Group 'Centre'. On 3 December, Hoepner had taken Kluge to task for the failure of his 4th Army to make any progress in their three-day attack on the Nara. Hoepner had reached a point 19 miles from the Kremlin

Winter-equipped German troops. Until the arrival of such equipment, the Germans had to strip Russian dead for their winter clothing and snow suits, especially the very efficient felt overboots.

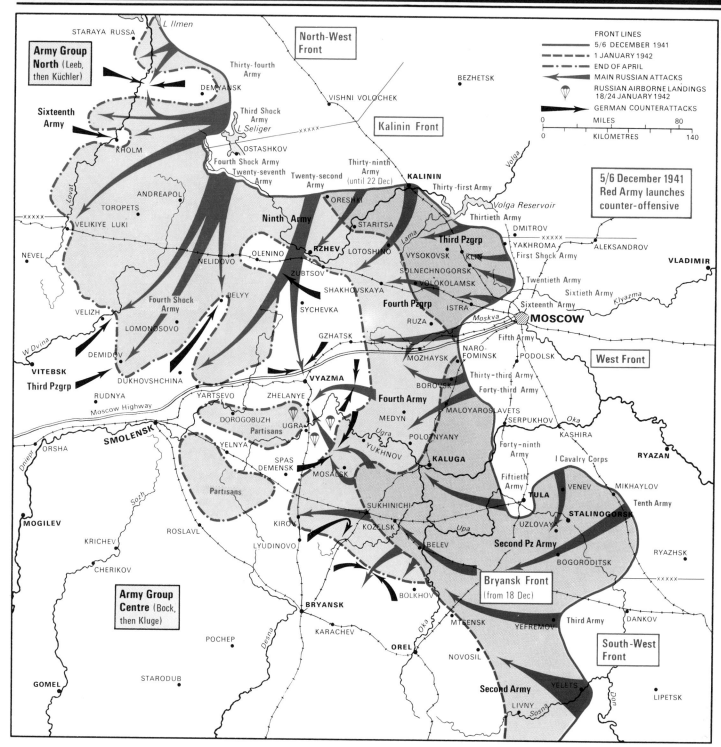

FRONT LINES
— 5/6 DECEMBER 1941
--- 1 JANUARY 1942
—·—·— END OF APRIL
◄—— MAIN RUSSIAN ATTACKS
RUSSIAN AIRBORNE LANDINGS 18/24 JANUARY 1942
▶—— GERMAN COUNTERATTACKS

	MILES	80
0		
0	KILOMETRES	140

5/6 December 1941 Red Army launches counter-offensive

and, feeling his men deserved more support from the 4th Army, suggested that both the 3rd and 4th *Panzergruppen* should be withdrawn from their 30-mile-deep salient in order to straighten the line. In the meantime, he said, he and his men would take three days rest while OKW made up its mind about what exactly it was trying to do.

Kluge, who had the nickname of *'der kluge Hans'* or 'clever Hans', had earned it not only for his military ability but also his skill in surviving the political and emotional hazards of serving under Hitler. Hoepner's comments about his superiors, and such dangerous phrases as 'civilian lleadership' were being noted by Kluge.

Dangerously frank, Hoepner sent a report to Kluge on 5 December in which he complained that the Ministry of Propaganda was incorrectly calling the Russians demoralised, defeated and without courage – in fact, he

said, they were fighting very well. He estimated that there were 19 rifle, four cavalry and 12 armoured units in front of the 4th *Panzergruppe*. Whilst some of these units had suffered severe losses, the Germans were nevertheless outnumbered. Moreover, he added that whilst his men were still in their summer-weight denims, the Russians were now appearing in excellent fur caps, felt boots, and quilted trousers and tunics. While the Germans were forced to scrape hollows in the snow, the Russians operated from prepared covered positions.

A day later, under the full shock of Zhukov's counter-offensive, Hoepner received an order from Kluge's 4th Army that he could withdraw from his salient back to the line of the Istra. As Hoepner commented, however, whoever drafted the order had absolutely no understanding of general staff work. He had orders to withdraw, but

Above: Russia's first proper counter-offensive of the war, prepared by General Zhukov to lift the immediate threat to Moscow. Although Hitler's order that no retreat was to be contemplated was completely right here, it set a disastrous precedent for dissimilar future occasions.

Above right: An 8.8-cm AA and anti-tank gun, and a vigilant sentry.

Right: A German sniper.

the 3rd *Panzergruppe* under Reinhardt, which was not under Kluge's command, had received no instructions. It would be out on a very dangerous limb if Hoepner withdrew. When Reinhardt did receive his orders from Army Group 'Centre', he found

that he was being attacked on his right flank and rear. Hoepner delivered a sharp protest to Kluge, and on 8 December the 3rd *Panzergruppe* was put under his command for easier command and control.

The *Stavka* was surprised by the speed of the German withdrawal, but as the German author Paul Carell explains, 'the German *Wehrmacht* had never learned the principles and methods of retreat. The German soldier regarded retreat not as a special type of operation, to be bent to his will, but as a disaster imposed by the enemy upon him.

'Even in *Reichswehr* days the practising of withdrawals had been looked upon askance. Somewhat contemptuously it used to be said: One does not practice withdrawals; it merely teaches the men to run away.

'Later, after 1936, even elastic resistance was deleted from the training programme.

"Attack" and "holding" were the only two techniques taught to the German soldier. As far as fighting retreats were concerned, the *Wehrmacht* went into the war unprepared.'

Pressed by the Russians, Hoepner reached his stop line at Istra on 12 December. He had lost a lot of equipment, including half his artillery, since it had been immobilised because of the death of horses or the lack of working prime-movers. In spite of this he was encouraged by reports that the men were still in good spirits and he had been able to move the 2nd Panzer Division into reserve now that the line had been shortened.

However, when he examined his position Hoepner realised that he could no longer defend it, for on his left Reinhardt was still in difficulties and his flank was in danger of envelopment. Hoepner decided that he would have to pull back to the River Ruza. On 20 December the 3rd and 4th *Panzergruppen* reached the line Ruza–Volokolamsk–Lama.

Two days earlier Hoepner had received Hitler's controversial 'stand and fight' order. On 24 December the commander of the 4th *Panzergruppe* drafted a reply, explaining simply that a static defence was beyond the capabilities of his men. They were without the equipment, weapons and logistic support, there were too few of them and those that were available were hungry and frozen. The Russians, however, were well-equipped and numerous, so it was doubtful if they could be worn down in a battle of attrition. Reasonable as this report sounds to a post-war reader, it was the sort of truth that was unacceptable to Hitler.

Hoepner's men remained relatively undisturbed until 3 January when Hitler ordered that they were to assume responsibility for part of the front held by the 4th Army. They were to close the breach made by the Russians at Maloyaroslavets.

Not only did Hitler give orders that were near impossible, but he even gave instructions as to how they were to be carried out. Neither the orders nor the instructions bore any relation to the reality of fighting in the East. Although Hoepner's front was secure, his flanks were under attack. To the left, 40 miles to the west, the 9th Army was still withdrawing, while to the right was the Borovsk–Maloyaroslavets gap which Hitler had ordered him to close.

Following Hitler's orders Kluge transferred XX Corps on the north shoulder of the gap from the 4th Army to the 4th *Panzergruppe*. Hitler explained that it was a quite simple operation: Hoepner had merely to stand fast and at the same time thin out his troops to provide a mobile reserve to plug the gap. He explained that the 5th Panzer Division could be moved from the northern flank down to the south and employed as the mobile reserve to attack into the gap.

The men on the ground, however, said that it was impossible. Hoepner spoke with the commanders of XLVI Panzer Corps and the 5th Panzer Division, and they both said that it could not be done in the time allowed. Not only were the road conditions bad, but they did not have enough fuel to move 100 miles. The only possibility would be to withdraw to the 'Winter Line' running

from Rzhev to Gzhatsk and Yukhnov. This would allow the 5th Panzer Division to move south – but all this would take time.

Making the best of what was available, Hoepner counterattacked with a small force. He was not allowed to use XX Corps since it was defending ground and Hitler had ordered that there be no further withdrawal. So it sat unused on the shoulder of the gap as Hoepner's modest reserves were swamped by the Russians.

Since the angry exchanges early in December, relations between Kluge and Hoepner had been very cool. They communicated by telephone or by aides, but never met face to face.

On 1 January Hoepner had sent a formal request that the 4th *Panzergruppe* should withdraw towards Gzhatsk starting about 5 or 6 January. He waited a week without a reply, and by then the Russians pressing through the Maloyaroslavets gap had begun to cut off and outflank XX Corps.

On 8 January there were a series of telephone calls between Hoepner and Kluge. The commander of Army Group 'Centre' even suggested that not just XX Corps but the whole of the 4th *Panzergruppe* might be able to withdraw to the Winter Line, but he gave no firm orders since they could only come from Hitler.

By the afternoon Hoepner was desperate. He tried to telephone Halder, but only contacted an aide who said that Halder would ring back. The call never came and Hoepner on his own responsibility gave XX Corps the order to withdraw.

Above: A German grave, seen in the brighter days of summer.

Right: Winter warmth somewhere on the Eastern Front.

Kluge did not hear of the move until the evening. He had a choice: either he could order that XX Corps move back to their position which was still being held by a rearguard, or he could endorse the order and support Hoepner. True to his nickname he managed to do neither. He rang Hoepner, upbraided him and reminded him that he had been warned of the consequences of disobeying the *Fuehrer*'s order.

The events of this day are still unclear. Some authorities say that Kluge had in fact given Hoepner the go ahead to withdraw, but realising how this would be received at the OKW covered himself with these warnings to Hoepner and then rang Hitler and reported to him the angry remarks that Hoepner had uttered about civilian leadership. Whatever the truth, Kluge broke the news to Hitler in tones that were guaranteed to fire the dictator's anger.

Though Hitler ordered that Hoepner be dishonourably discharged 'with all the legal consequences that it entailed' these orders were softened either by the intervention of Schmundt or by the judgements of the army lawyers who were ordered to investigate this unjust order. Hoepner lived in retirement, and even after his execution for his part in the July Plot his widow continued to draw a pension.

Analysis—
German Generalship in the East, from Minsk to Stalingrad

The five-month campaign waged against Soviet Russia by the armies of Germany between June and November 1941 is one of the most extraordinary military feats ever performed. Even the fact that it was launched with insufficient resources, too late and against an enemy whose capabilities had been completely misjudged cannot detract from the achievements of the *Wehrmacht*, especially the army and the air force.

Whilst on the part of the ordinary troops the campaign was a triumph of deter-mination and endurance against the enemy, terrain and climate, for the generals the campaign produced other difficulties. Some of these were caused by the enemy, and others by their own high command, in particular Hitler himself. Problems with the enemy were only to be expected. Problems with their own high command were not.

Although the Russian armies always seemed to be on the point of disintegration, with whole formations breaking and fleeing, and hundreds of thousands of demoralised troops being captured in the vast German pockets, there always seemed to be something preventing the wholesale dissolution of the Red Army, and always more troops forthcoming to try to plug the gaps torn in their defence lines by the German Panzer troops. For all that he was poorly trained and poorly equipped, and often led by officers of mediocre quality, the Russian soldier showed right from the outset of the campaign the qualities that have earned him admiration in every campaign fought by Russia in recent history: a dogged determination,

enormous physical resiliency, and the ability to make do with very little food and shelter. Yet in this campaign the Russian soldier fought to greater effect as he was better led than previously. Admittedly there had been terrible catastrophes at the beginning of the campaign, largely attributable to bad leadership; but combat had sorted out the worst of these offenders, and the others had been disposed of by an implacable Stalin. The senior commanders left quickly adapted them-selves to the new conditions and began to fight back with increasing ability and confidence. Russia was still in dire straits, but with the emergence of men such as Zhukov, Konev, Malinovsky and Rokossovsky some light could be seen on the horizon.

Decimated command

There were two reasons for the initial poverty of the Russian senior command. Firstly, the purges carried out by Stalin in the late 1930s had emasculated the officer corps from the level of divisional commander upwards. To fill the gap junior officers had been promoted early in their careers, and whilst all were politically reliable, their military abilities were not necessarily of the same order. Moreover, those who were able had had little time to get to know their formations and improve their efficiency. The second reason for the Russian officer corps' inefficiency was the result of misappreciations of the lessons of the Spanish Civil War, the border struggles with the Japanese in Siberia, and the 'Winter War' against

Above: German assault groups paddle across a river on Soviet Russia's frontier on 22 June 1941. The provision of inflatable rubber boats for such units proved a great boon in those days of swift advance, enabling the Germans to probe round the flanks of major Russian formations with little or no hindrance.

Left: German *Panzergrenadiers* debus from their SdKfz 251 halftrack. The man vaulting over the side has a *Gewehr* 98 rifle, and the man on the ground is just about to accept an MG 34 machine gun from his partner in the halftrack. *Panzergrenadiers* were the essential accompaniment to protect tanks from infantry attack.

Finland. The most important of these misconceptions had led to the breaking up of the homogeneous armoured formations built up in the early 1930s in favour of penny packets attached as support weapons to infantry formations. Some indication of this latter concept's disadvantages were gained in the Winter War, but little had been done to revise the older arrangement. The lesson was hammered home by the success of the German armoured formations, and Stalin immediately took steps to reintroduce armoured corps into the Red Army on a large scale.

Compared with the Red Army, the German army was well off in its officers, for although the army had been expanded enormously in the middle and late 1930s, with some trouble in finding adequate officer material, this problem had by now been solved. Most of the officers had combat experience in Poland, Denmark and Norway, the West, or the Balkans, and the senior commanders knew how to get the best out of their men. Combat tactics and doctrines had been tested, and the commanders from divisional level upwards developed considerable tactical flexibility. This last was a factor that amazed Allied commanders throughout World War II.

This is not to say that the Germans did not have their problems. The Panzer divisions, for example, were at low strength. This was because Hitler had divided each of the Panzer divisions involved in the campaign in the West to produce more armoured divisions. Thus each of the Panzer divisions involved in the Russian campaign of 1941 had only about half the strength of its 1940 counterpart. In addition to this, much of the German army was still dependent on horse transport, which posed considerable difficulties in Russia – the horses used were well bred European ones, ill-suited to the extremes of the Russian climate.

Time or space?

The most important single factor in the Russian campaign, however, was time. The Germans did not have enough of it – Hitler's adventure in the Balkans had cost 'Barbarossa' a vital month, for the Germans considered that they had to win the war by the onset of winter. They did not have the resources to fight a prolonged two-front war, and all was gambled on a swift, knock-out blow on Russia. The result in the short term was near disaster, for no winter clothing had been provided for the men, the animals perished in the extreme cold, and vehicles seized up for lack of proper oils for the low temperatures of winter. The Russians also needed time, but for a different reason. They had to evacuate the industries of western Russia to new sites behind the Urals, safe from German attack or air assault, and they had also to build up the defences of cities such as Moscow and Leningrad, as well as bring up reserves from deep inside Russia. To gain the time for these two objectives, Stalin was prepared to pay with space and lives: his forces would hold on until they

Above: A tank commander waits for the order to take his machine into battle. He is wearing the black battledress and beret issued to *Panzer* troops early in the war.

Left: Rumanian troops, accompanied by a German officer, march into Odessa on 16 October 1941. With the exception of the Finns, Germany's allies in the war against Russia proved of little fighting value, and were usually relegated to less important sectors of the front.

Right: A Vichy French poster urges Frenchmen to work in Germany. Similar posters were to be found in every occupied country, as well as posters calling for volunteers for men to 'fight against Bolshevism'.

LA RELÈVE *continue!*

IL EN RESTE... RELEVEZ LES!

Ils sont encore nombreux là-bas, et la France les attend avec une naturelle et légitime impatience. Leur présence est indispensable chez nous, car ils représentent les forces vives de notre pays.

•

Ouvriers, qui partez librement pour l'Allemagne, regardez ces hommes que vous croisez sur la route. Ils vous doivent leur liberté, ils ne l'oublieront jamais. La reconnaissance de la Nation toute entière monte vers vous.

•

Ces ouvriers qui partent me permettront de mieux défendre les intérêts de notre pays.

•

La fraternité — qui ne fut souvent qu'un grand mot — se traduit ici par une émouvante réalité.

P. LAVAL
Compiègne, 11 Août 1942.

were all but annihilated, and then fall back to another position. The Russians were thus able to save their industrial capacity, and thereby the war, at the cost of about $1\frac{1}{2}$ million dead and wounded and $1\frac{1}{2}$ million prisoners.

What finally lost the first stage of the Russian campaign for the Germans were Hitler's two changes of mind, first to make Leningrad and the Ukraine, instead of Moscow, the primary objective, and then exactly the opposite decision. It is interesting to speculate on what might have happened had Hitler not made these two decisions. Without Hitler's insistence the generals would not have contemplated invasion of Russia, but once the decision had been made, it was these same generals, who could have won his campaign for him, who were deprived of the chance to do so by others of Hitler's decisions.

The German field commanders were also hampered by the complete inadequacy of the German high command. The staff generals through whom the orders should have come and who would thus have been able to moderate the worst of Hitler's excesses, were so much nonentities that men such as Bock, Leeb, Guderian and Hoepner had to deal with Hitler directly. They could not convince the *Fuehrer* of the sense of their military ideas, and so such men resigned or were sacked, to the detriment of the army's fighting efficiency. The same problem was also prevalent in 1942 and 1943, before the more courageous of the generals evolved the method of agreeing with Hitler and doing what they themselves saw fit.

What of Germany's performance against Russia in 1941 and 1942? Firstly, the abilities of the ordinary fighting men must be mentioned as being quite superb under the most trying and difficult of conditions. The generals fall into two categories: those who had to deal with strategy, and therefore with Hitler, and those who dealt with tactics, and therefore had little occasion to deal with Hitler. The former performed creditably, although their success would have been greater had they been able to stand up to the *Fuehrer* with the aid of an efficient staff. The latter performed extremely well, showing great flexibility and speed of reaction, acting quickly as the situation demanded, without waiting for orders from higher up. It was these men, divisional and corps commanders in 1941, that were to prove so useful to Germany's defence in the desperate days of 1944 and 1945.

Left above: **Russian PoWs in a German camp plead for food. Such men were treated little better than the inmates of concentration camps.**

Left below: **A Russian KV-1 heavy tank knocked out in Rostov. This tank, with its excellent protection and adequate armament, came as a shock to the Germans, like the T-34.**

Left: **A German forward command post.**

The Campaigns in North Africa and Italy

A German convoy, led by an SdKfz 221 light armoured car, in the Western Desert. The amount of dust being thrown up makes it abundantly clear that secret daylight movement was all but impossible.

The German commitment of land forces to the North African theatre was an emergency measure prompted by Italy's expulsion from eastern Libya and the likelihood of the British capture of Tripoli in 1941. The redeployment of the *Wehrmacht* for the invasion of Soviet Russia had been ordered, and the sudden crisis created by the defeat of Mussolini's forces in Libya was a thorough nuisance. A small mechanised force, with a stiffening of armour, was scraped together, in all an under-strength corps: the 5th Light Division and 15th Panzer Division, whose final disembarkation at Tripoli was scheduled for the end of May. This purely German armoured force became known as the *Afrika Korps;* and its commander was Lieutenant-General Erwin Rommel, who after his brilliant career in France with the 7th Panzer Division was scheduled for a Panzer corps command.

Rommel arrived in Tripoli in mid-February and immediately deduced that there was every chance of bundling the British out of El Agheila and Benghazi. Although specifically ordered not to undertake any offensive until the end of May, he decided to use his own initiative and see how the British reacted to a series of limited attacks. By 25 March he had prodded the British out of their advanced positions and taken their advanced base at El Agheila. And on the 31st he set in motion a three-pronged advance into Cyrenaica which completely surprised the British, weakened as they were by the withdrawal of their best armoured forces for the Greek campaign. This, his first offensive in Africa, is still a classic of how an energetically-driven armoured thrust can set off a chain-reaction of disorganisation on the other side. On 7 April the three slim German prongs met at Mechili. Rommel had not only taken western Cyrenaica but Generals O'Connor, Neame, Gambier-Parry, Combe, and Rimington, all snapped up in the whirling advance. Only the narrowest of escapes prevented Rommel from capturing his opponent, Wavell, who also had the

defence of Greece to worry about during April 1941.

The Australian General Morshead's success in defending Tobruk ended Rommel's first run of luck. Precipitate attacks on the western sector of the perimeter caused needless losses to Rommel's scanty forces and consolidated the defence. By 2 May he had to accept the need for a prolonged siege. Meanwhile his superiors at OKH thought he had run amok. Halder considered Rommel's version of soldiering chaotic and wasteful, and he sent out General Paulus (destined for disaster at Stalingrad) to rein him in. Paulus relayed firm orders that Rommel was not to advance further to the east (his outposts stood on the Egyptian frontier, commanding the vital Halfaya Pass on the Sollum escarpment) until his lines of communication had been made good and Tobruk captured.

Legendary general

At the end of May a tentative British attack, Operation 'Brevity', pushed Rommel's forces out of their frontier positions for a time, but prompt counter-moves by the 5th Light and 15th Panzer (now arrived) Divisions recovered Capuzzo, Sollum and Halfaya. Fortifying Halfaya Pass with dug-in 8·8-cm AA guns, Rommel prepared for the inevitable British counter-offensive to relieve Tobruk. Churchill had rushed a tank-supply convoy ('Tiger') through the Mediterranean and nagged Wavell until the latter was forced to attack prematurely – with tanks that were not 'broken-in' to desert warfare and also inferior on most counts to the German machines. Operation 'Battleaxe', Wavell's attack, showed Rommel at his best in a defensive rôle. The clash lasted three days (15–18 June), in which Rommel kept concentrated, blunted the clumsy British attacks with his minefields and anti-tank guns, and forced back the British armour by hooking repeatedly at its flanks. Churchill replaced Wavell with Auchinleck on 22 June; and the next months saw both Auchinleck and Rommel preparing for new offensives, Rommel to take Tobruk, Auchinleck to relieve it and recover Cyrenaica.

By 18 November 1941, the date of Auchinleck's offensive, entrusted to the 8th Army under General Cunningham and code-named Operation 'Crusader', Rommel was already a legend. This was due not to the Nazi propaganda machine but to the British whom he had so roughly handled. Whether invoked with the blackest invective or with grudging admiration, Rommel's name was fast becoming synonymous with British discomfiture in the desert. Auchinleck, recognising this, took pains to issue a general order urging the men of the 8th Army to think more of 'the enemy' or 'the Germans' and less of bogeyman Rommel. No other German general of World War II had such a high (if indirect) compliment paid him by an opponent. And no other German general had a commando raid launched for his assassination. On the eve of 'Crusader' the gallant but totally misconceived 'Keyes

Raid' landed far behind the German lines to kill Rommel in what was believed to be his HQ – but he was not even there.

Despite this charisma, Rommel had to account 'Crusader' a defeat. Totally surprised at the outset, he rapidly concentrated the *Afrika Korps* and halted the British armoured thrust towards Tobruk, smashing the 5th South African Brigade. The battle became centred around the Sidi Rezegh airfield outside the Tobruk perimeter to the south-east, with the British getting the worst of it all along the line. Then on 24 November Rommel made a snap decision to slice across the 8th Army's rear areas with the *Afrika Korps* to try to panic his opponent into calling off the attack. It would have been called brilliant if it had worked – but while Rommel was out of touch with his HQ, raising havoc in the British rear areas along the Egyptian frontier, the New Zealand Division kept going and joined hands with the Tobruk garrison. Rommel had to race back to the westward and try to reimpose the siege. The ensuing fighting so depleted his forces that by 7 December he had to abandon the battle for Tobruk and withdraw to the west. Determined to preserve what was left of the *Afrika Korps* as a fighting force, he overrode belated and

Germany's two major Mediterranean theatres of action were North Africa and the Italian peninsula.

Above: A PzKpfw II light tank in desert camouflage and markings.

Right: German coastal defence on the island of Sicily.

ill-founded Italian objections and pulled right back to El Agheila. By 28 December he had brought the pursuing 8th Army to a definite halt. One of the hardest decisions he had had to make was to abandon the German garrisons on the Egyptian frontier, the last of which surrendered on 17 January.

Two factors combined to make Rommel's discomfiture a matter of only a few days. The first was the new crisis in the Far East, created by Japan's entry into the war on 7 December, forcing the British, once again, to pull vital forces out of the North African theatre. And the second was the timely arrival in Libya of German tank reinforcements – 45 on 19 December and 55 on 5 January. He immediately decided to repeat his former ploy of upsetting the British deployment in western Cyrenaica. By this time his bi-national force had been raised to the

status of *Panzergruppe Afrika* and was on the eve of additional preferment to that of *Panzerarmee*. Far more important was its recent reinforcement coupled with the weakening of 8th Army, which was still out of breath after the closing stages of 'Crusader'.

Rommel's second offensive (21 January–5 February 1942) bundled the 8th Army out of western Cyrenaica and pushed it back to a north–south axis hinged on Gazala on the coast. Both sides then began a mutual build-up for the decisive battle. There was another and far more crucial reason for the lull in the land fighting. The *Panzerarmee* and 8th Army both depended on seaborne supplies. Rommel's supply-lines were far shorter, but they had the British-held island of Malta commanding them. If Malta could be neutralised, or better still conquered, no further obstacle would remain to impede the Axis in North Africa. Logically, both Rommel and his colleague Field-Marshal Kesselring (German C-in-C South) agreed that the fall of Malta must precede an all-out offensive in North Africa. But this would be to ignore the activities of the British. By the end of April 1942 (when the attacks on Malta had reached their peak and Kesselring had concluded, prematurely, that the island had indeed been neutralised), Rommel was becoming uneasy about the pace of the 8th Army's build-up. The result was the compromise directive which authorised 'Theseus' (Rommel's offensive to take Tobruk) to precede 'Hercules' (Kesselring's airborne invasion of Malta). And on 26 May Rommel attacked the 8th Army's defensive positions in the open desert south of Gazala.

Rommel had set himself an impossibly optimistic deadline, planning for the defeat of the British armour on Day One, the smashing of the British infantry on Day Two, and the decisive assault on Tobruk on Day Three. He wheeled the *Afrika Korps* round the southern extremity of the Gazala line into the rear of the 8th Army's static defences only to find himself trapped. Only the piecemeal armoured tactics of the 8th Army commander, General Ritchie, saved him from disaster. Supplies for the trapped *Afrika Korps* (now a subsidiary formation of the *Panzerarmee*) were forced through in the nick of time on 1 June, hours before the deadline on which Rommel had already admitted to his prisoners that he would be forced to negotiate a surrender. After 10 desperate days, in which the last British reserves of armour were progressively squandered, the 8th Army had been levered out of the Gazala line. Rommel now flung himself against Tobruk, attacking the sector which had been marked down on the eve of 'Crusader'. The Tobruk defences had deteriorated since the 1941 siege, the garrison was improvised, and the perimeter was pierced with ease. Tobruk surrendered on 21 June. 'Theseus' had been accomplished; the road was clear for 'Hercules'; but now the road to Alexandria and Cairo seemed clearer still. Hitler and Mussolini agreed to give Rommel his head and invade Egypt – a move which Rommel himself later admitted to be a 'try-on'.

Savage riposte

In the first two weeks of July 1942 Rommel was fought to a standstill at El Alamein by Auchinleck, who employed the disorganised components of the 8th Army with very great skill. The pursuit effectively ended on 1/2 July, when

Above: A *Sturmgeschuetz* M43 *mit* 105/25 assault gun prepares to back into its concealed ambush position. The Germans made great use of foreign tracked chassis, in this case an Italian one, as the basis of self-propelled guns, here a German 10.5-cm howitzer.

Right: German ground troops watch the effect of artillery shells on typical Italian mountain terrain.

Rommel repeated his old mistake of attacking the first defences he came to and slowing himself down. Auchinleck riposted by savaging the Italian divisions of the *Panzerarmee* and forcing the *Afrika Korps* to wear itself out by doing all the work. By 5 June the tank strength of the *Afrika Korps* was down to 26. By the end of the month the situation was deadlocked. Now it was Rommel who was out on a limb and the 8th Army which had been backed up against its source of supply.

There were factors other than desperation behind Rommel's 'last throw' to break through at El Alamein via the Alam Halfa ridge (31 August–1 September 1942). Like Paulus at Stalingrad, he had been promised supplies which never turned up. German intelligence was faulty and produced a wildly optimistic plan (obliging the *Afrika Korps* to cover 30 miles in seven hours over difficult terrain and through uncleared minefields). But it was a costly failure. Rommel was a sick man; and his new opponent, Montgomery, refused to fritter away the British armour as his predecessors had done, and so won a heartening victory for the 8th Army.

After Alam Halfa Rommel could only prepare for Montgomery's inevitable

offensive, which broke on 23 October. It was the most unbalanced line-up of the entire desert war: 96,000 Germans and Italians faced 150,000 men of the 8th Army; 756 Axis tanks were confronted by 1,348 Allied. Such odds were decisive enough for the battle of attrition which Montgomery wanted; the *Panzerarmee*'s fuel shortage made them doubly so. Nevertheless Rommel kept the *Panzerarmee* in position despite Montgomery's grinding attacks until 3 November. He then seized upon Montgomery's caution to make good a staged withdrawal from Egypt which took the *Panzerarmee* clear across Libya to the Tunisian frontier without having to fight another set-piece battle.

This gruelling retreat was forced on him by the Allied landings in Morocco and Tunisia (Operation 'Torch') on 8 November. That the *Panzerarmee* was not cut off and annihilated by this crushing blow was due entirely to the vigilance of Kesselring, who had expected such a move and earmarked troops for a swift airlift across the Sicilian narrows to hold Tunis and Bizerta. The spirited counterattacks launched by Kesselring's blocking force raised faint hopes that it would after all be possible to hold a 'Tunisian bridgehead' which, in conjunction with Sicily, would still deny the Allies free passage through the central Mediterranean. On 23 January 1943, after the *Panzerarmee* had reached the comparative safety of the Tunisian frontier defences, the Mareth line, *Armeegruppe 'Afrika'* (Army Group 'Africa') was set up with Rommel as C-in-C, General von Arnim commanding the 5th *Panzerarmee* and the Italian General Messe commanding the 1st Army. It was all a far cry from Rommel's original tiny force of February–March 1941. But Rommel and Arnim planned two offensive moves to jam the Allied vice closing round the 'bridgehead'.

End in Africa

First came *Fruehlingswind* or 'Spring Breeze' (14–24 February) which was aimed at the green American II Corps and caused considerable initial havoc before it ran out of steam. This was followed by Rommel's last battle in Africa: a costly armoured assault on the 8th Army's prepared positions at Medenine which was a total failure. After Rommel's departure on 9 March Arnim took over Army Group 'Africa'. His contribution – the last Axis offensive on anything like a large scale in Tunisia – was *Ochsenkopf* ('Oxhead') between 26 February and 2 March, on the northern sector. All were fruitless, for with the forcing of the Mareth line (20–28 March) and the Wadi Akarit line (5–6 April), the 8th Army finally 'turned the corner' northward into Tunisia and left Arnim no further room in which to manoeuvre. Despite desperate resistance in the last weeks, the Axis collapse came suddenly on 6 May. Tunis and Bizerta fell simultaneously on the 8th; and by the 13th it was all over. In their leaderless and disorganised masses the men of Army Group 'Africa' were surrendering in their thousands – over a quarter of a million of

his 'ceiling' was a division, or at best a corps, and that he lacked the more placid qualities needed for commanding a full army. Certainly the brilliant successes won by his flair for improvisation amounted to a string of empty victories. Only the legend remained.

The disaster at Tunis could not have been worse timed, for coming as it did on the eve of the last German summer offensive in Russia it dashed all hopes of transferring large bodies of troops to Kesselring's southern command – and thus providing at least a chance of preventing the Allies from gaining a foothold in Sicily and southern Italy.

Kesselring was determined to make a fight for Sicily, but he only had the bare bones with which to do the fighting. It was a predominantly Italian defence, with Italian forces manning the obvious invasion beaches at the southern corner of the island and only two German divisions – 15th Panzer (reconstituted) and the 'Hermann Goering' – inland. (The German 1st Parachute Division was dropped into Sicily after the Allied landings went in on 10 July. But there was no chance of 'Dunkirking' the assault forces on the beaches; the Italian coastal defences collapsed on the first impact; and the British and American forces seized the opportunity to push inland and deploy for the overrunning of the island. The German troops used the natural defences of Sicily's terrain to full advantage and retreated in good order, but Kesselring had no intention of sacrificing them, as Army Group 'Africa' had been sacrificed, in a futile defence, and shipped them across to the Italian mainland before the Americans entered Messina on 17 August.

Combined landings

Italy was altogether different. The German high command got early intelligence that its erstwhile Italian allies were negotiating an armistice, and was determined to prevent the Allies from being presented with Italy at a single stroke. Initially, however, Kesselring was alone in wishing to try to keep the Allies as far south as possible; and even Rommel, appointed to the temporary command of Army Group 'B' in northern Italy, believed that the decisive stand should be made along the heights of the northern Apennines to defend the valley of the Po. Further confusion was caused by uncertainty as to whether the Allies would go straight for Rome with an airborne landing, push for Naples by landing in the Gulf of Salerno, or content themselves by crossing the Straits of Messina and advancing methodically up the 'leg' of the Italian 'boot'.

Moreover, when the Allies combined the latter two alternatives (3–8 September 1943) all German forces in Italy were fully engaged in disarming the adjacent Italian troops. Kesselring's genius for improvisation showed itself in the speed in which he drew the hodge-podge of airborne and armoured German units in Italy into a cohesive form (10th Army, commanded by General von Vietinghoff-Scheel), and fed

Above: The limit of an Allied beach-head in Sicily bounded and marked by the bursts of German heavy shells. The Italians, on whom the main burden of the defence of Sicily devolved, proved incompetent, and additional German troops had to be provided to bolster the defence. These forces fought a remarkably skilful campaign, and those that were left at its conclusion were also extricated with great flair, to fight again in the later Italian campaign.

Left: A PzKpfw VI 'Tiger', Germany's heaviest and most powerful fighting tank of World War II, was first encountered by the Western Allies in 1943 in Tunisia, where its armament and protection amazed the British and Americans.

them. At the most, 800 survivors escaped to Sicily.

For the British, North Africa was the only theatre where an initial decisive blow could be dealt at the Axis; for the German high command, it was a sideshow – especially after the invasion of Russia. Only Kesselring, on the spot, sensed the practical possibilities, and most of his energies were devoted to getting the best out of the Italians. 'Torch' turned the whole scene upside-down and made the eventual reinforcements a waste. The *Wehrmacht* lost more men in Tunisia than it did at Stalingrad.

Tactically, Rommel's troubles stemmed from the fact that he had too few German troops – and when Auchinleck concentrated on the Italian units at Alamein the result was near disaster. Rommel was without doubt a master of mobile warfare with small units; it has been said of him that in enough powerful forces at Salerno to bring the British and Americans who landed there to the brink of disaster (8–17 September). Cutting his losses on realising that the invaders were there to stay, and that Naples was therefore lost, Kesselring then supervised a fighting retreat to the superb natural defences across the narrowest neck of the Italian peninsula: the 'Gustav Line', centred on the Monte Cassino massif commanding the direct route to Rome.

Every stream and river, every ridge of high ground, favoured the retreating Germans – and so too did the foul weather and mud of the Italian autumn. By the middle of November the US 5th Army (General Clark) and the British 8th Army (General Montgomery, soon to be replaced by General Leese) were bogged down for the winter facing the Gustav Line. At its heart, Monte Cassino dominated Highway No. 6 and the Liri valley – the road to Rome.

The Allied attempt to lever the Germans out of the Gustav Line by landing at Anzio and Nettuno, far behind the front, failed completely (21 January). The landing, which was concerted with an all-out assault at Cassino, gained initial surprise but was contained by hastily flung-in forces, which were speedily reinforced from the German 14th Army (General von Mackensen) which Kesselring had formed in central Italy. While the Cassino attack was repulsed, the beach-head at Anzio was all but captured by energetic German counterattacks and reduced to a state of siege. Meanwhile, Monte Cassino monastery was bombed by the Allies, giving the Germans the excuse to occupy the ruins and so command the crest of the mountain – leaving the German front stronger than it had been before the attack began.

Cassino falls

The second battle for Cassino was fought between 15 and 23 March. Cassino itself was battered beyond recognition, but the German 1st Parachute Division under General Heidrich, holding Cassino town and abbey, held on against all odds. The Allies gained only vestigial advances and the German ring around the Anzio beach-head remained unbroken. Alexander, Allied supreme commander, decided to regroup for a decisive assault in April; but delays in redeploying the troops forced a postponement until May.

On 11 May the last Cassino battle began in the same way as its predecessors, with the Allied attacks blunted by a superb resistance. But the rapid penetration of the Aurunci mountains by French colonial troops unhinged the Cassino line in three days, and Kesselring had to agree to a withdrawal. The next three weeks were chaotic in both sides. The British and Americans had the chance of splitting the 10th Army and the 14th Army apart and destroying them piecemeal, but despite heavy and irreplaceable German losses Vietinghoff and Lemelsen (Mackensen's successor as commander of the 14th Army) managed to join up and pull right back to

the 'Gothic Line' across the northern Apennines, where Kesselring had his best remaining line of fixed defences. By mid-August the Allies had closed up to the line and another temporary stalemate settled over the Italian front.

Alexander now lost four French and three US divisions, earmarked for the landings in southern France. He made a desperate effort to unhinge the Gothic Line on the Adriatic sector, but failed to score a decisive breakthrough before the autumn rains came. Inch-by-inch progress during October and November took the 8th Army as far as Ravenna; on the left flank Clark's Americans were stopped short of Bologna. It was another strategic triumph for Kesselring, preventing the Allies from any chance of reaching the Alps until the spring of 1945.

The end in Italy

After a second miserable winter in the Italian mountains, Alexander's two armies prepared for the decisive breakthrough in April 1945. By this time the Allies were across the Rhine and the Red Army was preparing for its final assault on Berlin. But Kesselring had quitted Italy, appointed to the thankless task of presiding over the chaos in the West. He had been replaced as C-in-C Army Group 'C' (the 10th and 14th Armies) by Vietinghoff.

The final Allied push in Italy lasted just 17 days. It opened with an amphibious

Above: **Rommel at his first parade in North Africa, in Tripoli. Although under orders to wait until his full force had arrived, Rommel decided to strike at the British immediately, caught them off balance and drove them back hundreds of miles. That part of his career that was to make the name Rommel a household word, was about to begin.**
Right: **PzKpfw III tanks are swayed down from a transport ship onto Tripoli dock for Rommel's *Deutsches Afrikakorps.* Often considered an elite formation, the DAK was in fact nothing of the sort.**

assault across Lake Comacchio on 9 April. This completely unseamed the German left flank. By the time Vietinghoff finally ordered a staged withdrawal to the River Po, his last possible defence line, the British were already across (20 April). Secret negotiations between Allen Dulles of the CIA and the SS supreme commander in the south, Karl Wolff, accelerated the surrender of nearly a million men on April 29 (the German forces in Austria were included in the surrender). American forces had meanwhile raced north to join hands with their compatriots on the Brenner Pass – 12 months too late to have any effect on the Soviet domination of eastern and central Europe.

Field-Marshal Erwin Rommel

After a brief spell in Italy, Rommel took up command of Army Group 'B', which had the task of defeating any Allied attempt to land in northern France.

Rommel favoured a scheme to defeat the Allies on the beaches, but was overruled from above. He was in Germany at the time of the Allied landings, and was able to achieve little on his return to the front.

On 17 July 1944 Rommel's car was shot up by Allied fighters and the field-marshal was severely wounded. Rommel was implicated in the July Plot, and on 14 October, whilst he was still recovering from his wounds, he was persuaded to take poison.

Rommel still remains an enigmatic figure, commanding considerable respect even from his former enemies. He tended to place himself too far forward in battle, in a manner more suitable for a divisional, or perhaps even corps, commander than an army commander.

Erwin Rommel was born on 15 November 1891 at Heidenheim near Ulm, the son of a local school teacher. In July 1910 the 18-year old Rommel joined the 124th Regiment (6th Wurttemberg) as an enlisted man, being commissioned in March 1911 and subsequently attending the officer school in Danzig.

Rommel had a very distinguished career as a junior officer in World War I, serving in France, Rumania and Italy. During the Battle of Caporetto Rommel won the *Pour le Mérite*, Imperial Germany's premier decoration.

Between the two wars Rommel served mostly as an instructor at schools and academies, before being appointed to command Hitler's bodyguard in 1939. In the invasion of France he commanded the 7th Panzer Division, the first German formation to reach the French north coast.

Slated for command of a corps in 1941, Rommel was sent to the aid of the struggling Italian forces in North Africa. In this theatre, with steadily growing forces, he proved a considerable thorn in the side of the British in two major offensive drives before his defeat at El Alamein in October 1942. Rommel conducted an excellent fighting retreat back to Tunisia before being ordered home in March 1943.

Field-Marshal Erwin Rommel

Gazala-is justly hailed as Rommel's greatest victory in North Africa. It ended a three-month period of deadlock in Cyrenaica; it destroyed the cohesion of the British 8th Army and forced it into headlong retreat; it gave Rommel Tobruk and his field-marshal's baton; and it cleared the way for the invasion of Egypt. None of this can be contested. But it is also true that although he retained the initiative throughout the battle, Rommel had set himself an impossibly optimistic schedule. He brought his army to the brink of destruction through rashness, as he had done during 'Crusader' six months before. He won his battle with his flexibility and determination – but only by the narrowest of margins.

Rommel attacked at Gazala on 26 May to forestall the offensive which his opposite number, General Ritchie of the 8th Army, was obviously planning. It had always been fairly clear what Rommel would do – he had very little choice. The chain of 8th Army defences running south from Gazala on the coast ended in the open desert at Bir Hakeim (or Hacheim), a series of wired and mined defences known as 'boxes', each manned by a brigade. Behind the boxes and their connecting minefields was the killing-ground where the British and Axis armour would settle the final outcome of the battle.

Rommel's initial error was to assume that he could arrive in the 8th Army's rear completely by surprise and then fight the sort of battle he wanted. But the big wheel of the *Afrika Korps* southward round Bir Hakeim on the night of 26/27 May was spotted and observed. By nightfall on the 27th he had

had to accept that he had not gained surprise – and that he had also underestimated two other vital factors: the disruptive rôle of the boxes, which jeopardised his supplies; and the basic strength of the British armoured divisions. What saved him was the tactical adolescence of the British in tank warfare. Although Auchinleck had warned

A PzKpfw I light tank, in all probability modified to take a flame gun in place of the right-hand machine gun in the turret, moves up against the staunchly held Free French 'box' at Bir Hakeim. General Koenig's stand here, at the southern end of the Allied line at Gazala, was of crucial importance in the early stages of the Battle of Gazala.

Ritchie 'you should not break up the organisation of either of the armoured divisions. They have been trained to fight as divisions, I hope, and fights as divisions they should', they never did. And this saved Rommel from his initial errors.

The British armour had a superb chance on the 28th, but was repeatedly committed to battle in brigade packets. By the end of the day the *Afrika Korps*, the German 90th Light Division and the Italian 'Ariete' Armoured Division were concentrated but running dangerously short on fuel and ammunition. Attempts to solve the problem by running supplies past the Bir Hakeim box on the 29th proved inadequate and far too dangerous; and Rommel was forced to think again.

He decided to punch a hole through the Gazala line by reducing the British 150th Brigade Box at Sidi Muftah, which would give him a direct supply-line through the heart of the British defences, and shifted the *Afrika Korps* westward to a fine defensive position which was soon to earn the nick-name of 'The Cauldron'. Rommel then fell upon the 150th Brigade Box, where after desperate fighting British resistance ended on June 1. Once again, Ritchie made no move to intervene.

Although he had taken the first step necessary to compensate for his initial over-eagerness, Rommel was still in a most dangerous position. The *Panzerarmee* was split, with the *Afrika Korps* and 'Ariete' Division east of the Gazala line and the remaining Axis divisions – predominantly Italian – west of it. The obvious move for the British was to exploit this situation, but the next phase of the battle – a concentric attack on Rommel in the 'Cauldron' – failed to use the intact reserves still at Ritchie's disposal. Rommel's forces survived the attacks of 5 June with ease, and flung in a superb counterattack which resulted in the wiping-out of 10th Indian Brigade on 6 June.

During the 'Crusader' fighting the previous November, Rommel had thrown away

the methodical and damaging defensive tactics being waged by *Afrika Korps* by making his rash 'Dash to the Wire'. He did not make a similar mistake now. Having restored the dangerous situation created by his own misconception of the 8th Army's position, he now turned south to eliminate the terminal defences of the Gazala line: the Free French box at Bir Hakeim. Here he found that he had caught a tartar: the French troops under General Koenig held out against merciless Stuka attacks until, on 9 June, infantry units from 15th Panzer Division forced their way on to 'Point 186' – all-important high ground which commanded the main French position. The Bir Hakeim Box held out on the 10th but its days were clearly numbered; and the garrison broke out through the German lines on the night of 10/11 June.

Preliminaries over

But all these events were nothing more than the preliminary to the decisive phase of the battle: breaking the 8th Army's main strength in the field. The northern positions of the Gazala line were still intact, and a screen of defensive positions – of which the two most important were boxes at 'Knightsbridge' (201st Guards Brigade) and El Adem (29th Indian Brigade) – barred the approaches to Tobruk to the north-east. Moreover, Ritchie still had the advantage in armour: 330 cruiser and infantry tanks against 160 German and about 70 Italian machines.

To cope with this problem Rommel reverted to his original idea of a fan-shaped advance across the 8th Army's flank. This sacrifice of concentration was more than justified, and compensated for, by the failure of Ritchie's generals to concentrate their own armour. Rommel's new advance began on the 11th and had taken him up to the region of El Adem by the evening. Then came 12 June, a black day for the 8th Army, with the 21st and 15th Panzer Divisions

hammering the separated 2nd, 4th and 22nd Armoured Brigades and wiping out 120 tanks. The armoured balance had now swung dramatically and decisively in Rommel's favour. And with the *Afrika Korps* effectively dominating the desert 'no-man's land', the British did not even have the chance of salvaging their many tanks which had run out of fuel or suffered repairable damage.

Tactically, Rommel had reversed the 8th Army's initial tank advantage by his old trick of luring small British tank units on to the German anti-tank batteries and then scattering the survivors with well-timed tank attacks of his own. This was now the only tactic which offered the 8th Army the chance of fighting a draw at Gazala. But it could only have worked if a clearly-defined objective had been defined at once and the ensuing defensive battle fought by a single commander co-ordinating the efforts of what was left of the 8th Army's original strength. General Ritchie, the 8th Army commander, was constantly looking over his shoulder to the Middle East supreme commander, General Auchinleck, back in

Below: **A scene typical of the war in North Africa – a German PzKpfw III trundles past the burning wreckage of a 'brewed up' tank.**

Right: **The opening phase of the Battle of Gazala. Note Rommel's sweeping move round the southern flank of the Allied line, the Free French 'box' at Bir Hakeim, and the dispersed nature of the British armoured units.**

Below right: **Rommel's next move in the planning stage. Such preparations were likely to be made void, however, once Rommel got up towards the front line and started to take personal control of the battle.**

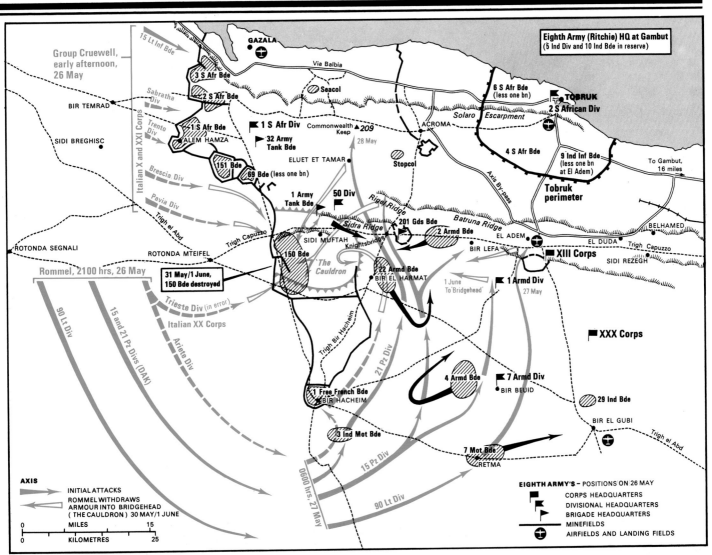

Group Cruewell, early afternoon, 26 May

15 Lt Inf Bde

GAZALA

Via Balbia

Eighth Army (Ritchie) HQ at Gambut
(5 Ind Div and 10 Ind Bde in reserve)

3 S Afr Bde

Seacol

6 S Afr Bde
(less one bn)

TOBRUK

2 S African Div

Sabratha Div

2 S Afr Bde

BIR TEMRAD

Trento Div

1 S Afr Bde

ALEM HAMZA

Solaro Escarpment

ACROMA

4 S Afr Bde

9 Ind Inf Bde
(less one bn at El Adem)

SIDI BREGHISC

1 S Afr Div

Commonwealth Keap ▲209

Brescia Div

151 Bde

32 Army Tank Bde

ELUET ET TAMAR

28 May

Stopcol

Axis By-pass

To Gambut, 16 miles

Pavia Div

69 Bde (less one bn)

1 Army Tank Bde

50 Div

Rigel Ridge

Tobruk perimeter

Trigh el Abd

Sidra Ridge

201 Gds Bde

Batruna Ridge

BELHAMED

ROTONDA SEGNALI

Trigh Capuzzo

ROTONDA MTEIFEL

SIDI MUFTAH

150 Bde

Knightsbridge

2 Armd Bde

EL ADEM

EL DUDA

Trigh Capuzzo

SIDI REZEGH

XIII Corps

Rommel, 2100 hrs, 26 May

31 May/1 June, 150 Bde destroyed

The Cauldron

22 Armd Bde
BIR EL HARMAT

BIR LEFA

1 June To 'Bridgehead'

1 Armd Div

27 May

90 Lt Div

15 and 21 Pz Divs (DAK)

Trieste Div (in error)

Italian XX Corps

Ariete Div

Trigh Bir Hacheim

21 Pz Div

4 Armd Bde

7 Armd Div
• BIR BEUID

XXX Corps

29 Ind Bde

BIR EL GUBI

Trigh el Abd

1 Free French Bde
BIR HACHEIM

3 Ind Mot Bde

15 Pz Div

7 Mot Bde
RETMA

0600 hrs, 27 May

90 Lt Div

EIGHTH ARMY'S — POSITIONS ON 26 MAY

AXIS

INITIAL ATTACKS

ROMMEL WITHDRAWS
ARMOUR INTO BRIDGEHEAD
(THE CAULDRON) 30 MAY/1 JUNE

CORPS HEADQUARTERS

DIVISIONAL HEADQUARTERS

BRIGADE HEADQUARTERS

MINEFIELDS

AIRFIELDS AND LANDING FIELDS

0 MILES 15

0 KILOMETRES 25

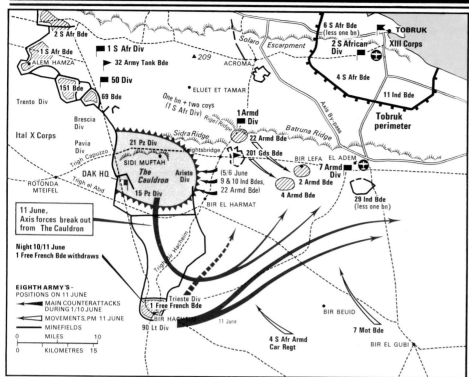

Crisis point in the Battle of Gazala as the Germans break out of the 'Cauldron'. The British were by now exhausted, and Tobruk's fall certain.

Egypt. Auchinleck himself was plagued by a series of constant queries from Churchill in Whitehall – and so, for that matter, was Ritchie. There was total confusion as to what was to be done with Tobruk. Should the perimeter be manned for another siege or not? Snap decisions and counter-orders in the heat of a fluid, armoured battle, especially when made by commanders not on the spot, are a sure recipe for defeat – and at Gazala they were a golden gift for Rommel.

On 13 June the main obstacle to Rommel's attacks during the tank battles of the previous 48 hours – the Guards at 'Knightsbridge', who had offered a fixed rallying-point throughout – was removed by their withdrawal. By the evening the British armour had been an inevitable additional beating and Rommel now had a tank superiority of two to one – an advantage which was still further increased by field repairs to retrieved tanks.

Then came 14 June, the day that dissolved the 8th Army. Ritchie announced his decision to pull out from Gazala and 'occupy the frontier defences', which meant accepting the investment of Tobruk, if only temporarily. Auchinleck's order that 'our forces will not be invested in Tobruk, and your army is to remain a mobile field army', was not much help. Their opponent, speaking from his front-line perspective, saw things clearest of all: 'Full speed ahead was ordered, as British vehicles were now streaming east in their thousands.' On the 15th he felt free to write to his wife: 'The battle has been won and the enemy is breaking up. We're now mopping up encircled remnants of their army . . .'

Three more days sufficed to make certain of Tobruk. The 29th Indian Brigade was forced off El Adem airfield on the 16th; the 4th Armoured Brigade, the last effective force which the 8th Army could field in the

Tobruk area, was smashed on the 17th; and on the following day Rommel, hounding his own exhausted troops like a slave-driver, pushed 20 miles east to Gambut while Tobruk itself was invested from the east. By keeping up this merciless pressure he had prevented Ritchie from making an effective stand west of the Egyptian frontier. Much more important, Tobruk itself, with its run-down defences and polyglot garrison, now lay at the mercy of the *Afrika Korps*. By nightfall on the 19th Rommel had put the 15th Panzer, 21st Panzer and '*Ariete*' Divisions into position at the south-eastern corner of the Tobruk perimeter – the assault sector he had marked down for the previous November, when Auchinleck's 'Crusader' attack had forestalled him.

Tobruk falls

Twenty-four hours sufficed to shatter the defenders of Tobruk and take the town, which had been an obsession of Rommel's since April 1941. He held all the cards – total air and armour superiority and artillery support – and he made no errors. General Klopper, commanding the garrison, made his formal surrender to Rommel in person at about 0940 hours on the 21st. In just under four weeks, Rommel had completed the task laid down for him by the Axis high command. He had beaten the 8th Army out of its defences and disrupted it as an organised fighting entity, leaving it with no alternative but precipitate retreat. He had captured the declared objective of the *Panzerarmee*'s offensive: Tobruk. With the surviving elements of the 8th Army retreating at full speed into Egypt, it seemed that the decisive battle of the desert war had been won.

Rommel's Gazala triumph had been nearly wrecked at the outset by bad intelligence and over-confidence. Of the all-important 150th Brigade Box at Sidi Muftah, General Bayerlein has stated: 'We never knew that it was there. Our first attacks on it failed. If we had not taken it on 1 June, you would

have captured the whole of the *Afrika Korps.*' And this would have been the result of Rommel's under-estimation of the inhibiting effect of fixed defences and minefields, which left the *Afrika Korps* out on a limb behind the Gazala line after the big encircling wheel on the night of 26/27 May. On 1 June, while putting out all his strength to smash the 150th Brigade, Rommel admitted to a British officer POW that 'we cannot go on like this. If we don't get a convoy through tonight I shall have to ask General Ritchie for terms.'

Rommel's measures to put matters to rights – moving the *Afrika Korps* into the 'Cauldron' and grinding down the Sidi Muftah and Bir Hakeim boxes – took 10 days to achieve but left him in the position he had wanted for the second day of his original offensive: soundly established in the base positions of the Gazala line, ready for the decisive clash with the British armour. In this ensuing phase he was helped immeasurably by the persistent small-scale armoured attacks which Ritchie's subordinates carried out. This is particularly noteworthy because the British in the Western Desert had been fighting Rommel for 14 months, and had been repeatedly discomfited by the concentrated power of the *Afrika Korps* under Rommel's hand: the 15th and 21st Panzer Divisions acting as a single unit.

Moving to the subject of the art of generalship, Gazala saw Rommel adopting the ploy of dividing his army in order to fix his enemy's attention with the weaker half and strike the enemy's weakest point with as much force as possible. Until Bir Hakeim fell, this meant that his *Panzerarmee* was effectively partitioned by the Gazala line and that Ritchie had been deliberately offered the initiative. And as far as tank tactics were concerned this was the *Afrika Korps'* favourite trick: luring British tanks against anti-tank guns as a prelude to a decisive counterattack. As General Bayerlein admitted, Rommel's initial leap behind the Gazala line's defences nearly proved fatal. But the assault on the *Afrika Korps*, when it came, was repulsed with ease because the defenders were concentrated and the attackers were not.

Another definite item in Rommel's favour was his leadership from the front line, which the 8th Army never had. Rommel was everywhere the crucial action happened to be, supervising minefield clearance, bringing through supply convoys and pressing home the pursuit. By the time Tobruk was cut off, the men of the *Panzerarmee* were as exhausted as their opponents in the 8th Army. Only Rommel's merciless hounding of his own men prevented stalemate by mutual fatigue on the Egyptian frontier.

Brilliant though it was, however, Gazala remained a Dead Sea fruit. It was not that classic military dream, a 'battle without a morrow'. Gazala was certainly Rommel's Austerlitz; but the sequel to his triumph was the Waterloo of El Alamein.

Above left: **A heavily laden PzKpfw III drives into fallen Tobruk.**

Left: **Part of the German 'bag' of British PoWs awaits removal.**

Colonel-General Juergen von Arnim

French North Africa had rendered the Axis position parlous in the extreme. Elevated to the rank of colonel-general, Arnim was given command of the 5th *Panzerarmee* on 3 December 1942. With the return of Rommel to Europe, Arnim on 9 March 1943 inherited command of Army Group 'Africa' in its last desperate days of resistance to the British 1st and 8th Armies. Arnim surrendered on 12 May 1943 and spent the rest of the war as a British prisoner.

Hans-Juergen von Arnim was born on 4 April 1889 at Ernsdorf in Schleswig, and joined the Imperial German Army as a cadet on 1 April 1908. He was sent to the 4th Regiment of Prussian Foot Guards as a lieutenant on 17 August 1909, and served as a junior officer throughout World War I. Arnim elected to remain in the army after the end of the war, and rose gradually in rank during the days of the *Reichswehr*.

Arnim reached the rank of major-general on 1 January 1938, and was given the command of the 4th *Heeres Dienstelle* (Frontier Zone Command) on 4 February 1938.

After the start of the Polish campaign, Arnim received command of the 52nd Infantry Division on 8 September 1939, and promotion to lieutenant-general on 1 December 1939. After the conclusion of the Western campaign in June 1940, Arnim was appointed to the command of the 17th Panzer Division on 5 October 1940. He led this formation, part of Army Group 'Centre', in the first stages of the war against Soviet Russia before receiving command of XXXIX Panzer Corps on 11 November 1941. Arnim had been promoted general on 1 October 1941.

Arnim was next moved to North Africa, where the Allied landings in

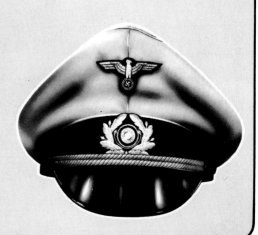

Colonel-General Juergen von Arnim

Operation 'Torch' – the Allied landings in Morocco and Algeria in early November 1942 – should have spelled doom to Rommel's *Panzerarmee*, which had just begun its long retreat from the battlefield of El Alamein. That this fate was averted was due entirely to the prescience of Field-Marshal Kesselring, who had feared such a move and earmarked a scratch collection of airborne units, plus the transport planes to airlift them to Tunis from Sicily. On hearing of the 'Torch' landings, Kesselring shot these forces across to secure Tunis and Bizerta, and the subsequent reinforcement of the 'Tunisian bridgehead' was swift and effective. Between 10 and 20 November both sides in Tunisia were pegging out claims as far forward as possible; and in the last week of the month the first head-on clashes occurred, between Sedjenane and Mateur, at Sidi Nsir and at Medjez-el-Bab. In this fighting the Germans in Tunisia won a clear first

round, halting the British and American probe towards Tunis and Bizerta and throwing the Allies on to the defensive.

At this stage, with Rommel still retreating across Libya, it was vital to win enough time for the battered *Panzerarmee* to pull back into Tunisia itself; and the result was a series of spoiling attacks to make this possible. German troops continued to pour into Tunisia, the most important reinforcement being the 10th Panzer Division, whose advance units on 1 December began a series of successful probes which continued until the 6th, when Colonel-General Juergen von Arnim arrived in Tunisia to take command of the newly-formed 5th *Panzerarmee*, ultimately intended to hold Tunisia together with Rommel's *Panzerarmee Afrika*.

Arnim's first move, naturally enough, was to keep up the existing pressure. Repeated attacks towards Medjez were held, but in Christmas week the Germans successfully

recovered the strategic heights of 'Longstop Hill', key to the Medjerda valley leading down to the sea between Tunis and Bizerta. Further to the south, attacks against the French-held sector of the Allied front won the Pichon pass, 75 miles south of Tunis. It was of vital importance to gain Rommel as much room as possible in the southern sector and for this Arnim wanted all key passes across the range known as the Eastern Dorsale. A further series of limited attacks in January was completely successful, securing not only the Pichon pass (3 January) but

German *Panzergrenadiers* watch with satisfaction from their tank as a small party of British prisoners is marched through Tebourba in December 1942. The end of this year, and the beginning of the next, were marked by some significant successes for the Germans in Tunisia.

Pont-du-Fahs (18 January) and the Faid pass (30 January). By this series of small offensives in his first month of command in Tunisia, Arnim had deepened and strengthened the Tunisian bridgehead just in time for Rommel's arrival in the Mareth line with the 8th Army at his heels.

By this time Arnim's reinforcements had raised the total German and Italian strength in Tunisia to about 100,000, and to this figure were now added the surviving 70,000 of Rommel's *Panzerarmee*. This gave the Axis forces in Tunisia a splendid chance to counterattack, first against the strung-out British, French and Americans in Tunisia, then against Montgomery in front of the Mareth line. But now the muddled set-up created by the *Comando Supremo*, the Italian high command in Rome, ruined all real hopes for concerted and decisive action. Rommel had already been told he was to quit the *Panzerarmee* after reaching the Mareth line: newly entitled the 1st Army, it would be taken over by the Italian General Messe. But Rommel was left to decide when he should actually go. The decision had been taken to create an Army Group 'Africa' to combine the operations of the 1st Army and the 5th *Panzerarmee* in the bridgehead – but no C-in-C had yet been designated. In the meantime friction was rapidly growing between Rommel and Arnim. The former wanted to tear open the Allied right flank by an armoured smash through the Western Dorsale, with the faint possibility of capturing Bône on the coast if the Allied flank could be rolled up. The Axis forces could then turn about and fall on Montgomery. Arnim saw his rôle as purely defensive. The result was the compromise plan which unleashed the Kasserine offensive on 14 February. This hammered an ominous dent in the American positions. The plan came to nothing because of Arnim's caution – he withdrew the 10th Panzer Division at the crucial moment, leaving Rommel facing stiffening Allied resistance at the tip of the salient. By the end of the month the Germans were back at their start-line, having achieved little else but giving a sobering lesson to American troops about coping with Panzer attacks.

Timing essential

Before the Kasserine attack petered out, Army Group 'Africa' had been brought into being and Rommel had accepted the command. Messe took over the 1st Army, and Rommel prepared for his 'back-hand' punch at the 8th Army. But Arnim's excessive care for the strength of his own front in keeping a tight hold over the 10th Panzer Division meant that the new attack on the 8th Army could not be dealt with the speed originally envisaged by Rommel. Montgomery had a full week to prepare for Rommel's attack against the 8th Army's positions at Medenine; and the ensuing battle saw the British make excellent use of the time-tested methods of the *Afrika Korps*. On 6 March 1943 Rommel's armour was allowed to crucify itself on a dense shield of anti-tank guns. The attack was a total failure – and Rommel's last battle in Africa. A sick man, he quitted Tunisia on 9 March; and the command of Army Group 'Africa'

passed to Arnim.

Whatever chances of success existed for Rommel's double-blow plan, time was the vital factor. Pinpoint timing was required for the shuttling of the armoured forces between the Kasserine and Mareth fronts, which was not achieved. This was largely due to the half-baked Axis command structure in Africa, which left Arnim outside Rommel's sphere of command. Not only did Arnim deny Rommel the total co-operation of the 5th *Panzerarmee* necessary to make the Kasserine attack a success: his own offensive in the northern sector came to nothing. This was the aptly-named *Ochsenkopf* ('Oxhead'), which had as its objective the Allied bases of Béja and Medjez, and was scheduled for 26 February. Other attacks were to be made at Abiod on the extreme Allied left. The best that can be said for Arnim's idea of attack was that it

Above: German heavy artillery in action during January 1943.

Above right: The closing stages of the Tunisian campaign. With Rommel recalled to Europe, and the Allied 1st and 8th Armies linked up, the final defeat of the Axis forces in Tunisia was certain. The Allied task was considerably eased, however, by Arnim's lack of tactical and strategic flair.

Right: A German paratroop MG 34 machine gun crew. In the Tunisian campaign the elite *Fallschirmjaeger* troops were used as conventional infantry, and continued to add to their laurels as excellent, tough and aggressive fighting men, as did the British airborne forces.

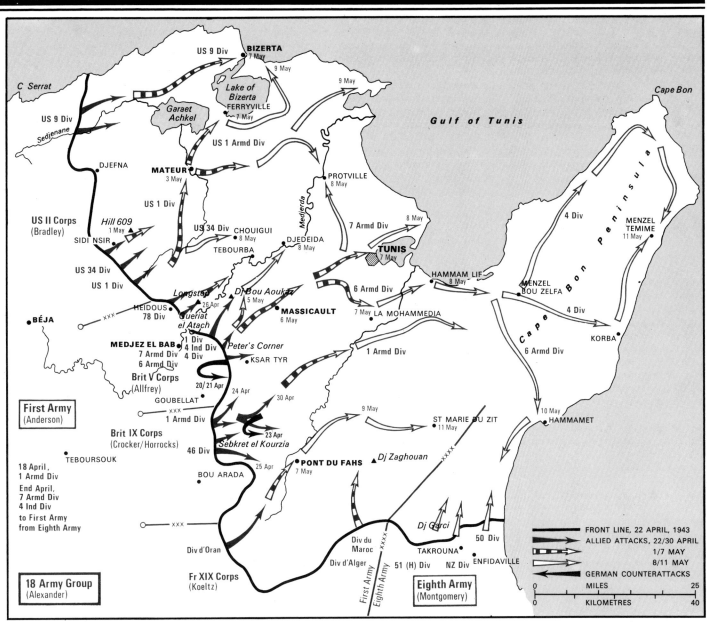

C Serrat

US 9 Div
BIZERTA
7 May
9 May
9 May

Lake of
Bizerta
Garaet
Achkel
FERRYVILLE
7 May

Gulf of Tunis

Cape Bon

US 1 Armd Div

DJEFNA

MATEUR
3 May

PROTVILLE
8 May

US 1 Div

Menzerda

7 Armd Div
8 May

US 34 Div
CHOUIGUI
8 May

US II Corps
(Bradley)

Hill 609
1 May
SIDI NSIR

TEBOURBA
DJEDEIDA
8 May

TUNIS
7 May

4 Div

MENZEL
TEMIME
11 May

US 34 Div
US 1 Div

Longstop
26 Apr

Dj Bou Aoukaz
5 May

MASSICAULT
6 May

6 Armd Div

HAMMAM LIF
8 May

MENZEL
BOU ZELFA

Cape Bon Peninsula

HEIDOUS
78 Div

Queriat
el Atach

7 May LA MOHAMMEDIA

4 Div

BÉJA

MEDJEZ EL BAB
7 Armd Div
6 Armd Div

1 Div
4 Ind Div
4 Div

Peter's Corner

KSAR TYR

1 Armd Div

6 Armd Div

KORBA

Brit V Corps
(Allfrey)

20/21 Apr

24 Apr

30 Apr

First Army
(Anderson)

GOUBELLAT

1 Armd Div

23 Apr

Sebkret el Kourzia

9 May

ST MARIE DU ZIT
11 May

10 May
HAMMAMET

Brit IX Corps
(Crocker/Horrocks)

46 Div

25 Apr

PONT DU FAHS
7 May

Dj Zaghouan

TEBOURSOUK

BOU ARADA

18 April,
1 Armd Div
End April,
7 Armd Div
4 Ind Div
to First Army
from Eighth Army

Dj Garci

50 Div

FRONT LINE, 22 APRIL, 1943
ALLIED ATTACKS, 22/30 APRIL
1/7 MAY
8/11 MAY
GERMAN COUNTERATTACKS

Div d'Oran

Div du
Maroc

Div d'Alger

TAKROUNA

51 (H) Div

NZ Div

ENFIDAVILLE

First Army
Eighth Army

0   MILES   25
0   KILOMETRES   40

18 Army Group
(Alexander)

Fr XIX Corps
(Koeltz)

Eighth Army
(Montgomery)

did follow the pattern which he had so successfully set in December and January. But the arrival of Rommel's *Panzerarmee* had transformed the whole situation; and after the failure at Kasserine, Arnim's scheme for the other end of the Allied line was strategically wasteful. None of the *Ochsenkopf* attacks attained their objectives, and all of them had been soundly repulsed by 1 March. As Rommel was soon to find at Medenine, a notable feature of the British defence was the furious and accurate concentration of artillery.

Rommel had spent much of his remaining time in Tunisia in vainly trying to get the *Comando Supremo* to tell him what the overall strategy for the theatre might be. He pressed for a shortening of the line in Tunisia, abandoning the Mareth line, pulling Messe's 1st Army north to Enfidaville for a higher concentration of the two armies. When Arnim took over as army group commander, his opponent General Alexander sharpened the Axis dilemma by launching attacks on the Gafsa sector. Thus Arnim was never certain whether the next main Allied attack was going to be at Mareth or Gafsa; and by keeping Messe's 1st Army exposed at Mareth he risked its destruction. Arnim's limited determination to hold as much of the original bridgehead as possible was totally unrealistic and certainly helped to accelerate the pace of the Allied advance.

In March, Montgomery squared up to the Mareth line, in blissful ignorance of the fact that Rommel had actually left Tunisia. Messe, facing the oncoming attack, was deceived by American attacks on the Gafsa sector into holding back the 10th Panzer Division from the Mareth front. The actual battle of Mareth lasted from 20 to 28 March and was a fine achievement for the 8th Army, the 1st Army being forced out of the Mareth line. Montgomery, however, had promised his men before the battle that they would destroy their enemy; and that this was not achieved was largely due to a legacy of Rommel. Although the latter had accepted the fact that an Italian general would take over his old *Panzerarmee*, Rommel had provided that General Bayerlein should remain as liaison officer – in effective command of the German forces of the 1st Army. As the Axis hold on the Mareth line was prised away, the surviving German forces conducted their own brand of fighting retreat. It was a paradoxical situation, again created by the muddled and bi-national chain of command. Mareth should have destroyed the 1st Army, but the professional insubordination of its German components kept it in being. Yet the Axis losses were serious. Never again would the 1st Army be able to launch a counterblow of the weight which Rommel had unleashed at Medenine.

Thus it is clear that the turning-point of the battle for Tunisia was in fact Medenine on 6 March. This was the last time that the Axis defenders of the bridgehead had the luxury of the initiative, turning from the Allied 1st Army to Montgomery's 8th Army with separate, heavy counterattacks. Conversely, Medenine was the last battle which saw the 1st and 8th Armies fighting separately. From Mareth onwards, the two armies would be advancing in close co-ordination.

This was proved by the immediate postscript to Mareth: the 8th Army's head-on penetration of the 'Gabes Gap' across the Wadi Akarit (5/6 April). Once again, Messe escaped total destruction, but this time pressure from both Allied armies caused a minor Axis landslide. American forces from Gafsa joined hands with 8th Army forces on 7 April, and on the same day a 1st Army assault on the Fondouk Pass began to batter open to the door to Kairouan from the west. Sfax fell to the 8th Army on 10 April, and on the following day British troops from the 1st and 8th Armies met in Kairouan. Sousse was added to the 8th Army's bag on 12 April. But then the pace of events slowed and halted. Army Group 'Africa' had been driven back into the Tunis–Bizerta litoral, and its line was now correspondingly easier to defend. Once again, Alexander had to sit down before the enemy lines and plan a set-piece attack.

No evacuation

Now the total failure of the Axis high command to take the North African theatre seriously came home to roost with a vengeance. Army Group 'Africa', a quarter of a million strong, had been created two years too late to have any strategic vitality as an offensive weapon. It now lacked so much as an inch of spare ground in which it could manoeuvre against its enemies; and its leader, Arnim, was a wooden and limited commander who never realised that his short-sightedness in the vital month of

February had brought him and his armies into this deadly trap. With the small-scale attacks of December and January, Arnim had done very well. But that was his limit. His mind recoiled from the daring opportunism which alone could have transformed the Kasserine attacks into one of the most daring Panzer operations of World War II. Nor was Arnim the man to accept the strategic enormity which alone made sense after Kasserine: getting as many men as possible out of North Africa to fight again.

The men of Army Group 'Africa' did all that fighting men could do, when the Allied attack was resumed on 22 April, to hold their last perimeter. Continuing until the end of the month, these attacks battered the German and Italians out of their front-line positions on the vital heights. The final assault on 6 May shattered Army Group 'Africa' like a glass block hit with a hammer. Arnim's insistence on commanding by the book totally deprived his men of any meaningful order after Tunis and Bizerta fell on the 7th, rupturing the chain of command. The hundreds and thousands of milling Axis troops, well armed and supplied, never even received an order to take to the hills and carry on guerrilla warfare from there, which they could easily have done for months. The formal surrenders of Arnim and Messe – on 12 and 13 May respectively – were accompanied by the usual punctilio. They set the seal on what can most accurately be described as a colossal piece of waste – of strategic opportunity, of *matériel* and, most important of all, of men.

A Hawker Hurricane IID swoops down in a firing pass at an Axis tank. By 1942 obsolete as a first-line interceptor fighter, the Hurricane was very successfully converted into a ground-attack aircraft in two major roles: as a fighter-bomber, armed with cannon and bombs (rockets were later added to the underwing inventory of the 'Hurribomber'), and as a tank-busting fighter, armed with two 40-mm cannon under the wings. No German tank up to the end of 1942 could take such a 40-mm shell without taking considerable damage, and so the Hurricane IID became an invaluable weapon in the predominantly armoured warfare fought in North Africa.

Field-Marshal Albert Kesselring

Albert Kesselring was born at Markstedt on 20 November 1885, like Rommel the son of a school teacher. He joined the 2nd Bavarian Foot Artillery Regiment in 1904, and served with this army first in the field and later on the staff during World War I.

In the first years of the *Reichswehr*, Kesselring held a number of staff posts, anf from 1930 to 1931 was the commander of the 4th Artillery Regiment in Dresden.

Kesselring had long been fascinated by air power, however, and on 1 October 1933 he was discharged from the army to take up the position of head of the Administration Office of the *Luftwaffe*, as yet still a secret organisation. Although in his late 40s, Kesselring learned to fly.

In the Polish war Kesselring commanded the 1st Air Fleet, and was awarded the Knight's Cross of the Iron Cross at the end of the campaign. In the war against the West he commanded the 2nd Air Fleet, which also took part in the Battle of Britain before moving east for the invasion of Russia in June 1941. In Russia the 2nd Air Fleet operated very successfully in support of Army Group 'Centre'.

Early in 1942, however, Kesselring and his air fleet were transferred to Italy. Kesselring was made Commander-in-Chief South, with authority over all German forces in the Mediterranean. In this capacity he gave Rommel much help. Realising the object of the Allied landings in French North Africa in November 1942, he airlifted German forces across the Mediterranean to create a bridgehead in Tunisia.

After the Allies had taken Tunisia and crossed to Sicily and then to Italy, the Germans fought a good defensive campaign up the Italian peninsula, superbly co-ordinated by Kesselring.

In March 1945 Kesselring was moved to the Western Front, to replace Rundstedt in the hopeless task of holding back the Western Allies from the German heartland. Captured by US troops, Kesselring was tried, condemned to death and then had his sentence commuted as a result of ill-health.

Field-Marshal Albert Kesselring

A natural comparison can be drawn between the attempt of Rommel and Arnim to defend Tunisia after El Alemein, and the attempt of Kesselring to halt the Allies at Monte Cassino after the invasion of Italy in September 1943. Both episodes lasted about the same time: seven months. Both episodes saw periods of marked German success; and both episodes helped prolong the life of the Third Reich and thus inhibit the Allied planning for final victory. As we have seen, however, the Axis position in Tunisia was basically hopeless. This was not the case in Italy, where every feature of the peninsula was ideally suited to a planned defence. Much more important, the defenders in Italy had a clear brief and a simple and effective chain of command. Thanks to Field-Marshal Albert Kesselring and his dogged defence at Cassino, the Allies were kept out of Rome for seven months. This took the victors past the spring of 1944 – the deadline when the armies in Italy must yield their strategic precedence to the forces preparing for the cross-Channel invasion of France – and ended all hopes of a runaway Allied victory in Italy.

Such in essence was the nature of Kesselring's achievement at Cassino. The battle itself tends to overshadow the fact that he had been on the verge of being overruled in his demands to hold central Italy, that

Rommel himself, commanding in the Po valley, had believed that the only chance would be to make a decisive stand along the northern Apennines – in short, that there might never have been a stand-up fight at Cassino at all. Kesselring had had to fight for his strategy, which was basically to keep the Allied bomber bases as far away from the Reich as possible. Originally, Hitler backed

Rommel. But although the *Fuehrer*'s lack of interest in the southern theatre had never really been modified since Rommel's first victories in Africa back in the early part of 1941, two concurrent events in the autumn of 1943 caught his imagination. They were the battle of Salerno, in which Kesselring's miscellany of Germany troops nearly succeeded in forcing the invading Allies back

Above: **A PzKpfw IV medium tank in the ruins of Cassino. This was the single most daunting German defence position to be overcome by the Allies in Italy.**

Left: **Abbot Georgio Diamere is escorted from his abbey on top of the commanding heights of Monte Cassino.**

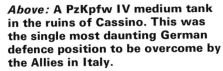

into the sea, and the rescue of Mussolini from his mountain-top prison by Otto Skorzeny's paratroops. These were heartening achievements against which Kesselring's optimistic strategy looked well; and in November 1943 Kesselring was appointed C-in-C of Army Group 'C', responsible for the defence of central and southern Italy.

By this time the Allies had survived the traumatic shock of Salerno, had taken Naples and were inching painfully through one of the foullest Italian autumns for years along the road to Rome. But although his appointment came late, Kesselring did not have to start from scratch. His foresight a year before had enabled him to save Tunisia from the Allies; and during the fight for Sicily in the high summer of 1943 he had taken steps to counter the next obvious Allied move against southern Italy. The narrowest section of the Italian peninsula between Naples and Rome was only 85 miles wide and was studded with perfect natural defences. South of this line, rivers and other suitable ridges of high ground offered the defenders parallel outer lines of defence. Throughout November 1943 the German troops fell slowly back towards the main line of defence, which had been code-named the 'Gustav Line' and whose main features were the Garigliano and Rapido rivers on the right, the Sangro river on the left and in the centre, commanding Route No. 6 and the road to Rome, the *massif* of Cassino itself.

1st Cassino

The defence of the Gustav Line was entrusted to the 10th Army under General von Vietinghoff-Scheel, and it was composed of superb if polyglot troops under equally good commanders: Hube and von Senger of XIV Panzer Corps, Heidrich of the 1st Parachute Division, Fries of the 29th *Panzergrenadier* Division and Ringel of the 5th Mountain Division. But the 10th Army did not wait for the advancing US 5th and British 8th Armies behind static defences. The opening phase of the Cassino campaign was in a fact a fighting retreat from the Volturno river (crossed by the 5th Army in mid-October) to the outer bastion of the Gustav Line proper. This was the 'Reinhard Line', a miniature Cassino, with the formidable heights of Monte Maggiore and Monte Sammucro commanding Route No. 6; it took the 5th Army the whole of December and the first fortnight of January 1944 to batter through the Reinhard Line and close up to the Garigliano and Rapido, under the heights of Cassino. Meanwhile, on the Allied right flank, Montgomery's 8th Army (taken over on 30 December by General Leese) struggled forwards across the Sangro river, painfully taking Ortona after a set-piece assault before being halted short of the Arielli river. But Kesselring could afford to give ground on the Sangro front. The decisive fight had to be made at Cassino, against the 5th Army.

What became known as the first battle of Cassino opened well for the Allies, with the German right flank on the lower Garigliano rapidly losing ground. The Allied attack at Cassino was co-ordinated with the celebrated landing at Anzio-Nettuno, deep behind the Gustav Line and posing a direct threat to Rome. Although Kesselring had his hands full at Cassino, and was totally taken by surprise by the Anzio stroke, he managed to contain the latter danger without withdrawing any troops from the Cassino front, where his reserves had already been committed on the lower Garigliano. Once again his foresight saved the day. Rome had always been an obvious goal for a surprise Allied attempt, and Kesselring had earmarked nucleus units to stand in readiness to enter the battle if need be. Thus he managed to seal off the beach-head with an extraordinary collection of battle-groups and

special detachments from just about every German division in Italy. Another invaluable factor was the caution of the first Allied commander at Anzio, General Lucas, whose road to Rome was wide open on 22/23 January. By the time he started probing cautiously inland it was too late. The ring round the beach-head was secure.

At this point it is necessary to state that the Allies had attached a secondary purpose to the Italian theatre, apart from the obvious advantages of closing in on the Reich from the south. This was to compel the Germans to feed in as many troop reinforcements as possible – troops which would otherwise be sent to France to defend the Channel coast against invasion. Kesselring's improvisations had been made without such a reinforcement – but once again the shadow of Salerno touched the scene. Hitler and OKW wanted a counterattack that would succeed where that at Salerno had failed, and packed four divisions off to Italy, thus indirectly aiding Allied strategy. This fact was certainly not apparent to the wretched troops in the beach-head, who had to fight for their lives to maintain their position and then endure over three months of siege warfare worthy of the trenches in World War I.

Despite the initial danger on the lower Garigliano, the German positions along the Rapido held well and inflicted heavy losses on the Allied attacks during January. During a three-day battle (20/22 January) the US II Corps, and in particular the 36th 'Texas' Division, suffered bloody losses in its attempts to burst through the Gustav Line across the Rapido, and the attacks had to be called off.

Although the fighting on the Rapido was

Top: **The shattered ruins of Cassino after the Allied raid of 15 March 1944, in which over 1,400 tons of bombs were dropped.**

Above: **Monte Cassino Abbey in February 1944, before it was almost totally razed in the disastrous raid of March. The decision to bomb the abbey is still one of the most controversial aspects of World War II history, as the abbey was not used by the Germans until after the bombing raid.**

Right: **German paratroops in defensive position at Cassino.**

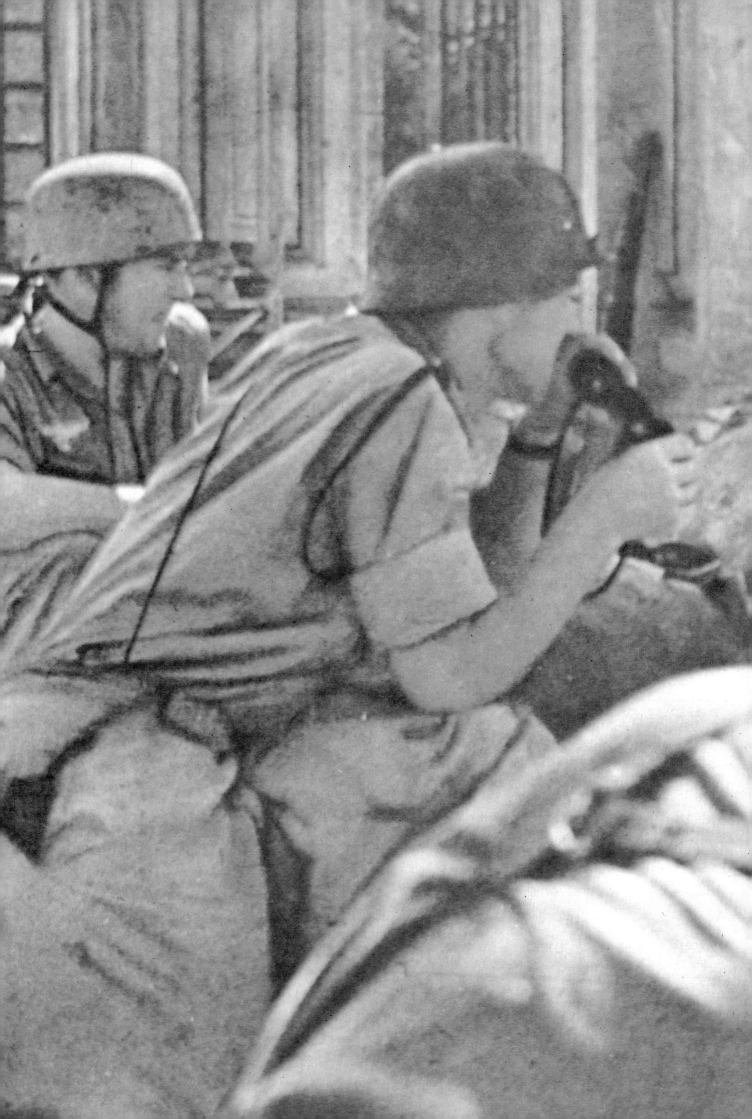

fierce, it was nothing to that seen during the third phase which now ensued: the attempt to force the Germans out of their positions on the heights of Monte Cassino itself. Ten days of intense fighting carried the troops of the US 34th Division to the verge of success on Monte Cassino before desperate counterattacks by German paratroops drove them off. This was a two-level fight, waged with equal intensity up on the heights and down in the shattered ruins of Cassino town.

To bomb or not?

Meanwhile, Alexander had pulled three of the best 8th Army units out of the line on the Adriatic sector and formed them into a special shock corps under the command of the famous New Zealander, General Freyberg. Final-gasp attacks by the US II Corps on 11 and 12 February petered out just over a mile away from Highway No. 6 in a welter of persistent counterattacks. The Americans had fought themselves out; and Freyberg's newly-formed New Zealand Corps took over the job of pressing home the offensive.

There now followed one of the most controversial events of the war: the decision to bomb the venerable Abbey on the crest

of Monte Cassino. This was a definite Allied miscalculation. There were in fact no German troops in the monastery, for all Freyberg's protestations to the contrary. Indeed the Germans, fearing for the safety of the priceless objects of art and devotion in the monastery, had evacuated the latter to the safety of the San Paolo monastery in Rome, after which Kesselring had drawn a 400-yard perimeter around the abbey precincts at Monte Cassino and issued the strictest orders that no German troops were to violate it. Freyberg's refusal to assault the heights until the monastery had been razed by bombers was an act of military shortsightedness, to say the least. Apart from being mistaken, he should have known that a heap of ruins is far easier for infantry to defend than an undamaged building. It is, after all, impossible to construct an invisible machine gun nest in a smooth and unbroken wall. And the bombing of the abbey on 15 February merely gave the Germans the excuse to move into the ruins and defend them in earnest. Even the pulverising effect of the bombardment was wasted, for Freyberg did not send in a heavy attack until 18 hours after the bombardment. It was handled roughly by a spirited German

counterattack; and on 18 February a temporary silence settled on the Cassino battlefield. Kesselring's defenders, although frequently brought to the brink of defeat, had won a resounding victory; and the Allied attempt to dislodge them by the Anzio stroke had also failed.

The second battle of Cassino lasted from 15 to 23 March, and in it the Allies repeated every mistake they had previously made. The assault on Cassino town and abbey was preceded by the biggest air bombardment ever seen in the Mediterranean theatre, with 575 heavy and medium bombers taking part. Manning the crucial eight-mile Cassino sector of the Gustav Line were the crack paratroops of 1st Division under General Heidrich. Like the men of the German army on the Western Front in World War I, they once again proved that heavy bombardments do not mean that every soldier in the target area is killed. The heaped ruins acted as perfect anti-tank traps for the Allied armour, and also slowed the advance of Freyberg's infantrymen to a crawl. It was another sobering defeat for the Allied armies at Cassino.

The keynote of the month and a half after the second clash at Cassino was a regrouping

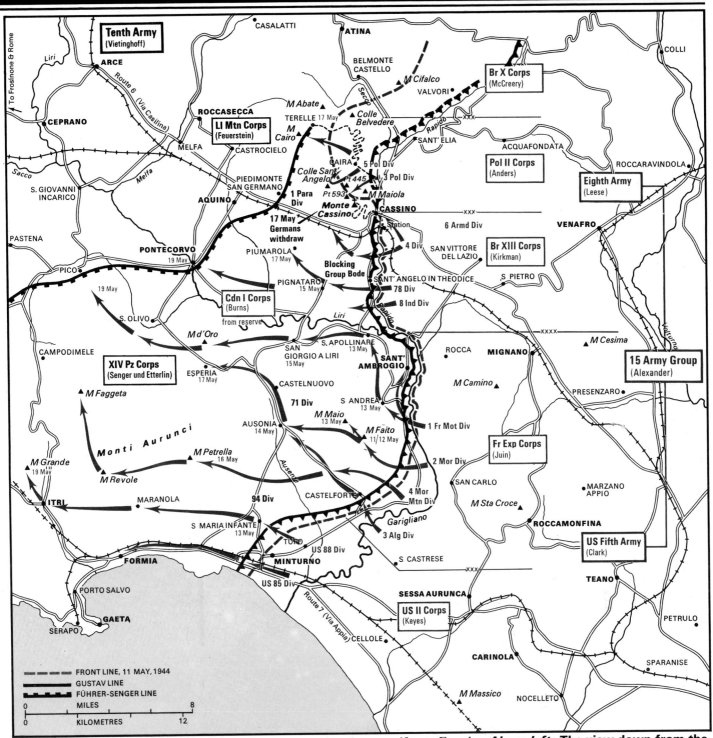

FRONT LINE, 11 MAY, 1944
GUSTAV LINE
FÜHRER-SENGER LINE

MILES 0 — 8
KILOMETRES 0 — 12

on both sides, and an Allied air bombing offensive – Operation 'Strangle' – aimed at a total disruption of Kesselring's supply-lines in Italy. The latter aim was never achieved, although the repeated raids got a good deal of optimistic press coverage – 'Bombs blast enemy HQ', and so forth. Essentially Kesselring's dilemma remained unchanged. The Allied armies had the choice of making their main attack at Cassino, from the Anzio beach-head, or by means of yet another seaborne hook further north up the Italian coast. In fact Alexander planned for a decisive breakthrough at Cassino, having decided that the forces of the US 5th Army alone were inadequate. Massive reinforcements were brought across from the 8th Army; and by the opening of the third and final battle of Cassino at 2300 hours on 11 May, 21 Allied divisions faced 14 German divisions.

The story of the third battle is soon told.

It was won by the magnificent French colonial mountain troops of General Juin's French Expeditionary Corps, who swarmed through the hills and took the Monte Maio *massif*, opening the Liri valley from the south. The Germans held on at Monte Cassino for four days, but the uninterrupted advance of the French to the south unseamed the entire Gustav Line position, and the monastery was finally evacuated on the night of the 17th. When the breakout from Anzio was launched on 22 May it seemed that nothing could prevent the destruction of the retreating German 10th Army, but Allied failure to co-operate – and, some have said with justice, General Mark Clark's anxiety to be first into Rome – served as an unbelievable reprieve for Kesselring. On the very eve of the invasion of Normandy, the Allied armies at last entered Rome after seven months of frustration before the Gustav Line. But Alexander's objective of

Above left: **The view down from the mountain up which the Allies had to fight their slow and bloody way.**

Above: **The Allied forces finally break through at Cassino. The 10th Army, led by Vietinghoff under the overall command of Kesselring, had put up an excellent defence, but finally Allied strength had won the day, and the way north was open.**

'destroying the enemy south of Rome' had not been achieved.

Very few commanders have ever been as well served by their officers and men as was Kesselring at Cassino, yet the credit for that amazing defensive battle remains his. Never was Alexander's verdict on the man – that he could be easily out-thought, but only with the greatest difficulty be out-fought – so emphatically proven.

Colonel-General Heinrich von Vietinghoff

suffering from intense nervous strain. He returned to his army at the end of 1943, but soon advised Kesselring that he thought the German forces should pull back to the Gustav Line. Vietinghoff was then primarily responsible for the German defence in the Garigliano and Cassino battles up to the end of March 1944.

Vietinghoff stayed with the 10th Army during the defensive battles north along the Apennine mountains. Between 24 October 1944 and 14 January 1945, and then between 10 March to 2 May 1945, Vietinghoff was German supreme commander in Italy, but failed to display the verve and initiative that had been the hallmark of Kesselring.

Vietinghoff was a good, if uninspired, soldier, better as an army than as an army group commander. He was conservative and correct, and disapproved of the secret surrender negotiations carried out by SS General Karl Wolff.

Heinrich-Gottfried von Vietinghoff-Scheel was born on 6 December 1887, and joined the German army, as a junior officer in the Prussian Guards, in 1906. After an average career up to the end of World War I, Vietinghoff decided to remain in the army, and gradually rose in rank.

Vietinghoff's first major command was XLVI Panzer Corps, which he led in the Balkan campaign of April and May 1941, and in the invasion of Russia starting a month after the conclusion of the Balkan war.

Between June and December 1942 another advance brought acting command of the 9th Army in Russia. On 15 December 1942, however, Vietinghoff received his own army, the 15th, which he kept until 22 August 1943.

It was on this date that Vietinghoff was given the command of the 10th Army in south Italy. Just over a fortnight later, his new command was in action when the Allies landed at Salerno.

Vietinghoff's problems were now added to when Rommel fell ill on 20 September and he had to stand in as deputy commander of Army Group 'B' for eight days. During October Vietinghoff was concerned with the retreat to the Winter Line, but then had to take nearly two months off as he was

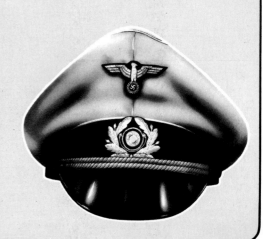

Colonel-General Heinrich von Vietinghoff

When the Allies entered Rome on 4 June 1944, the German 10th and 14th Armies were still conducting so chaotic a retreat that there seemed every likelihood of cutting them off and destroying them before they could re-form and establish another defensive front. That this was not achieved was due to the magnetic influence of the Italian capital, which had come to obsess the 5th Army ever since the Allies had been fought to a halt at Cassino the previous November. Kesselring's shaken forces were given just enough time to get clear of the trap which never closed.

When Kesselring ordered the retreat to the northern Apennine *Gruen-Linie* (or Gothic Line, as it was more familiarly called) he was in a unique position. He had to retreat fast enough to prevent a débâcle in the Rome area, but not so fast that his armies got to the Gothic Line before its defences were ready. (This was scheduled for the autumn of 1944.) He was helped that he still had the terrain on his side as he retreated along the line of the Apennines, Italy's spine; and on either side of Lake Trasimene he had drawn the 'Albert Line', where he intended to make another stand.

Kesselring was also helped by a dramatic switch in the balance of forces in Italy. His opponent, General Alexander, was about to lose 97,000 men – the US VI Corps and the French Expeditionary Corps – which were required for the 'Dragoon' landings in southern France. This meant that Kesselring would not only be spared from having to face the markedly superior masses which had assailed him in the third battle of Cassino: he would also no longer have to worry about

A camouflaged Sherman medium tank of the Allied 15th Army Group motors up the dusty road to Mondaino in typical Italian hot summer conditions.

the best troops to serve on the Allied side in the Italian theatre. At the same time, OKW was sending him reinforcements: a paper strength of eight divisions in all, of which the most bizarre were the mounted Cossacks of the 162nd Turkestan Division. The first Allied withdrawals of troops came just in time to take the pressure off the 14th Army, on the German right flank, and enable it to reach the Albert Line in safety (20/23 June).

During the Cassino fighting, Vietinghoff's 10th Army had borne the brunt, drawing on reinforcements from 14th Army. The keynote of operations between 20 June and 3 August reversed this pattern, for Alexander's objective was a powerful thrust up the western side of the Apennines with Florence as its first objective. This was the 14th Army's front, and it was now the 10th Army's turn to do the reinforcing. While Vietinghoff and Lemelsen handled the operations of the 10th and 14th Armies, Kesselring presided like an anxious chef who knows that he is short of ingredients, 'doling out the appropriate reinforcements as required. The assault on the Albert Line commenced on 20 June, and by 2 July the Allies were through to Foiana, north of Lake Trasimene, and Cecina on the west coast. The Albert Line was breached.

During the next 14 days Lemelsen and Kesselring were helped by the constant withdrawal and replacement of Allied troops for the 'Dragoon' venture, but the 5th Army and its attached 8th Army divisions continued their northward crawl against stubborn resistance. Leghorn fell on 19 July; Pisa on the 23rd. On the night of 2/3 August the Germans evacuated Florence without a fight, and the city was entered by the British on the following day. By the end of the first week of August, the Allied armies had closed up to the approaches to the Gothic Line.

No 'Blitz attack'

Alexander knew that there could be no question of a 'Blitz attack' on this new and formidable belt of German defences. For his initial attack on the line he planned for nothing less than a complete switch of mass across to the Adriatic sector and the British 8th Army/German 10th Army front. His first attack would be launched here, and much was expected from it; but if it got bogged down Alexander planned to unleash his 5th Army against the 14th Army and tie down all Kesselring's reserves.

The Allied redeployment was a godsend for Kesselring as many of the key defence positions in the line were still not ready. To make matters worse, the German 71st Division was pulling back from the Metauro river to the Foglia when Alexander's attack opened on the night of 25/26 August, and at first both Vietinghoff and Kesselring believed that the 8th Army's attack was only a limited follow-up. Their disillusionment was rapid and appalling. By the last day of the month the 8th Army was battering at the Adriatic sector of the Gothic Line, capturing German troops who were in the process of occupying their positions. By 3 September the leading 8th Army forces were across the Conca river, over 10 miles to the rear of the Gothic Line.

Kesselring hauled three divisions across from 14th Army to take the sting out of the Allied offensive. Two factors alone saved the 10th Army: the difficulty of getting the Allied tanks through the gap won by the infantry, and the eternally fickle Italian weather, which broke on the night of 4 September. The 8th Army's advance faltered and died; and Alexander promptly ordered the 5th Army to push into the mountains and come to grips with Lemelsen's 14th Army, weakened as it now was

Vietinghoff – the Defence of the Gothic line

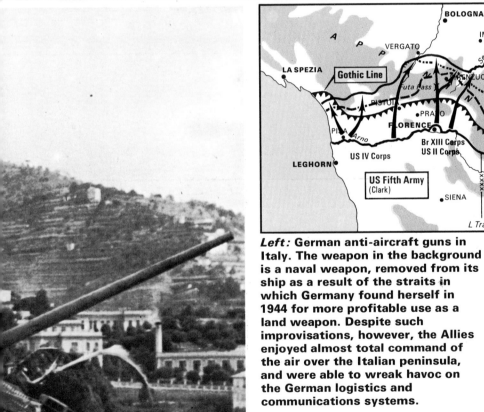

by the reinforcements drawn off for Vietinghoff. Clark opened his attack on the Imola axis on 12 September, and after a superb initial defence by the green young troops of the 4th Parachute Division, the 5th Army began to make ground. By 27 September the 5th Army forward positions were within 10 miles of Imola, and Kesselring, aware that he had yet another crisis on his hands, threw in units from four German divisions on both sides of the Allied salient. After a week of desperate fighting, Clark accepted the position and began to plan a new thrust in the direction of Bologna.

Back on the 8th Army sector, a new attack opened on 12 September along the lowland coastal strip. A rapid advance was out of the question as the attacking forces were now entering the Romagna plain, which is basically an enormous reclaimed swamp watered by innumerable parallel watercourses. On 20 September Rimini fell and the Marecchia river was crossed on the following day, but ceaseless rain throughout the last week of the month brought the advance to another halt.

Further desperate efforts in October and November halted the 5th Army nine miles short of Bologna and the 8th Army south of Ravenna. Never had the foul winter weather

Left: German anti-aircraft guns in Italy. The weapon in the background is a naval weapon, removed from its ship as a result of the straits in which Germany found herself in 1944 for more profitable use as a land weapon. Despite such improvisations, however, the Allies enjoyed almost total command of the air over the Italian peninsula, and were able to wreak havoc on the German logistics and communications systems.

Top: The crew of a German self-propelled gun, based on an Italian tank chassis, prepare a camouflaged defensive position. But by now the German armoured forces had been decimated by Allied air power, and the vehicles left them were very short of fuel. All they could do was try to slow up the Allied advance.

Above: The Allies break through the Gothic Line defences. These were formidable defensive positions built in excellent sites, and caused the Allies heavy casualties.

of Italy been of such help to Kesselring: at one stage floods carried away every Bailey bridge carrying 8th Army supplies across the swollen rivers of the Romagna. A series of limited attacks in late December and early January carried the 8th Army to the southern tip of Lake Comacchio and forced the Germans back behind the Senio river, losing Ravenna in the process; but Kesselring's obstinacy allied to the adverse weather forced the Allies to contemplate another winter south of the line of the River Po.

The remaining months of the winter of 1944–45 were months of preparation on both sides for the final campaign in Italy. There were command changes all round. McCreery had already replaced Leese as commander of the 8th Army; Alexander moved to the post of Supreme Commander, Mediterrean, and Clark took over the Allied 15th Army Group; Truscott, who had saved the day at Anzio, took over the 5th Army from Clark. On the German side, Kesselring finally left Italy in March to try to sort out some order from the hopeless situation in western Germany, and was replaced by Vietinghoff. General Herr took over the 10th Army, while Lemelsen stayed on with the 14th Army. Before he left, Kesselring had been doing the only thing he could: setting his forces to create as many defences as they could on the river lines of the Po valley, the last natural defences left to Army Group 'C' between the northern Apennines and the Alps. Clark's army group, on the other hand, teemed with preparations for the coming offensive. There were lavish supplies of amphibious armoured transports and 'Kangaroos' – turretless tanks to serve as armoured troop-carriers. Allied training stressed the need for complete teamwork between infantry and armour. The lessons taught by the experiences before the Gothic Line last August had been well learned, and there was certainly no underestimating the gravity of the task which lay ahead.

The new German army group commander, Vietinghoff, was an old 'Italy hand', but his character was strikingly – and depressingly – similar to Arnim of Tunisia. He was a dour and methodical ex-Prussian guardsman who fought his battles by the book. He was precisely the sort of German general who could be guaranteed to produce an early defeat by sticking to the letter of Hitler's orders not to retreat an inch – and that was what happened in the campaign of April 1945.

Standard tactics

The pattern of the last Allied attack contained many elements which had been familiar throughout the Italian campaign. Vietinghoff was led to expect another Allied amphibious landing in his rear, this time in the Venice area. In fact, the 8th Army would attack across the Senio around Lugo before the 5th Army resumed its drive towards Bologna. Then the 8th Army would switch direction, sending an amphibious push across Lake Comacchio and striking north through the 'Argenta Gap' to pen Vietinghoff's forces in the central Po valley.

On 9 April Alexander and Clark opened their offensive. At first definite progress was achieved only slowly, with Truscott's US II Corps managing to advance a mere two miles in three days – but between 15 and 20 April Vietinghoff's defences cracked. The 8th Army's attack poured through the Argenta Gap and closed to within 15 miles of Ferrara. Bologna fell at last on 21 April. Vietinghoff, who had struggled manfully, if myopically, to keep to Hitler's 'no retreat' order, accepted the inevitable on the 20th and ordered a general retreat to the Po, but by now it was too late. In the Gothic Line fighting of the previous autumn, Kesselring had managed to delay until the last minute before giving ground because the difficulties of the terrain prevented the Allies from moving fast enough, but matters were very different down in the Po valley. And this time dominant Allied air power, unhampered by weather, struck at the German bridges across the Po and wrecked them, keeping up constant air strikes, as in Normandy, and making the German withdrawal across the Po a near-suicidal operation by day.

The pursuit was mercilessly pressed and the leading 8th Army troops were up to the Po by the 23rd. On 24 April three British divisions got across. Foremost in the pursuit was the US 10th Mountain Division, which had leaped forward 55 miles in two

days to reach the Po. It pounced forward to seize Verona on the 25th and headed up Lake Garda towards Trento and the Alps. Meanwhile, on the extreme left and right of the shattered German front, the Allies fanned out to the north-west and north-east with a relentless symmetry. Genoa fell on the 27th, Turin and Milan on 2 May; the 8th Army took Venice on 28 April and had reached Trieste on 2 May.

Vietinghoff's forces had lost nearly all of their artillery, armour and transport in the retreat across the Po, and there was not even a chance of making any kind of last stand on the north bank. Individual units had already begun to surrender when weeks of undercover negotiations between the SS in Italy and CIA virtuoso Allen Dulles in Switzerland bore fruit. The great fear in the Allied supreme command had been the mythical *Alpenfestung* – a non-existent bastion in the Alps and southern Bavaria and Austria where the last stand of the Third Reich would be fought. The Dulles negotiations, however, provided for the surrender of all German forces in Italy and Austria, and the capitulation came into force on 2 May, the day Turin, Milan and Trieste fell. It involved nearly a million men and is generally agreed to have shortened the course of the war by weeks. As it was, the surrender in Italy was made only six days before the European war came to an end.

Above: **Churchill infantry tanks of the 51st Royal Tank Regiment move up in support of an attack by men of the 139th Infantry Brigade north of Isola del Piano.**

Right: **One of the crew of a *leichte Selbfahrlafette (2-cm Flak 30) SdKfz 10* light self-propelled AA gun scans the sky for signs of Allied air activity. In action the sides of the halftrack were dropped to facilitate all-round traverse.**

Yet at one stage it had seemed most likely that the Italian campaign would have Allied troops knocking at the door of Austria by the summer of 1944 at the latest. That this was thwarted was due primarily to the energy and skill of Kesselring, whose achievements in 1943 and 1944 need little further comment. He was admirably served by competent subordinates – Vietinghoff, Mackensen, Lemelsen, Herr, von Senger, Fries and Heidrich. He had all the luck any general could ever hope to have: repeated mistakes made by his enemy and foul weather practically on order to slow him up. Kesselring's own mistakes were many, and led him repeatedly to the edge of disaster. But his true greatness lay in his talent for repairing them and looking to the next battle, the next day.

Analysis–
German Generalship in North Africa and Italy

In the high summer of 1942, with Kleist's Panzers advancing towards the Caucasus in southern Russia and Rommel in Egypt menacing Alexandria and Cairo, it was easy to imagine that the German 'master war plan' for the conquest of the Middle East was on the verge of realisation. Of course, no such plan existed. The German army in World War II tackled its successive enemies according to the whims of Hitler, not according to an army blueprint. And it would probably never had got involved

in North Africa at all had it not been for the military uselessness of Germany's partner in the 'Pact of Steel': Italy.

Mussolini's ignominious defeats in Greece, Albania, Egypt and Libya created a situation which not even Hitler dare ignore. The original *Afrika Korps* was not, as was widely believed, an élite force seasoned for desert warfare by months of training in hot-houses and synthetic sand-storms: it was a scratch force of armour and infantry to save Tripoli for Mussolini.

There was a strong parallel between the formation of *Afrika Korps* and the formation of the expeditionary force which took Denmark and Norway in April 1940. Both were maddening distractions for OKH, which in 1940 was concentrating on the imminent assault on the West and in 1941 was concentrating on the imminent invasion of Soviet Russia.

Rommel's thoroughly insubordinate reconquest of eastern Libya for the Axis created far more problems than it solved. It still comes as a surprise to many that Brauchitsch and Halder sent out Paulus to keep Rommel under control, not to help him, in April 1941. North Africa was still irrelevant to OKH and OKW. Not so to the British. It was the only possible land theatre where they could actually fight the Germans.

OKW obligation

For OKW, Rommel's victories in Libya created the obligation to keep him supplied, to reinforce success despite themselves – an obligation which was never honoured. The 'parallel war' mushroomed in the Mediterranean, with convoy routes, shipping tonnage and the vexing question of Malta nagging at the planners of OKW and OKH as they struggled to get on with

Left: German infantry in their individual foxholes in North Africa. The outcome of any action eventually depended on such men, and so their welfare and morale was always of the utmost importance. Note the two 'stick grenades' ready for use in the foreground.

Right: A British infantryman sets about taking over as his foxhole a dug-in tank turret abandoned by the retreating Germans.

destroying the Red Army in Russia.

Even when a compromise was reached – that Rommel should attack at Gazala, take Tobruk, then wait for the conquest of Malta – the unpredictable, off-the-cuff nature of the desert war triumphed in the end with Rommel's invasion of Egypt. Rommel went so far that he put himself beyond the reach even of basic supplies, out on a limb where one slip would leave him hanging. He had made mistakes before, and he made one of the most disastrous mistakes in history when he made his initial heads-down rush at the strongest nuclei of the El Alamein defences in early July 1942. Rommel found himself, moreover, faced by Auchinleck, who actually wrested the initiative from him against all expectations.

Once halted at El Alamein, Rommel's every prospect depended on supply. He was not the first German general who was promised supplies which never turned up, and he found himself trapped by the results of his own successes earlier in the year. He had to attempt a breakthrough at Alam Halfa; he had no choice but to await the inevitable from Montgomery at El Alamein.

Rommel's defeat at El Alamein, and the Allied landings in Algeria, finally woke OKW up to what was going on in North Africa. On his own initiative, Kesselring had prevented the likelihood of Rommel's *Panzerarmee* being destroyed simultaneously with the 6th Army in Stalingrad. OKW decided to reinforce the initial small-scale successes won in Tunisia. Now, far too late, they came – Tiger tanks, *Nebelwerfer*, and above all, manpower. It was all for nothing; it was all wasted. Once they were penned into the Tunisian bridgehead there was nothing that the generals could do.

A very good nickname for Kesselring would be 'the great delayer of defeat'. His lightning seizure of Tunisia had staved off the end in Africa. His stiffening of the Italian garrison of Sicily delayed the Allied conquest of the island. And his equally brilliant takeover of the strategic centres of the Italian mainland when Italy quit the 'Pact of Steel' in September 1943 was the fitting prelude to the long ordeal of the Italian campaign – the protraction of which was Kesselring's finest achievement.

Extemporised units

From a scatter of miscellaneous units dotted all over Italy to forestall a variety of possible Allied moves, Kesselring welded a solid and formidable defensive front. His deployment, apparently haphazard, dealt out an initial shock to the Allies at Salerno, where Kesselring pushed home the attack on the Allied beach-head until he saw that there was no point in trying further. Nor was Kesselring remotely interested in defending Naples, the first major Axis city on the European continent to fall to the Allies. He ordered a fighting retreat back to the Reinhard and Gustav Lines, where he intended to hold for as long as he could.

His best ally during the winter fighting at Cassino was the terrain, which not only

Left: A German heavy gun in the Western Desert, camouflaged with scrap to look like debris.

Below left: A halftrack for the German forces under Rommel's leadership in Libya. Note the barrel of the tank in the foreground, to the right of the sailor in the striped shirt. Each ring round the barrel indicates the destruction of an enemy vehicle or tank.

Below: Although the desert offered some excellent fighting country, conditions at times could be very distressing for the combatants. Principal amongst these conditions were the fine sand that covered men and machines, especially when the wind blew up, and the almost total prevalence of flies and other such creatures.

favoured the defenders but made it impossible for the Allied armies to move fast. Indeed, Alexander had only one unit which worried Kesselring: Juin's French colonials, the men who finally cracked open the Cassino front in May. And he had the best possible troops to hold the town of Cassino and the monastery heights: paratroops. They were not soldiers who depended on orthodox supply-lines and command echelons: they were superbly-trained individual fighting men, used to working in small units virtually on their own.

The controversial Anzio stroke was only a surprise for Kesselring in that he had no way of knowing where and when the landing would be made. The Allies gained total surprise, only to waste it by excessive caution. Kesselring's ingenuity in sealing off the beach-head without fatally weakening the Cassino front was an altogether admirable feat. But he was unable to prevent the Allies from building up the beach-head force and making it a

miniature 'second front' against Kesselring when the big push went in at Cassino in May.

When the French swarmed through the mountains and shattered the Cassino front, the 10th Army teetered on the verge of total dissolution. Here again, as in the initial stages of the Anzio landing, Kesselring was lucky in the mistakes made by his opponents. Rome, not the destruction of the German forces which had held up the Allies for so long, was the chief 5th Army objective. This alone enabled Kesselring to pull his 10th and 14th Armies together again and take them north to the last natural defence-line in the mountains of Italy: the 'Gothic Line' across the northern Apennines. Had Alexander been left with the full strength with which he had broken through at Cassino, the story of the August fighting along the Gothic Line would have been very different. As it was, Kesselring was able to fight the Allies to another muddy standstill in the autumn of 1944, while

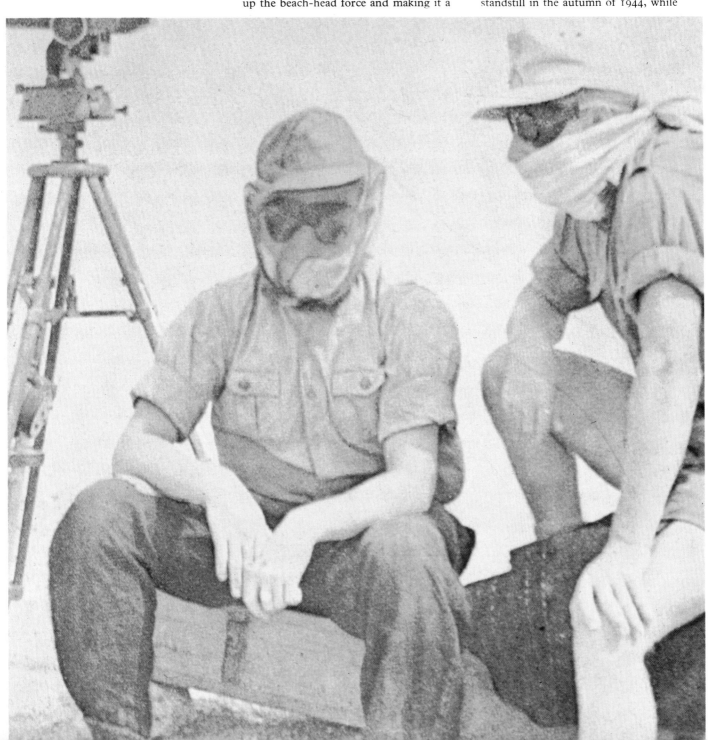

The Mediterranean Fronts

invaluable French and American units fought their way up the Rhône valley in southern France to form Eisenhower's right-wing army group.

This halting of the Allies along the Gothic Line was Kesselring's last major achievement in Italy. It coincided with the halting of the Red Army along the Vistula and with the petering-out of Eisenhower's advance on the Western Front. For the last time, Hitler's high command had time to take stock behind fronts which were everywhere stable. This respite only produced the Ardennes gamble of December 1944 and the subsequent acceleration of the Allied advance, but set against the overall disasters of 1944 the stabilisation of the Italian front was a notable success.

In a way, the Sicilian and Italian campaigns, twin sequences to the collapse in Africa, were the disastrous fruits of Hitler's decision to make an ally out of Fascist Italy. For over four and a half years German forces fought on the 'southern front', first shoring up the inadequacies of their Italian ally and then holding the breach left by Italy's surrender. Territorially speaking, however, the whole story – Africa, Sicily and Italy – amounts to the defence of the biggest outer bastion by which any nation at war has ever sought to keep the enemy from her gates. The biggest, that is, apart from German-occupied Russia, to which Africa, Sicily and Italy remained of secondary importance in any case.

Above: A self-propelled 2-cm anti-aircraft gun is worked on by its German crew.

Left: A German paratrooper prepares for action with his sub-machine gun. He has taken up a position on the lip of a shell or bomb crater. Hitler was loathe to commit the airborne forces in their intended role after their losses in the capture of Crete, so they were used as elite infantry for the rest of the war.

The Campaign against Russia, from Kursk to Berlin

A Russian town begins to burn as German and Soviet troops fight for it – all too common a sight in 1942 and 1943.

On 12 January 1943, as the grim battle for Stalingrad was drawing towards its conclusion, the Russian armies on the southern front took the offensive against the German, Italian, Hungarian and Rumanian forces of Weichs' Army Group 'B' and Manstein's Army Group 'Don', driving them back from the River Don near Voronezh to a line along the central Donets and Oskol. The Bryansk, Voronezh, South-West and South Fronts resumed their offensive on 2 February, driving the Germans back to a line between Kursk in the north and Kharkov in the centre, and in a great salient towards Dnepropetrovsk in the south.

Manstein decided on a bold counter-offensive to throw back the Russians. In the centre Corps 'Raus' of *Gruppe* 'Kempf' counterattacked on 18 February and on 14 March retook Kharkov, whilst in the south II SS Panzer corps of *Gruppe* 'Kempf', acting in concert with the

1st and 4th *Panzerarmee* from the south, wiped out the salient towards Dnepropetrovsk, restoring the front to the line of the Donets. In the north the battle swayed to and fro for some time before the spring thaw settled matters, leaving the Russians in control of the great salient to the west of Kursk after 20 March. Manstein's forces, although outnumbered by about seven to one, had halted the powerful Russian thrusts, and had even thrown back a considerable portion of the central and southern ones with great losses. It was a quite remarkable feat, and perhaps the crowning glory of Manstein's distinguished career. Nevertheless, the Russian drive and the German riposte had hurt the German cause very considerably. Communist estimates put the German casualties at over one million, together with 5,000 aircraft, 9,000 tracked vehicles and 20,000 guns. Russian losses have never been revealed, but must have

been in the same order of magnitude, if not greater.

Manstein's losses had been so great that a major German offensive in the summer of 1943 was completely out of the question. All that could be attempted was a limited offensive to put the Russians off their balance and iron out the salient around Kursk left by the cessation of hostilities with the spring thaw. The offensive, known to history as the Battle of Kursk, was a disaster for the Germans. They had delayed too long so as to in introduce significant numbers of their latest armoured fighting vehicles, and the Russians, whom agents had warned of the exact time and location of the German pincer offensive (by the 4th *Panzerarmee* of Army Group 'South' and the 9th Army Group 'Centre'), had prepared formidable defences. The German offensive went in on 4 July, and resulted in the greatest tank battle of history. The

Germans made virtually no progress, and lost 70,000 men, 5,000 vehicles, 3,000 tanks, 1,400 aircraft and 1,000 guns, according to the Russians.

As their forces in the salient were halting the German offensive, the Russians launched the fronts holding the German salients around Orel and Kharkov, to the north and south of the Russian salient of Kursk respectively, in a counter-offensive. Despite strenuous German efforts to stem the Russian offensives, both the Orel and Kharkov salients had been overrun by 23 August. Manstein had been ordered by Hitler to hold on to Kharkov at any cost, but refused to do so, conducting a masterly retreat back to the line of the River Dniepr.

Manstein retreats

Manstein found it necessary to pull back so far because the local Russian offensives for Orel and Kharkov had on 23 August been joined by a general Russian summer offensive by all the fronts west and south of Moscow – the Kalinin, West, Bryansk, Central (later Belorussian), Voronezh (later 1st Ukrainian), Steppe (later 2nd Ukrainian), South-West (later 3rd Ukrainian), South (later 4th Ukrainian) and North Caucasus Fronts. By 16 September the Russians had advanced an average of 50 miles all along the front, the Central Front under Rokossovsky doing best in reaching Nezhin, only some 60 miles from the Ukrainian capital of Kiev after an advance of 100 miles. By the end of September the Russian armies had pressed on yet further, retaking Smolensk in the north on 25 September and reaching the line of the Rivers Sozh and Dniepr as far south as Zaporozhye, the front running down to the Sea of Azov from there. In fact bridgeheads over the Dniepr had been gained downstream from Kremenchug, between Bukin and Kanev, and in two places upstream from Kiev. Between the beginning of November and 23 December the Russians continued to advance, recapturing the key city of Kiev on 6 November, encircling Vitebsk in the north, driving Army Group 'Centre' back to the Pripet marshes, and cutting off the 17th Army in the Crimea. This last had evacuated its beach-head in the Kuban by 9 October, but Hitler would not hear of its leaving the Crimea as this would provide a good jumping-off point for another attempt in the Caucasus when the German armies recaptured southern Russia! By the end of December the 17th Army was completely cut off, the 4th Ukrainian Front having advanced to Kherson at the mouth of the Dniepr.

As with all previous Russian offensives, German casualties in men and *matériel* had been extremely heavy, and the Third Reich was finding it increasingly difficult, if not impossible, to find replacements. Even when the required replacements were forthcoming, they were far inferior in quality to the troops who had played so important a part in gaining Germany's victories up to the end of 1941. The Russians, however, were in a far better situation. Although they were still

suffering very heavy casualties, they were still able to replace them, to a great extent with conscripts from the liberated areas. *Matériel* was also in better supply, both from the factories behind the Urals and from Lend-Lease from Great Britain and the United States. Of Lend-Lease supplies, perhaps the most important items were the 80,000 trucks supplied by the United States. These gave the Russians a far greater degree of mobility than they had possessed previously, and permitted their commanders to employ more daring tactics. The skill of the Russian commanders continued to improve rapidly with their growing combat experience.

Leningrad freed

In the north Leningrad, which had been under German siege since October 1941, was finally freed from German threats in January 1944. A corridor had been driven through to the city along the southern shore of Lake Ladoga in January 1943, but it was not until the concerted drive by Govorov's Leningrad Front and Meretskov's Volkhov Front between 14 and 31 January 1944 that the citizens of Leningrad could be sure that they would not come under German shelling or bombing attacks. Popov's 2nd Baltic Front, which had played a minor part in the first stage of the offensive, played a more prominent part in later stages, which only ended when Model, who had taken over Army Group 'North' from Kuechler on 29 January, halted the Russian advance

Above: A snow-camouflaged *Panzergrenadier* on heavily fought-over ground in February 1943.

Above right: An MG 42 machine gun provides covering fire. A Russian T-34 tank, comprehensively knocked out, dominates the background.

Right: German sappers prepare to blow a railway line during the autumn retreats of 1943.

along the line of the River Narva, Lake Peipus and River Velikaya by 1 March. The spring thaws now intervened to prevent any further movement.

In the Ukraine the Russians had launched another winter offensive on 29 January. The major early event was the trapping of two German corps at Korsun-Shevchenkovsky by the 1st and 2nd Ukrainian Fronts. The weather prevented any success by the relief force and also the breakout by the trapped forces, and Manstein lost another 100,000 men when the pocket was overrun on 17 February. It was now the turn of the 1st *Panzerarmee* to receive the Russians' attentions. Under the command of General H. V. Hube, the 1st *Panzerarmee* was cut off, but on instructions from Manstein and supplied from the air by the *Luftwaffe* (which was making one of its few significant contributions since its losses in the Battle of Kursk), it operated behind the Russian lines, severely hampering Russian supply and communication lines. With the aid of the 4th *Panzerarmee*, the 1st *Panzerarmee*

The Eastern Front, February 1943 – May 1945

finally broke out to the west on 10 April, with its forces intact. It had played an important part in slowing down the Russian offensive. Along the north coast of the Black Sea Army Group 'A' was having a bad time of it at the hands of Konev's 2nd, Malinovsky's 3rd and Tolbukhin's 4th Ukrainian Fronts. Odessa had to be given up on 10 April. Hitler was so infuriated by these constant retreats in the south that he sacked both Manstein and Kleist, replacing them with Model and General F. Schoerner respectively. The two army groups involved were renamed Army Groups 'North Ukraine' and 'South Ukraine'. The whole of the western part of the Ukraine had now been liberated from the Germans, and Konev's forces were almost in a position to threaten eastern Hungary. It is worth noting here how the Russians had by now developed their offensive tactics into a fine art. Using their massive numerical and *matériel* superiority, and closely controlled by the *Stavka* or high command in Moscow, the Russians steamrollered the Germans, accepting heavy losses, but feeding fresh troops into the battle as quickly as possible. Against such tactics the Germans found that there was little that they could do except attempt to slow down the Russian advance.

Disastrous tactics

Such was Hitler's preoccupation with holding ground and thinking of offensive action that when the Russian summer offensive of 1944 broke upon the hapless Axis forces in Russia, there was no way to halt the Russian tide. No defensive positions had been chosen or prepared, and German troops were deployed as far forward as possible, with no thought for the expediency of the positions. Thus

Above: The Russian advance into eastern Poland and the Baltic states of Latvia and Lithuania.

Left: Weary retreat for a group of German *Panzergrenadiers*. Note the first and third men, who have *Panzerfaust* anti-tank weapons.

Right: A *Panzerschreck* anti-tank weapon in action.

Zhukov's offensive in Belorussia, and thence into Poland, was a total disaster for the Germans.

Zhukov, now deputy supreme Russian commander, had prepared his plans carefully, with even more massive concentrations of tanks, artillery and aircraft than was usual. The offensive, directed in a south-westerly direction from Smolensk towards Warsaw in Poland, opened in fine weather on 22 June against Colonel-General E. Busch's Army Group 'Centre'. Busch's communications had been cut by partisans, and his air units had been removed to the West to help in the struggle against the Western Allies, who had just landed in Normandy. Busch's forces had not a chance against the Russians, and a 250-mile gap was ripped through the German defences. Zhukov's

armour pressed on, leaving the encircled towns of Vitebsk, Bobruysk and Minsk to be overrun by the infantry on 25 June, 27 June and 3 July respectively. Army Group 'Centre' was in ruins, with three-quarters of its 33 divisions destroyed or cut off. German losses totalled 381,000 killed, 158,000 captured, and 2,000 armoured vehicles, 10,000 guns and nearly 60,000 vehicles lost. Busch was immediately replaced by Model. By 10 July Zhukov's forces had cleared Belorussia, and were preparing to debouch into Poland and the Baltic states. Lvov fell on 27 July, Brest Litovsk on the 28th and Vilnyus on the 13th. Rokossovsky's 1st Belorussian Front threatened Warsaw until a desperate counter-attack by Model's forces halted it, leaving the Polish insurgents in Warsaw to be crushed by the

SS in a heroic two-month struggle in August and September. By 7 August Zhukov's forces had pushed on some 450 miles and were exhausted; the summer offensive was over. Later in the year Germany suffered another shock when Finland dropped out of the war as a result of a truce with Russia on 4 September. Another near disaster for German arms was the Russian autumn offensive into the Baltic states. Schoerner's Army Group 'North' had nearly been cut off in Latvia by the advance of Chernyakovsky's 3rd Belorussian Front at the end of July. It was in fact cut off in the autumn offensive, in which the Russians retook all the Baltic states with the exception of the Kurland peninsula in Latvia, held by Schoerner's army group. Although fighting continued until

15 December, the Russians made no important gains after the end of October. An offensive into East Prussia was repulsed. The 20 divisions of Army Group 'North', trapped in Kurland, are a good example of Hitler's strategic stupidity. By refusing to allow them to pull back in good time, Hitler condemned these good divisions to a type of captivity, and one in which they could play no further part in the attempt to rescue Germany's fortunes.

Back in the south, the Crimea had been cleared between 8 April and 9 May by Tolbukhin's 4th Ukrainian Front. Most of the 17th Army, however, managed to get away from Sevastopol by sea. The 2nd and 3rd Ukrainian Fronts now attacked across the River Prut into Rumania, which was defended by General J.

Friessner's Army Group 'South Ukraine'. The offensive started on 20 August, and when Rumania threw in her lot with Russia on the 25th, the Rumanian 3rd and 4th Armies, part of Friessner's command, went over to the Russians, trapping most

Balkan fiasco

of the German 6th and 8th Armies. The Russians reached the River Danube south of Bucharest on 1 September, completely outflanking the German defence and causing considerable losses in men and *matériel*. When Bulgaria also defected to the Russian side on 4 September, the whole of the German flank in the Balkans was exposed. The Russians rushed on towards Belgrade, which fell on 19 October, in an effort to cut off the retreat of Army Groups 'E' and 'F' from Greece and southern Yugoslavia respectively. The two army groups managed to escape, however, by veering to the west, and linked up with Friessner's forces, now designated Army Group 'South'. The Russians got a bridgehead over the Danube on 24 December, and invested Budapest on 24 December. The Hungarian capital, however, fell only on 14 February 1945. But Hitler's unwillingness to allow retreat had very nearly lost him his forces in the southern Balkans.

12 January 1945 witnessed the penultimate act in Germany's defeat, when the Russian armies from the Danube

The Eastern Front, February 1943 – May 1945

Above left: **A youthful guard detail for an 8.8-cm anti-aircraft gun on the borders of Germany. Judging by the gun's low elevation, its crew clearly expect their weapon to be used in the anti-tank role.**

Above: **So dire were Germany's straits in 1945 that even the very old and the very young were called up. Here a grandfather and his grandson wait with their *Panzerfausts* for the Russian onslaught on the capital city of Berlin.**

Left: **A demolition team sets about its task. Like the Russians before them, the Germans implemented a totally ruthless 'scorched earth' policy in the wake of their retreat.**

valley in the south to the Baltic in the north once again went over to the offensive. In the north Chernyakovsky's 3rd Belorussian and Rokossovsky's 2nd Belorussian Fronts pressed into East Prussia and pushed back Army Group 'Centre' (redesignated Army Group 'North' on 25 January) to the Baltic. The Germans put up a brave defence, but as usual in this late stage of the war, there was nothing the Germans could do but attempt to delay the Russian advances. Koenigsberg and several other isolated beach-heads held out until the end of the war.

Further south, the left flank of

Rokossovsky's 2nd Belorussian Front drove to the north-west after capturing Warsaw, whilst Zhukov's 1st Belorussian Front attacked due west, and after an advance of some 300 miles reached the River Oder, only about 40 miles from Berlin, on 31 January. Further south again, Konev's 1st Ukrainian Front advanced from the River Vistula line to the River Oder–Neisse line by 15 February. At this point the portion of the winter offensive north of the Carpathian mountains halted, Russian logistics being unable to supply front-line units any further from their supply bases.

South of the Carpathians, the Russian advance had been checked by the splendid defence of Budapest, which fell only on 14 February. After the vain attempt to secure the Hungarian oilfields in the Battle of Lake Balaton in March, the Germans were unceremoniously bundled out of Hungary into Austria, whose capital, Vienna, fell to troops of Tolbukhin's 3rd Ukrainian Front on 14 April.

Germany invaded

Meanwhile, in the north the 1st and 2nd Belorussian Fronts cleared Germany's Baltic coast, which had been left in the Russian advance to the River Oder. The defence of the coastal strip was entrusted to the so-called Army Group 'Vistula', a hotch-potch collection of *Volkssturm*, SS units, police and military remnants under the command of *Reichsfuehrer*-SS

Heinrich Himmler, then of General G. Heinrici, and finally of General K. Student. The 1st Belorussian Front attacked northwards towards Kolberg on 16 February, as did the 2nd Belorussian Front towards Gdynia and Danzig. The coast, with the exception of some pockets, had been cleared by 15 April, leaving the northern group of Russian armies free to launch their final offensive – on Berlin.

The last act

This final offensive began on 16 April, with advances by Konev's 1st Ukrainian Front and Zhukov's 1st Belorussian Front, commanded in this last offensive by General V. Sokolovsky, allowing Zhukov to co-ordinate the whole offensive. Rokossovsky's 2nd Belorussian Front went over to the offensive on 20 April. The German defence was desperate, but ill co-ordinated, and the Russians reached Berlin on 22 April and invested the city on the 25th. In the north men of Rokossovsky's front had come into contact with troops of the British 21st Army Group in Wismar on 3 May, and in the south contact was made between Konev's front and men of the US 12th Army Group in Torgau on 25 April. Hitler, after appointing Doenitz his successor, committed suicide on the 30th. Meanwhile the Russians were fighting a savage battle for Berlin, which finally capitulated on 2 May.

The last actions of the war against Germany were fought in Czechoslovakia, where Schoerner's Army Group 'Centre' was putting up a final, defiant resistance. Completely surrounded, and attacked by Konev's 1st Ukrainian Front, Petrov's 4th Ukrainian Front, Malinovsky's 2nd Ukrainian Front, the US 1st Army and the US 3rd Army, Schoerner finally called it a day in a pocket between Prague and Pardubice on 11 May 1945.

According to Russian sources, in all probability correct, the last three months fighting had cost Germany at least one million dead and 800,000 prisoners, together with 12,000 AFVs, 6,000 aircraft and 23,000 guns. Hitler's folly had bled Germany white. What was all the most distressing from the German point of view was that given the situation at the beginning of 1943, the Germans could have fought their war far more efficiently with a supreme leader other than Hitler, and even had the war still been lost, as was entirely probable, casualties would have been far less.

Above right: **A horse-drawn field kitchen – but by the end of 1944 there was very little food for the German army, let alone German civilians, to live on.**

Right: **The dreaded flamethrower in action. This was a weapon invented in World War I, improved and almost universally adopted for close-range anti-personnel and anti-tank work in World War II. It was quite horribly efficient, and quite ghastly in its results.**

Field-Marshal Erich von Manstein

Erich von Lewinski von Manstein was born on 24 November 1887 in Berlin. During World War I he held the rank of lieutenant, later captain, in a variety of staff appointments in West and East.

Manstein stayed in the army after the war, and in 1921 was the commander of the 6th Company, 5th *Jaeger* Regiment, with the rank of captain. In 1927 he was promoted to major; by 1939 he had attained general rank and was employed as a staff officer.

Hitler's attention was drawn to Manstein by the latter's daring 'Sickle' plan. During the execution of this plan in May 1940, its originator commanded an infantry corps with distinction during the advance through the Ardennes.

From September 1941 to November 1942 the 11th Army in Russia was led by Manstein, who was promoted field-marshal in July 1942 for the capture of Sevastopol.

Between 28 November 1942 and 14 February 1943 Manstein was in command of Army Group 'Don', entrusted with the hopeless task of trying to break through to the 6th Army trapped in Stalingrad. Manstein next moved to the command of Army Group 'South', which he held until 30 March 1944. During this period he achieved considerable tactical successes in the recapture of Kharkov and in the abortive Battle of Kursk. After Kursk he conducted a series of masterly retreats, principally to the River Dniepr. Hitler by now distrusted Manstein, whose realistical demands for permission to retreat had earned him Hitler's disapproval as a 'pisspot strategist'.

After his dismissal in favour of Model, Manstein lived for the rest of the war in retirement. Sentenced in February 1950 by a British court to 18 years' imprisonment, later commuted to 12 years, Manstein was freed on 6 May 1953.

Liddell Hart said of Manstein that 'he was a man who combined modern ideas of manoeuvre, a mastery of technical detail and great driving power'. He was also afforded great respect and loyalty by those who served under him.

Field-Marshal Erich von Manstein

In March 1943, the Germans needed a spectacular victory in the East to make up for the defeat at Stalingrad.

Manstein's plan for such a victory was presented to Hitler as early as February 1943. He believed there was much to be gained from a strategy of manoeuvre and he thought the Germans should await the expected Russian offensive to recover the Donets basin and then hit them hard. He envisaged surrendering the whole Donets basin and luring the Russians as far as the lower Dniepr. The whole weight of the German Panzer force would then strike south-east at lightning speed from Kharkov and pin the attackers against the Sea of Azov. For Manstein, mobile defence was very important. Static defence was useless in his opinion as the Germans had too few troops to defend such an enormous front.

This sound plan was rejected by Hitler on vague political grounds, although the real reason lay in the fact that he would never consider giving up territory.

Others, including Zeitzler, thought that a limited offensive should be waged against Kursk, which would be less risky than simply waiting for the Russians to attack and did not contain a preliminary sacrifice of land.

Dangerous salient

The Kursk salient was a huge and menacing-looking bulge, 9,000 square miles in area, lying between Orel in the north and Belgorod in the south. It had been captured by the Russians the previous winter. Geographically, it was a far-flung plain, broken by valleys, copses, villages, rivers and streams. Fields of corn made visibility difficult and the ground rose to the north, a fact which was to favour the defenders. Roads were simply tracks through the sand, which became channels of mud when it rained and were thus impassable for motor vehicles. The Russians had large troop concentrations here.

To the Germans, Kursk was a suitable target because simultaneous attacks from north and south could be made, thus trapping large numbers of Russians, including reserve formations.

The plan was that Colonel-General Walther Model's 9th Army of Army Group 'Centre' should attack southwards towards Kursk from Orel while Colonel-General Hoth's 4th *Panzerarmee* and *Gruppe* 'Kempf' of Army Group 'South' should attack northwards from Kharkov to meet Model at Kursk. The enemy encircled in the Kursk salient was then to be destroyed. This was to be Operation 'Zitadelle' (Citadel) and Zeitzler was the main architect of the plan. Detailed planning began in March, but delays blighted the operation from the start. Manstein urged the attack be made straight after Kharkov in March, but it was delayed by the difficulties in assembling the necessary troops. D-day was then fixed for mid-April, but by now Model, who approved the plan in principle, had doubts about the adequacy of his resources, and asked Hitler for a postponement until reinforcements arrived. Guderian had recently been recalled from retirement to take up the post of Inspector General of Mobile Troops. He opposed 'Zitadelle', anticipating heavy tank losses when tanks were desperately needed on the Western Front. Guderian's task was to invigorate the Panzer forces, and prepare them to break through the Russian numerical superiority. Field-Marshal von Kluge, commander of Army Group 'Centre', and Manstein, commander of Army Group 'South', were both in favour of the plan, but Manstein soon became wary of the delays. Hitler could not make up his mind what to do, and so the weeks passed. The new Panther tanks – for which Model was waiting – were beset with technical difficulties and only about 12 were being produced each week.

With time, the concept of Operation 'Zitadelle' changed from a short, sharp,

German infantry on the move in Russia. In the battle around Kursk, Model used his infantry to lead his armour, while Manstein used his to back up the main armoured punch into the Russian defence lines in the south.

surprise blow to a head-on trial of strength, for the Russians had not been idle while the *Fuehrer* vacillated.

The Russian defences had been organised with the utmost speed. To co-ordinate the arrangements, *Stavka* (the Russian high command) sent Marshals Vasilevsky and Zhukov to Kursk at the end of April. The northern part of the Kursk salient was held by General Rokossovsky's Central Front with the 48th, 13th, 70th, 65th and 60th Armies deployed from north to south; the 2nd Tank Army and three corps lay in reserve. The southern (Voronezh) front was commanded by General Vatutin with the 6th and 7th Guards Armies, with the 38th and 40th Armies under orders and the 1st Tank Army and the 69th Army in reserve.

The Russians fully expected the attack against Kursk. They received accurate information from a spy in OKW and decided to postpone their own planned offensive and await that of the Germans.

Good planning

Rokossovsky recommended that their main reserve strength be centrally deployed east of Kursk, from where it could counter the thrusts of Manstein and Model, but where it was unlikely to be cut off. The reserve became known as the Steppe Front, and it was placed under the command of Colonel-General Konev. It comprised five armies, including one tank army and one tank, one mechanised and three cavalry corps. The Steppe Front was also to provide fresh troops for a counter-offensive. And should the battle take a turn for the worse, it was to establish a line across the neck of the salient, so that the attacking Germans would again have to rupture the Soviet line.

Earthworks and parallel trenches made up an important part of the Soviet defences. The main forward defensive zone was three miles deep with at least five lines of trenches, one behind the other, interlinking and containing shelters. The second zone was seven miles further back; the third line lay 20 miles behind the second – and so on. Trenches stretched for hundreds of miles. Anti-tank defences were formidable. Large areas were mined and anti-tank defences were formidable. Large areas were mined and anti-tank strongpoints were set up. Half a million mines were laid on the Central Front alone – 2,400 anti-tank and 2,700 anti-personnel mines per square mile. The Artillery Reserve of the High Command was in support, and the two fronts had 13,000 guns, 6,000 anti-tank guns and 1,000 Katyusha multiple rocket-launchers. All defending units were subjected to an intensive and repetitive course of training.

The Russian armour comprised mostly T-34s, but the KV tanks available now mounted the 85-mm gun. Also in service were the new tank destroyers – the self-propelled SU assault gun. The 2nd and 16th Air Armies provided 2,500 planes for support.

D-day for '*Zitadelle*' was eventually fixed for the beginning of July. Manstein felt that it was too late, and that the operation was no longer feasible. Model urged that the operation be abandoned because he felt the

Russians expected the offensive, but Hitler had now decided to go ahead, even though he confided to Guderian that the thought of '*Zitadelle*' made him feel sick.

The northern pincer movement was to be executed by Model's 9th Army with three Panzer corps, two army corps and supporting infantry. The southern pincer, under Manstein's command, had the 4th *Panzerarmee* (Colonel-General Hoth) with Hausser's II SS Panzer Corps (including the divisions '*Leibstandarte*', '*Das Reich*' and '*Totenkopf*'), and Knobelsdorff's XLVIII Panzer Corps (including the army's '*Grossdeutschland*' division); Ott's LII Corps and also *Gruppe* '*Kempf*', whose task it was to guard the eastern flank of the 4th *Panzerarmee* as it moved northwards. Thus some of the finest

Above: **A German armoured sub-unit manoeuvres in the Kursk salient to find an advantageous firing point. But so well thought out and built were the Russian anti-tank defence lines around Kursk that even in the few places the Germans managed to punch through they had suffered very heavy casualties and lost all momentum.**

Right: **A German gun in a counter-battery shoot. At Kursk the German artillery was outclassed and outnumbered by that of the Russians, which also had all the advantages of the higher ground and good observation positions.**

divisions of the Reich lay shoulder to shoulder within a 30-mile front.

This southern arm alone had 1,500 tanks and self-propelled guns (including 94 Tigers and 200 Panthers) and 2,500 guns and mortars. Model had approximately 900 tanks. In all, the Germans had 70 divisions, totalling almost one million men, and 1,800 aircraft, under command of the 4th and 6th Air Fleets, for the battle of Kursk. Aerial photographs were available of the whole salient. Troops were carefully briefed and rested. The Germans, however, did not have precise knowledge of the weather or the location and strength of the Russian reserves.

Model was to use the traditional method of using the infantry to achieve penetration for the armour – but to Manstein, this seemed too costly and time-consuming, because of the extent of the front in the south and also because of the depth of the Soviet defences. Tactically, therefore, Manstein decided the rapid breakthrough should be made by armoured formations.

The battle commenced at 1500 hours on 4 July, a hot, sultry afternoon with thunder threatening. The 4th *Panzerarmee* manoeuvred to gain possession of the hills in front of the German lines. Probes by Ott's LII Corps and Knobelsdorff's XLVIII Panzer Corps directly south of Oboyan pushed home attacks despite resistance by Chistyakov's 6th Guards Army.

The Russians, however, were waiting with their reserves behind the 6th Guards Army, having realised the German initial thrust would be made at this point. At 2230 hours Soviet artillery opened up heavy firing all over the area. Rain fell during the night, too, and the roads and tracks turned into mud sloughs, which delayed the German tanks.

At 0500 hours on 5 July the German attack was resumed by XLVIII and II SS Panzer Corps. XLVIII Corps broke through the first line of the Soviet defences with little trouble. The Germans had to watch out for mines, however, and the Russian artillery kept up a constant barrage – Luftwaffe attacks on enemy gun emplacements not having much effect.

By nightfall on 5 July, Hausser's SS divisions had also breached the Soviet lines, but nowhere were the penetrations deeper than six or seven miles. Where their lines were breached, the Russians simply moved men and equipment back to behind the second line of defence.

Manstein's instructions said he should achieve the link-up with the 9th Army at Kursk by direct penetration via Oboyan. General Hoth and he agreed, however, that the Russians would expect this and so they decided to meet the expected counter-attack at Prokhorovka before continuing north to Kursk. This was a good decision and, to a certain extent, upset the Russian defensive plans.

German tactics involved thrusts by a succession of armoured wedges (*Panzerkeil*) with Tiger tanks at the tip of the wedges and Panthers and Pzkw IVs fanning out behind. Light infantry followed the tanks and the heavier forces with mortars followed at the rear in personnel carriers.

Russian fire control was in the form of *Pakfronts* – groups of up to 10 anti-tank guns under one commander concentrating on one particular target at a time. The Germans underestimated the number of *Pakfronts* and found the Russian guns difficult to knock out, as they were protected by machine gun and mortar nests. Manstein found that his guns were unable to saturate the Russian defences, nor were they able to clear a safe route through the minefields. German tank crews were instructed not to stop to help disabled tanks, which the Russians picked off without difficulty. By the evening of 5 July, the nature of the Soviet defences was alarmingly obvious and the German tactics were in disarray.

Worn out

On 6 July, 4th *Panzerarmee*'s attack in the general direction of Oboyan continued. Katukov's 1st Tank Army was now behind the Soviet 6th Guards Army in the second defence zone, dug in amongst the latter's rifle divisions to thicken up the artillery and anti-tank fire. Hausser's II SS Panzer Corps had now advanced about 20 miles into Chistyakov's front. Hausser continued this drive with great dash, and on 7 July, the situation looked a little alarming for the Russians on the Voronezh Front. More artillery was therefore transferred to it, and Rotmistrov's 5th Guards Tank Army and Zhadov's 5th Guards Army from the Steppe Front also moved in to the Voronezh Front. *Gruppe* 'Kempf' was able to harass the reinforcements.

By 8 July, the ground had dried out considerably and the German armour continued to make good, though slow, progress, with individual divisions making their own dents in the Russian line.

By 9 July, Hoth's forces had been in continuous action for five days, and their ammunition and supplies were running out. A rectangular salient, approximately nine miles deep by 15 miles across, had been driven into Vatutin's front. This was not much after nearly a week of armoured warfare. By 11 July, after establishing a bridge-head on the River Psel and getting close to Oboyan, the 4th *Panzerarmee* had advanced 18 to 20 miles through the Soviet lines.

Meanwhile, in the north, Model had fared much worse. The 9th Army had made some progress on 5 July, but by 6 July the Russians had moved up more tanks and the Germans found it impossible to make any headway against the Soviet artillery. On 7 July, Model switched his attack from the Orel–Kursk road to the area of Ponyri village, further east. Here, for three days, the Germans pounded away without result. By 10 July, Model was on the defensive. Obviously, he was not going to formulate the northern pincer movement on Kursk. In this short time, he had suffered tremendous losses – 50,000 men, 400 tanks and guns and 500 aircraft. To add to his troubles, the Russians were preparing to counterattack around Orel on 12 July.

Back in the south, on the night of 11/12 July, the Russian reserve armour was moved forward towards Prokhorovka to check the German easterly drive. Consequently, the two armoured forces clashed on the afternoon of 12 July, during intense, stifling heat and under an enormous cloud which greatly hindered air operations. This was the greatest tank battle of World War II.

The opponents were roughly equal in numbers – but the Russians were fresh, their machines unworn and with the full complement of ammunition. They had the new SU-85, a self-propelled 85-mm gun mounted on a T-34 chassis as an answer to the Panthers and Tigers.

In contrast, the Germans had just come from fierce fighting with patched up tanks. The new armour – the Panther, the Tiger and the Ferdinand (or *Elefant*) assault gun – all proved disappointing to the Germans at Kursk. The Tiger and Ferdinand had no machine gun and were therefore unable to provide their own short-range defensive fire. There was a shortage of ammunition for both Panther tanks and Ferdinand main-calibre guns. Also, the tactical employment of the large new tanks was at fault. The Germans failed to exploit their long-range

guns and stationed the tanks in the foreground of the battle. At close range a T-34 could hole a Tiger as effectively as a Tiger could destroy a T-34.

On 10 July, the Allies landed in Sicily. This introduced a new element into the *Fuehrer*'s thinking. On 13 July, Manstein and Kluge were summoned to East Prussia to hear Hitler's decision to break off Operation '*Zitadelle*' immediately and to redirect a large number of troops to Western Europe to contain the Allies.

Manstein, however, believing that the Red Army's armoured reserves were quickly running out, thought it essential that the offensive be continued and the Russians be defeated. Manstein still believed victory was possible, and he proposed to Hitler that Model should retain sufficient troops in the north to tie the Russians down, and that the offensive should continue in the south. In effect, this would complete half the '*Zitadelle*' plan. Hitler agreed that Hoth and Kempf could continue, but he would not sanction Model retaining a large force. Despite heavy rain, further successes were gained in the south by Manstein's group, resulting in the Soviet 69th Army and two tank corps being trapped between Rzhavets, Belenikhino and Gostishchevo. Hitler then decided to call a complete halt to '*Zitadelle*'; II SS Panzer Corps was transferred to Italy and two Panzer divisions were dispatched to Army Group 'Centre' in view of the worsening situation at Orel. Manstein could not now hold his position and a general withdrawal began at the beginning of August. He had had tactical success and since D-day had taken 24,000 prisoners and destroyed or captured 1,000 tanks and over 100 anti-tank guns.

Manstein's insistence on continuing with the offensive may well have been right, for the Voronezh Front was certainly not very secure, and the whole of the Steppe Front was committed to its support.

With '*Zitadelle*' the Germans lost the initiative in the East and were never to regain it. They had used up all their armoured reserves. With the German retreat, the threatening Russian defeat turned to victory as they vigorously pursued the retreating Germans.

Left: A German motorcycle reconnaissance crew pauses to watch the Russian city of Orel going up in flames as Kluge's Army Group 'Centre' pulls back in the face of determined attacks by Sokolovsky's West Front, Popov's Bryansk Front and Rokossovsky's Central Front.

Right: The Battle of Kursk, known to the Germans as Operation 'Zitadelle' or Operation 'Citadel'. This was Germany's last major offensive on the Eastern Front, and was one of the major turning points of the war. It is still disputed whether or not Manstein should have been allowed to go on with the southern half of the attack, which he considered to be close to a major victory, after Model's attack in the north had been halted and then turned back.

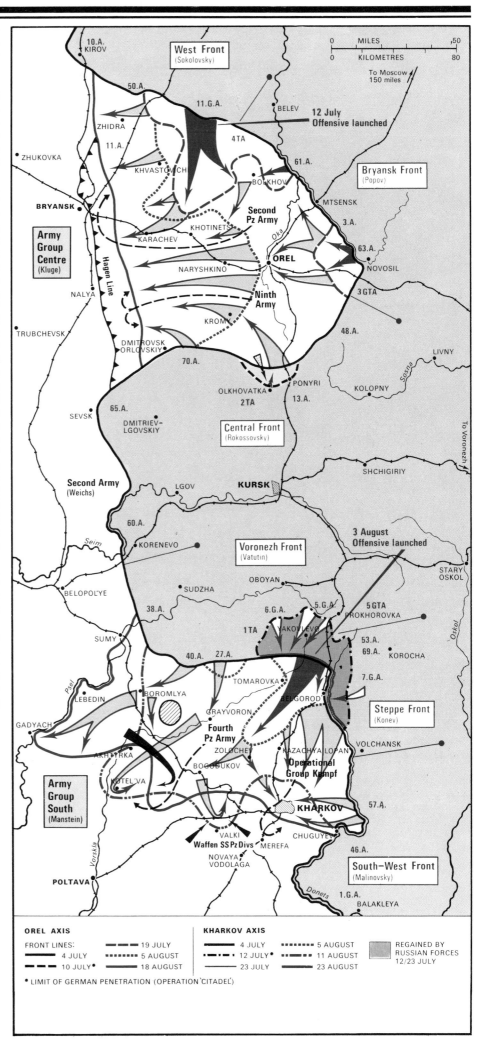

Field-Marshal Walther Model

June 1944 Model was switched to command of Army Group 'Centre', where again he had considerable success in halting the Russian advance before Warsaw.

Hitler on 18 August 1944 now moved Model to the West to take over from Kluge as Commander-in-Chief West. On 5 September, however, he moved to the command of Army Group 'B', which soon found itself faced with the problem of the Allied airborne landings at Arnhem. Model then helped in the planning of the Ardennes offensive.

By the spring of 1944 Model's army group had had to pull back to the Ruhr, where it was trapped. On 15 April Model disbanded his command, and six days later he shot himself rather than surrender. He was buried in a forest near Wuppertal.

Model worked both himself and his men very hard, but only within the limits of what was possible. He had a considerable knack of being able to scrape up reserves.

Walther Model was born on 24 January 1891 in Genthin, and joined the army in 1909. He moved up the promotion ladder steadily during World War I and during the *Reichswehr* period, and the opening of World War II found him chief-of-staff to IV Corps for the invasion of Poland. By the time of the campaign against the West in May 1940, he was chief-of-staff of the 16th Army.

Model's next task was as commander of the 3rd Panzer Division in Operation 'Barbarossa', during which he led the thrust beyond the River Dniepr. He quickly rose to command of XLI Panzer Corps. In October 1941

Model was promoted to general, and in January 1942 he received command of the 9th Army. In this command Model won swift recognition as a master of flexible defence.

This ability stood Model in good stead, for in October 1943 he was given command of Army Group 'North', and had to lead it in its retreat to the 'Panther' line. On 1 March 1944 Model was promoted to field-marshal.

On 30 March 1944 Model replaced Manstein as commander of Army Group 'South', and succeeded in blunting the Russian advance towards the Carpathian mountain passes into Hungary. In

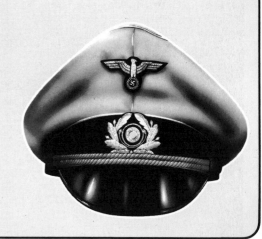

Field-Marshal Walther Model

On 22 June 1944 Stalin launched an all-out offensive against Army Group 'Centre'. The commander of 'Centre', Field-Marshal Busch, had four armies holding a salient which stretched from Vitebsk to Mozyr: the 3rd *Panzerarmee* under Colonel-General Reinhardt; the 4th Army under General von Tippelskirch; the 9th Army under General Jordan; and the 2nd Army led by Colonel-General Weiss. However, there were only 38 front-line divisions and the majority of these were understrength. There were three Panzer and two infantry divisions in reserve,

and three Hungarian and five special service divisions at the rear.

By contrast, the Russians had amassed 14 armies, amounting to nearly 200 divisions, which gave them a numerical superiority of six to one. They also had the advantage in weaponry in a ratio of 10 to one, and overwhelming air superiority. The Germans could not hope to hold an attack of this magnitude.

The 1st Baltic and 3rd Belorussian Fronts opened the offensive with a pincer attack either side of Vitebsk, taking 3rd *Panzer-*

armee completely by surprise. The Russians stormed through, and with the help of the 6th Guards Army closed in on the town. On 23 June, the 2nd and 3rd Belorussian Fronts moved toward Orsha and Mogilev, almost breaking the 4th Army. On the following day, the 1st Belorussian Front smashed into the 9th Army and penetrated its northern and southern boundaries. Busch tried to uphold Hitler's policy of inflexible defence and fortress-holding. But it was the wrong strategy. By the fifth day of fighting, Army Group 'Centre' had used up its reserve forces without stopping the Soviet advance. The fortresses of Vitebsk, Orsha, Mogilev and Bobruysk were soon encircled by pincer movements while the mass of Russian armour swept on westward towards Minsk. Hitler's 'fortified locality' policy had failed. Field-Marshal Busch received all the blame.

On 28 June, Hitler and OKH finally admitted that the Belorussian offensive was more serious than they had previously thought. But they still felt that an attack against Army Group 'North Ukraine' was imminent. So Hitler sacked the loyal Busch and appointed Field-Marshal Model to the command of Army Group 'Centre', whilst at the same time retaining him as commander of 'North Ukraine'. It was hoped that this dual command would facilitate troop movement between the two groups. Model was probably the best tactician apart from Rundstedt in active service at the time, and he was still in favour with Hitler after his successful improvisations at Orel, Rzhev and Leningrad. But the task of limiting the disaster facing Army Group 'Centre' was surely one of his greatest tests.

Army Group 'North', despite being in a desperate position itself, was ordered by Hitler to hand over three divisions to Model. But the new commander-in-chief was unwilling simply to wait for these reinforcements and himself order the transfer of ten divisions, including four Panzer divisions, from Army Group 'North Ukraine' to

Above left: **Russian dead, victims of German machine gun fire after being caught in the open during an ill-planned attack.**
Left: **German pioneers hitch a lift on a PzKpfw V Panther tank. The man standing on the right of the rear decking is holding the flame gun portion of a flamethrower. The rough, ridged appearance of the tank's outer surfaces is caused by the *'Zimmerit'* paste applied to the metal. This was put on to prevent magnetic mines from being attached to the tank by attackers. The paste could be painted over for camouflage.**

'Centre'. On assuming command, Model changed the rigid policies of Busch in favour of a more elastic system of defence. His only hope was to plug the most dangerous holes in his lines, try to re-establish contact with the 4th and 9th Armies and generally stiffen the overstretched front.

But for all this new-found aggression and flexibility, the Russians advanced relentlessly. Perhaps Model's appointment had been made too late. Whatever the case, his actions were all in vain. He could not hold the Polotsk–Berezina–Slutsk line and by 2 July he admitted that he had lost the bulk of the 4th and 9th Armies, trapped by Russian pincers between Minsk and the Berezina. It was estimated that 100,000 men had been cut off.

Part of the 9th Army managed to escape to the west, but most of the 4th Army was truly trapped in a pocket between the Berezina and the Volma rivers. The latter pocket was split into two groups, one under Lieutenant-General Traut and the other under Lieutenant-General Mueller. Marshal Zhukov ordered a colossal bombardment of the 4th Army with rockets, shells and bombs. German resistance was short-lived, and Mueller surrendered to the 2nd Belorussian front. The 57,000 prisoners were paraded through the streets of Moscow on 17 July. Minsk itself, the Belorussian capital, fell on 3 July to Chernyakhovsky's and Rokossovsky's troops. In 12 days, Army Group 'Centre' had lost the most part of 25 divisions.

Defeat at Minsk

In order to salvage what he could, Model proposed to halt the enemy along a new front some way behind Minsk, west of the Molodechno–Baranovichi line. This could only be done with new formations plus those Model had obtained from Army Groups 'North' and 'North Ukraine'. He urged OKH to send more reserves from Army Group 'North' to defend Molodechno. These were not forthcoming as Army Group 'North' was also in a desperate situation. Its right flank was held at Polotsk, another of Hitler's fortified areas. Between it and the left flank of the 3rd *Panzerarmee* north-east of Minsk there was a gap of 50 miles. A similar gap opened between the *Panzerarmee*'s right flank and Molodechno. The *Panzerarmee* could be pincered at any time the Russians wanted, and the road to Riga would be opened. But Hitler insisted that Army Group 'North' continue to hold Polotsk, despite Model calling it a 'futile experiment' and urging the *Fuehrer* to withdraw Army Group 'North' to Riga itself. As a result of this policy – and despite the dangers facing the 3rd *Panzerarmee* – no forces could be released to Model to form a new front.

Defeat at Minsk meant that only the flanks of Army Group 'Centre' remained. (According to Guderian the defeat signified the end of Army Group 'Centre'.) A 200-mile break in the German line opened up the Soviets' way to the Baltic states and East Prussia.

Stavka was determined to exploit this opportunity, and so the Russian tank formations moved rapidly westwards from Minsk on a broad front and harried the sparse German forces before the defence could be organised properly.

The Russian strategy was for the 1st Baltic Front under Bagramyan to advance through Dvinsk and on to Lithuania and Latvia after crossing the Dvina river. Chernyakhovsky's 3rd Belorussian Front was to develop a two-pronged attack, one from Molodechno through Vilnyus to Kaunas in Lithuania, and the second to the border of East Prussia via the River Niemen The 1st Belorussian Front under Rokossovsky was to push through Baranovichi to the River Bug, north-east of Warsaw. Here he was to meet the 2nd Belorussian Front, which was to arrive by way of Białystok and Grodno.

Hopeless situation

Those divisions that Model had managed to scrape together, for example the 14th and 95th Infantry Divisions, were unable to alter the depressing situation. Russian troops were east of Molodechno by 6 July and the way was open to Vilnyus. Under the tireless command of Marshal Zhukov, General Batov's 65th Army reached the rail junction of Baranovichi the following day, and despite resistance by the German 2nd Army, the town was liberated. On the 8th, the town of Lida also fell. The German front joining Baranovichi and Molodechno had vanished.

Model faced a hopeless situation. The Russians for the next 20 days covered 10–15 miles per day, often side-stepping the depleted units which Model threw in to plug his broken lines. Model's task was now to try to harass the enemy in order that the necessary time might become available for OKH to form a new and continuous line strong enough to turn back the Russian offensive. One significant success he did achieve at this stage was to persuade Hitler to order the evacuation of a whole series of fortified areas which otherwise would have become death-traps to the encapsulated German defenders.

By 8 July, Model reported that the line Vilnyus–Lida–Baranovichi had also been broken. All three towns were taken. Without reinforcements, he could not stop the Russians anywhere, and had no choice but to sacrifice considerable areas of territory.

The implications of the Soviet successes were not confined to the central area. The German retreat enabled the Russian high command to extend operations to the north and south flanks, against the German Army Groups 'North', and 'North Ukraine' and 'South Ukraine' respectively. On 9 July, Model accompanied the new commander of Army Group 'North', General Friessner, for an interview with Hitler. They tried to persuade him to withdraw from Estonia and so provide badly needed reinforcements. Hitler refused this suggestions although he did promise to give Model two divisions from Army Group 'North'. For the next few days, the position of Army Group 'Centre' continued to deteriorate as the front drifted west to Kaunas, the Niemen and Białystok. The divisions which Model expected from Army Group 'North' did not arrive, as Friessner was himself threatened with imminent encirclement should the Red Army break through the gap between Army Group 'Centre' and Army Group 'North', to the Gulf of Riga.

Model's Army Group 'North Ukraine' also retreated westward in the face of Russian pressure. On 14 July, Rokossovsky enveloped Pinsk and then moved on to Kovel and over the River Bug. He took the Polish town of Lublin on 24 July. Part of his force turned toward Brest Litovsk while the remainder pushed on to the Vistula, which they reached on 2 August. On 27 July, the Russians took Lvov, but the Germans retreated safely to the Carpathians and the Vistula. The situation facing Army Group 'Centre', and to a lesser extent, Army Group 'North Ukraine', began to improve as the tempo of the Russian attack slowed down. Having advanced so far so quickly, the Russians were outreaching their supplies. Their artillery and supply depots were far from the new front lines and the advance

Model – the Retreat into Poland

Left: The retreat from the Russians continues as weary and ill equipped German troops flood back towards the frontiers of Germany. Horse transport is again well in evidence.

Below: German infantry gingerly manhandle a light infantry support gun *(Infanteriegeschuetz)* across a collapsed bridge. Although obsolete in design, these guns gave German infantry a useful light artillery component for use immediately upon meeting the enemy, or where heavier support might be inappropriate or too slow in arriving. A similar type of gun would have been greatly appreciated by British and American infantry.

guard lacked petrol and munitions. At the same time, Model had managed to obtain reinforcements, including 10 new Panzer divisions to bolster the 'North Ukraine' front. He also received another six battle-proven armoured divisions, including the 'Hermann Goering' Division. Model's forces were gaining strength and the possibility soon arose of initiating small-scale counter-attacks.

Short-term safety

By 3 August, Model was able to send Hitler a relatively good situation report. He confirmed that a continuous front had been established from Siauliai in the north to the Vistula at Puławy in the south. The 420-mile stretch was covered by only about 40 German divisions, but nevertheless it seemed that it could be held for the time being and some room for light offensive manoeuvring made available, particularly the relief of Army Group 'North'. Model had fulfilled the job of repairing the situation in the East even if the repairs were only temporary. On 16 August, he was appointed to the command of the Western theatre.

Model was one of a new breed of German general, blindly loyal to Hitler, seldom disputing his orders and appearing to have the happy knack of minimising the catastrophic effects of the *Fuehrer*'s policies. He did not possess the strategic genius of Manstein, but had well-earned his reputation as being a highly competent tactician in defensive situations prior to his appointment to Army Group 'Centre'. Mellenthin considered that he was too prone to interfere in matters of detail, and tell his corps and army commanders exactly where they should deploy their troops. Even so, in the face of the Russian offensive he clearly adopted the correct tactics and his eye for detail, his efficiency and hard work surely contributed to his military efficacy.

He had little option but to withdraw and one of his successes was to convince Hitler of the futility of defending fortified areas as the Russians would simply bypass them. One of his strengths was his ability to stand up to Hitler. During the withdrawal of Army Group 'Centre' his deployment of those forces and reserves at his disposal was of sufficient quality not to tarnish his reputation as the master of flexible defence. He created and stabilised a new Eastern Front and was then whisked away to deal with the crisis in the West.

Paratroops follow in the lee of a PzKpfw VI 'Tiger' heavy tank. Apart from their special helmet, with its shorter 'skirt' round the nape of the neck, paratroopers could often be distinguished by their one-piece combat smock, as in this photograph. This was camouflaged, and came down to mid-thigh level. The Tiger has been covered in 'Zimmerit' paste, and has spare track links attached to the rear of its turret as extra protection and as replacements. Although it was excellently armed and armoured, the Tiger suffered from an unreliable transmission and an underpowered engine.

Colonel-General Georg-Hans Reinhardt

General Erich Hoepner's 4th *Panzergruppe*, with the task of taking the spiritual centre of Communism, Leningrad. Before this could be achieved, however, the *Panzergruppe* was given to Army Group 'Centre' for the reduction of the Vyazma pocket and the drive on Moscow.

With the sacking of Colonel-General Hermann Hoth, Reinhardt on 5 October 1941 received command of the 3rd *Panzergruppe*, elevated to the status of *Panzerarmee* on 1 January 1942, the date on which Reinhardt was promoted to colonel-general.

Reinhardt kept the command of the 3rd *Panzerarmee* until the Russian autumn drives of 1943. On 16 October 1944 Reinhardt received command of Army Group 'Centre', faced with the impossible task of stemming the Russian advance through northern Poland towards East Prussia. Reinhardt fought his campaign well, but fell foul of Hitler and was relieved of his command on 25 January 1945.

Georg-Hans Reinhardt was born on 1 March 1887 at Bautzen, and joined the Imperial German Army as a cadet on 25 March 1907. He was posted to the 107th Infantry Regiment as a lieutenant on 14 August 1908. Reinhardt served as a junior officer in World War I, and after that decided to stay in the army, by now named the *Reichsheer*, part of the German Republic's *Reichswehr* or Armed Forces. Reinhardt was promoted lieutenant-colonel on 1 October 1931, colonel on 1 February 1934 and major-general on 1 April 1937. In this last rank Reinhardt received command of the 1st Assault Brigade on 12 October 1937, and of the 4th

Panzer Division on 10 November 1938. He led this formation during the Polish campaign of September 1939, and was promoted lieutenant-general on 1 October 1939.

On 5 February 1940 Reinhardt received the command of XLI Panzer Corps, which performed with great distinction as part of *Panzergruppe* 'Kleist' during the defeat of France in May and June 1940. In the middle of this campaign, on 1 June 1940, news of his promotion to general reached Reinhardt.

In the opening phase of the campaign against Soviet Russia, Reinhardt kept command of XLI Panzer Corps as part of Colonel-

Colonel-General Georg-Hans Reinhardt

At the end of 1944, the Russians were planning the winter offensive in which they intended to drive on from Warsaw, which they had reached but not taken in August of that year, to the River Oder, only some 40 miles from Berlin. Whilst Marshal of the Soviet Union G. K. Zhukov's 1st Belorussian Front drove straight on in the centre, and Marshal of the Soviet Union I. S. Konev's 1st Ukrainian Front pushed on from the upper reaches of the River Vistula into the German industrial region of Upper Silesia, Marshal of the Soviet Union K. K. Rokossovsky's 2nd Belorussian Front was to take Warsaw and then drive up to the Baltic Sea, splitting Germany in two. East Prussia was then to be crushed by the combined forces of the 2nd and 3rd Belorussian Fronts, the latter commanded by General I. D. Chernyakovsky, with help from General I. Kh. Bagramyan's 1st Baltic Front along the River Niemen.

The German defence of East Prussia was entrusted to Army Group 'Centre', commanded by Colonel-General Georg-Hans Reinhardt. The army group consisted of three armies: the 2nd Army (Colonel-General W. Weiss) in the sector north of Warsaw; the 4th Army (General F. Hossbach) in the centre east of the Masurian Lakes; and the 3rd *Panzerarmee* (Colonel-General E. Raus) in the northern sector. As usual with German formations of the time, the armies had a fair number of divisions, but these were all at low strength, and the fuel, ammunition and *matériel* available to them was very limited. Reinhardt also had

Warmly clad Germans watch a Russian shell exploding in a snow field in front of them. Russian artillery fire was normally of a far more formidable nature, the Red Army placing great faith in the efficacy of massive artillery bombardments along great sectors of the front before any major offensive was launched. Technically, and in *materiel,* the best combat arm possessed by the Russians was their artillery, which was used intelligently as well as massively.

179

the uncertain help of some 200,000 police and *Volkssturm* units. In the event, the latter were to fight with great stubbornness until demoralised by the desertion of various non-German units serving in the area. Reinhardt had realised early in 1945 that the area with whose defence he was entrusted was far too great for the weak forces under his command, and begged Hitler to allow the evacuation of Army Group 'North' from its bridgehead in Kurland, these forces to be added to those of Army Group 'Centre' for the defence of East Prussia. At the same time Reinhardt noted that the mobility enjoyed by the Russians, combined with the geographical situation of East Prussia (defended in the centre by the Masurian lakes) meant that the Russians would almost certainly launch a huge pincer attack aimed from the south at Elbing, and from the east at Koenigsberg. Such an attack would leave the 4th Army out in a salient in front of the Masurian lakes, where it could not contribute to the defence battle and where it could be mopped up at leisure by the Russians. Reinhardt therefore urged Hitler to allow him to pull the 4th Army back into East Prussia itself. Hitler refused both the request to evacuate Kurland and the plan to pull back the 4th Army.

Growing forces

As noted above, the Russian forces by this stage of the war had a considerable quantity of motor transport, and could therefore employ their forces to take full advantage of their mobility. The Soviet armour and artillery was also well up to strength, and had sufficient ammunition to fight a large-scale offensive. Rokossovsky's one real worry was his lack of infantry. This arm, as was often the case with the Russians in World War II, had been used with little imagination or thought for casualties, and had suffered very heavy losses against stubborn German defence. However, the 2nd Belorussian Front received some 125,000 reinforcements in infantry at this time. These were Russians returning from hopital or combed out of the rear echelons, together with some 10,000 recaptured prisoners-of-war and 53,000 Polish, Ukrainian and Balt men forcibly conscripted into the Red Army.

The Russian plan was a large-scale one: whilst the 47th Army captured Warsaw (which it did on 17 January), the 70th and 65th Armies, with an attached tank corps, were to drive towards Pomerania via Torun, and the bulk of the 2nd Belorussian Front (2nd Shock, 48th, 3rd, 49th and 5th Guards Tank Armies) were to press on towards Elbing via Mlawa, Deutsch Eylau and Osterode. In the east, Chernyakovsky's 3rd Belorussian Front (using principally the 39th, 5th, 28th and 2nd Guards Armies, together with two attached tank corps) was to attack along the line of the River Pregolya towards Koenigsberg. With the help of the 43rd Army from the 1st Baltic Front, this second thrust was intended to destroy the German forces along the River Niemen.

The southern arm of the pincer moved in to the attack on 14 January in appalling weather. In fact the snow was so thick that the Russians advanced on an unsuspecting enemy, and did not need the planned artil-

lery barrage. Once the initial shock had been overcome, however, the Germans began to fight back in their usual determined way, causing the Russians very heavy losses, and slowing down the pace of Rokossovsky's advance very considerably. With the committal to the battle on 15 January of the army group reserves, the 7th Panzer and 'Grossdeutschland' Panzergrenadier Divisions, the Russian advance was slowed to a snail's pace. Reinhardt might indeed have completely halted the Russians had not Hitler seen fit to remove the 'Grossdeutschland' Panzer Corps for service with Army Group 'A' in an effort to stem the advance of Zhukov's 1st Belorussian Front past Lodz. But as Hitler removed Reinhardt's last hope, the Russian commander committed another two tank corps, and this enabled the Russians to start moving forward again. The bad weather also lifted at this juncture, allowing Colonel-General K. A. Vershinin's 4th Air Army to fly some 2,500 missions in support of the ground forces. By the 19th

Above: **Three German paratroopers, the centre one with a *Panzerfaust*, double through a ruined building to find cover.**

Right: **Considering the plight in which Germany found herself in 1945, these *Panzergrenadiers* appear quite remarkably cheerful. The man with the MG 42 machine gun slung over his shoulder is a *Gefreiter* or lance-corporal, as shown by the chevron on his sleeve. Note the 'stick grenades', or 'potato mashers' as they were sometimes referred to, in the background. By 1943 leather for boots was in short supply, so the old pattern boot up to the knee was abandoned in favour of ankle boots together with green canvas, reinforced with leather, gaiters. Both boots and gaiters are clearly visible in this photograph.**

Above: **A warm welcome ready for any Russians coming the way of this German sentry. Apart from the four 'stick grenades' on top of the parapet of his trench, the German has some 27 'egg' grenades on the rear slope of the parapet and his rifle.**

Left: **A PzKpfw VI 'Tiger' (foreground) and a 7.5-cm *Sturmgeschuetz* 40 assault gun move against the Russian spearhead advances.**

the Russians had broken through on a wide front, and had crossed the East Prussian frontier. The German 2nd Army was retreating in considerably disarray, and was close to breaking point. Rokossovsky continued to press on, his forces reaching the outskirts of Elbing on 23 January, and the Baltic Sea north of this town on the 26th. East Prussia was now cut off from the rest of the Third Reich. Further to the south, the left wing of Rokossovsky's pincer had also made good progress along the north bank of the River Vistula, capturing Torun and pressing on towards Grudziadz.

To the north-east, Chernyakovsky's forces had attacked on 13 January, the day before Rokossovsky's front. The Russians used a variety of deceptive measures to fool the Germans as to the true nature of their intentions, but progress was slow, the Germans fighting with great courage and determination. Tilsit was not taken until the fifth day after the start of the offensive. Unlike the 2nd Army to the south, the 3rd *Panzerarmee* fell back in good order. Reinhardt had pressed for the 4th Army to be allowed to pull back right from the moment the Russian offensive broke, but Hitler refused to sanction the move until the 21st, when Hossbach was ordered to pull back his army to Loetzen on the Masurian lakes and form a

defence line facing westwards, to cover the gap left by the destruction and disintegration of the 2nd Army. The position of Army Group 'Centre' was by now so desperate, however, that even the 4th Army's new positions would be untenable, and Reinhardt pressed for the evacuation of the military and civilian population of East Prussia. Had this been started early enough, Reinhardt thought, most of the Germans in East Prussia might have escaped to the west before Rokossovsky's troops cut off the province. Hossbach also thought this the only possible course, and pulled back behind the Masurian lakes to prepare to fight his way out towards northern Pomerania. Hitler, who had expressly forbidden any attempts at an exodus, grew suspicious, and on 26 January dismissed Reinhardt and Hossbach, replacing them with Colonel-General L. Rendulic (late commander of Army Group 'North' in Kurland) and General F. W. Mueller respectively. Rendulic's place in Kurland was taken by W. Weiss, lately C-in-C 2nd Army. Hitler ordered that Koenigsberg and as much of East Prussia's north coast as possible be held at any costs; this task Rendulic achieved under Germany's capitulation in May. In the meantime, some 500,000 Germans were evacuated from the various beach-heads by the *Kriegsmarine* in a quite remarkably able rescue operation.

The task that Hitler had entrusted to Reinhardt had been an impossible one made even more difficult by Hitler's complete intransigence about sensible defence measures. Yet Reinhardt fought an able defensive battle, and had it not been for the disintegration of the 2nd Army, he might have inflicted even more grievous losses on Rokossovsky's forces than he did. In the north the 3rd *Panzerarmee* had handled the 3rd Belorussian Front very hard whilst retaining its cohesion.

The Eastern Front, June 1941 – February 1943

General Otto Woehler

Otto Woehler was born on 12 July 1894 at Grossburgwedel, and entered the Imperial German Army as a cadet on 1 February 1913. He was posted to the 167th Infantry Regiment as a lieutenant on 20 May 1914, and served as a junior officer during World War I.

Woehler remained in the army, now designated *Reichsheer*, after the signing of the Treaty of Versailles, reaching the ranks of lieutenant-colonel and colonel on 1 June 1935 and 1 January 1938 respectively. He was appointed Chief Operations Officer (Ia) of the newly-formed 5th *Gruppenkommando* (Army Group Headquarters) on 1 April 1938. By the beginning

of World War II, Woehler was Chief Operations Officer of the 14th Army, under the command of General Wilhelm List, former head of the 5th *Gruppenkommando*. This army spearheaded the German advance into southern Poland.

On 18 December 1939, Woehler received the appointment of chief-of-staff to XVII Corps, and served in this capacity during the Western campaign of May–June 1940. Woehler was further advanced, to chief-of-staff of the 11th Army, on 1 October 1940, and served in Manstein's army in the opening stages of the campaign against Soviet Russia.

On 1 January 1942 Woehler was

promoted major-general, and served as chief-of-staff to Field-Marshal von Kluge's Army Group 'Centre' between 1 April 1942 and 1 March 1943. He was promoted to lieutenant-general on 1 October 1942.

Next Woehler received a fighting command, I Corps, on 1 April 1943. This was later expanded into *Gruppe* 'Woehler', which fought with some distinction during the summer of 1943. Woehler was promoted general on 1 June 1943, and received command of the 8th Army on 15 August 1943, just in time to lead it in a skilful retreat in front of the Russian autumn offensive from the Dniepr bridge-heads towards Rumania. As the Axis forces pulled back into Rumania, the 8th Army and the Rumanian 4th Army were grouped as Army Group 'Woehler', which the commander managed excellently, despite the defection of the 4th Army at the time of Rumania's surrender on 23 August 1944. As the Germans fell back into Hungary, Woehler on 28 December 1944 received command of Army Group 'South', which he held until 25 March 1945.

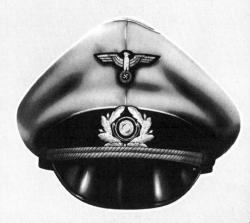

General Otto Woehler

By the end of February 1945, the Russian armies were poised in two major groupings for the final destruction of the Third Reich. In Germany herself, along the line formed by the Rivers Oder and Neisse, were the 2nd Belorussian Front, 1st Belorussian Front and 1st Ukrainian Front, whilst further south, in Czechoslovakia and Hungary, were the 4th, 2nd and 1st Ukrainian Fronts. These last three fronts had advanced from the Carpathian mountains–River Dniestr line on 20 August 1944, and having swept south and then north-west through Rumania, destroying Army Group 'South Ukraine' *en route*, reached a line half-way through Hungary by 31 January 1945. Here the Russian forces had halted to rest and redeploy before pushing on into the rest of Hungary, Austria and Czechoslovakia.

Guderian, now OKH chief-of-staff, warned Hitler that the Russians' main thrust, once they resumed their offensive, must come in the northern sector, aimed at Berlin itself. Therefore all the available resources and reserves should be deployed to counter this threat. Hitler, however, with his constant preoccupation with oil, saw a chance for a major counterstroke in Hungary. Army Group 'South', commanded by General Otto Woehler, was to strike through the gap between Lakes Balaton and Velencei with the aim of cutting off the part of the 3rd Ukrainian Front between the Rivers Danube and Drava, destroying it, and then swinging north to retake Budapest, cross the River Danube and recapture eastern Hungary.

Further to the south, pinning attacks on the cut-off portion of Marshal of the Soviet Union F. I. Tolbukhin's 3rd Ukrainian Front were to be made by General M. de Angelis' 2nd *Panzerarmee* of Army Group

Above: Defence forces dug in, albeit only lightly, on the 'reverse' slope of a railway line in Hungary. Aiding the predominantly SS *Panzergrenadier* units in the area were police and *Volkssturm* detachments, the latter two of uncertain combat efficiency.

Left: Two members of a *Jaeger* (light infantry) unit raised in the Schleswig-Holstein area duck into their trench for cover as a Russian mortar and artillery barrage begins to burst overhead. Such cover was in fact remarkably efficient unless a shell burst immediately above the trench.

'South' and a corps of three divisions from Colonel-General A. Loehr's Army Group 'E' in Yugoslavia. The success of the whole operation, Hitler was convinced, would safeguard the vital oil supplies Germany was getting from Hungary and Austria. These by now made up some 80 per cent of Germany's oil.

The major element of the offensive, codenamed '*Fruehlingserwachen*' or 'Spring awakening', was to be the drive to the Danube from the Lake Balaton–Lake Velencei gap. This was to be the task of a formidable strike force, formed against the strongest protestations from Guderian, who felt that these forces should be deployed against the Russian threat against Berlin. Some 10 Panzer and five infantry divisions from the 6th SS *Panzerarmee* (*Oberstgruppenfuehrer* Sepp Dietrich), 6th Army (General H. Balck) and the Hungarian VIII Corps were to drive to the River Danube between Dunapentele in the north and Baja in the south.

Although the German force, totalling 10 Panzer and 12 infantry divisions, appeared strong on paper, its real strength in men and tanks was low. Dietrich's force, in particular, had been severely handled in the 'Battle of the Bulge'. The Russian forces, however, were truly formidable. Tolbuk-

hin's 3rd Ukrainian Front consisted of five armies, with one cavalry, one mechanised and two tank corps, together with 37 Russian and six Bulgarian rifle divisions. In all, Tolbukhin had at his disposal more than 400,000 men, 400 tanks and self-propelled guns, and 1,000 aircraft. The Yugoslav 3rd Army was also co-operating on the Russians' left flank.

Attack essential

Hitler was so insistent on the offensive that considerations of terrain and weather were not allowed to intervene. The area over which the 6th Army and 6th SS *Panzerarmee* were to advance was low-lying, swampy and criss-crossed by a multitude of canals and small watercourses. These made progress for the infantry difficult, and for the armoured forces all but impossible. These conditions also made life difficult for the Russians. Although they greatly helped in front-line defence, they made the problem of supply and communication very difficult. The Russians' problems were exacerbated by the fact that ice floes were still coming down the Danube, threatening to sweep away the pontoon bridges so vital for Russian supplies. The construction of an overhead wire track across the Danube was

of great use, as was the pipeline for fuel, the first used by the Russians. Finally the weather, with extremely heavy rain and low temperatures, further reduced the Germans' chances of success.

The German build-up had not gone unnoticed by the Russians. As the latter were planning a major offensive, Tolbukhin decided not to deploy his forces so as to be able to launch a counterattack, but instead to deploy in depth, allow the Germans to advance, hold them and then launch his own offensive once all his preparations were complete. Confirmation of the German intentions was supplied by deserting Hungarians.

The German offensive opened on 5 March, when Angelis' four divisions advanced against Lieutenant-General M. N. Sharokhin's 57th Army, and Loehr's three divisions against the Bulgarian 1st and Yugoslav 3rd Armies. By the 15th of the month, none of these thrusts had advanced more than 10 miles. Loehr's and Angelis' drives were subsidiary, and the main German offensive started on 6 March.

After a 30-minute artillery bombardment, the main German forces pushed forward, the 6th Army on the left against Lieutenant-General N. D. Zakhvataev's 4th Guards Army, and the 6th SS *Panzerarmee* on the

Woehler — the Battle of Lake Balaton

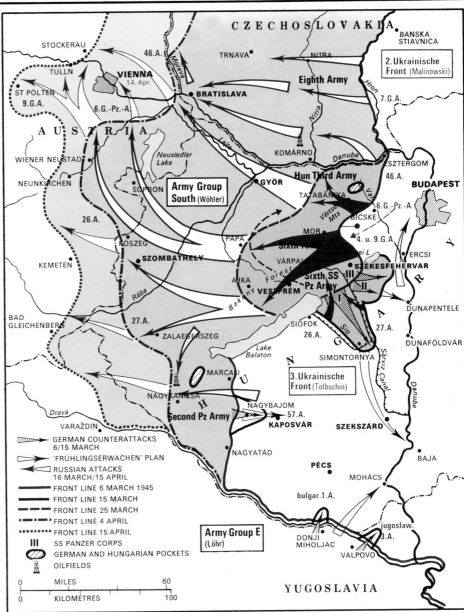

Map labels:

CZECHOSLOVAKIA

BANSKA STIAVNICA

STOCKERAU · 46.A. · TRNAVA · NITRA · 2. Ukrainische Front (Malinowski)

TULLN · VIENNA 14. Apr. · Eighth Army · 7.G.A.

ST PÖLTEN · 9.G.A. · 6.G.-Pz.-A. · BRATISLAVA · Hron

AUSTRIA · KOMÁRNO · Danube · ESZTERGOM

WIENER NEUSTADT · Neusiedler Lake · GYÖR · Hun Third Army · 46.A. · BUDAPEST

NEUNKIRCHEN · SOPRON · Army Group South (Wöhler) · TATABÁNYA · 6.G.-Pz.-A.

26.A. · KÖSZEG · PAPA · Vértse Mts · BICSKE · 4. u. 9.G.A.

SZOMBATHELY · Sixth Army · VÁRPAL · ERCSI

KEMETEN · Rába · AJKA · Forest · Sixth SS III · SZÉKESFEHÉRVAR

VESZPRÉM · Pz Army · II · I

BAD GLEICHENBERG · 27.A. · Bakony · DUNAPENTELE

ZALAEGERSZEG · SIÓFOK · Sió · 27.A.

26.A. · Lake Balaton · SIMONTORNYA · DUNAFÖLDVÁR

MARCALI · 3. Ukrainische Front (Tolbuchin) · Sárviz Canal · Danube

Drava · NAGYKANIZSA · NAGYBAJOM

VARAŽDIN · Second Pz Army · KAPOSVÁR · 57.A. · SZEKSZÁRD · BAJA

NAGYATÁD · PÉCS · MOHÁCS

bulgar.1.A.

Army Group E (Löhr) · DONJI MIHOLJAC · jugoslaw. J.A. · VALPOVO

YUGOSLAVIA

Legend:

- GERMAN COUNTERATTACKS 6/15 MARCH
- 'FRÜHLINGSERWACHEN' PLAN
- RUSSIAN ATTACKS 16 MARCH/15 APRIL
- FRONT LINE 6 MARCH 1945
- FRONT LINE 15 MARCH
- FRONT LINE 25 MARCH
- FRONT LINE 4 APRIL
- FRONT LINE 15 APRIL
- III SS PANZER CORPS
- GERMAN AND HUNGARIAN POCKETS
- OILFIELDS

0 · MILES · 60
0 · KILOMETRES · 100

Above left: **PzKpfw VI 'Tiger' heavy tanks *en route* for the front in Hungary.** Although qualitatively more than a match for any but the latest Russian tanks, the 'Tiger' was vulnerable to flank attack by the masses of tanks the Soviet forces now had, and was also capable of being bested by Russian ground-attack aircraft. The latter could roam the skies at will, so close to complete collapse was the *Luftwaffe*.

Above: **The Battle of Lake Balaton,** also known to the Germans as Operation *'Fruehlingserwachen'* or 'Spring Awakening', was Germany's last major offensive of the war, and reflected Hitler's preoccupation with oil. But the German forces committed were exhausted, and the plan's strategic ambitions were impossible, as any but a madman could have seen.

Left: **Exhausted troopers of the *Waffen-SS* rest from their labours.** Hitler was incensed in the extreme by the performance of the SS units committed at Lake Balaton, and ordered their armbands be removed.

187

right against Lieutenant-General N. A. Gagen's 26th Army. The one factor that might have given the Germans a greater chance of success, tactical air support, was limited by the small number of aircraft available and the appalling weather. Nevertheless the Germans drove forward slowly, making nearly five miles in the first two days and just over 15 by the end of the fourth day. But the German advance was gradually slowed and stopped as Tolbukhin sent in his artillery reserves (Colonel-General N. I. Nedelin) and the 27th Army (Colonel-General S. G. Trofimenko) to plug the gap between the 4th Guards and 26th Armies. Tolbukhin was refused further reinforcements, and when Woehler committed his one reserve Panzer division, the 6th, with some 200 tanks and self-propelled guns, on the 14th, the Russian situation began to look serious. But losses on both sides had been extremely heavy, and the Germans were running out of fuel and momentum. On the 15th they were forced to a halt.

Now it was the turn of the Russians, who planned a general counter-offensive by the 2nd Ukrainian Front (Marshal of the Soviet Union R. Ya. Malinovsky) as well as the 3rd Ukrainian Front. But instead of the drive on Vienna originally envisaged, Marshal of the Soviet Union S. K. Timoshenko, who was co-ordinating the offensive for the

Stavka, decided that the 9th Guards Army (Colonel-General V. V. Glagolev) and 6th Guards Tank Army (Colonel-General A. G. Kravchenko) should be allocated to Tolbukhin to cut off and destroy the 6th Army and 6th SS *Panzerarmee*. The Russian counter-offensive was launched on 16 March, from positions north-west of Lake Velencei. At first all went the Russians' way, Hitler refusing to sanction the abandonment of *Fruehlingserwachen* in favour of a flank attack on the Russian advance until it was too late. By the time the *Fuehrer* consented on the 19th, the German escape corridor to the north-west was narrowing hourly. In some of the bitterest fighting of the war, most of the men of the 6th SS *Panzerarmee* managed to escape. Many retreated without orders, and most of the 6th Army and all the two armies' heavy equipment was lost. Hitler was infuriated, and ordered that all SS units in the rout be stripped of their armbands. As no defensive preparations behind Lake Balaton had been set in hand, the Germans were unable to make another stand, and fell back in complete disorder. The Battle of Lake Balaton can be said to have ended on 25 March with the fall to the Russians of Papa. Woehler was dismissed from his command, being replaced by Colonel-General L. Rendulic. Meanwhile, the Russian offensive had been extended in the north and south, and by 4 April most of

Above: Russian troops push on into Austria in the direction of Vienna during April 1945. The swastika flag over which they are marching had in all probability been put there by the camera team, Russian propagandists being very keen on the symbolism of such occasions. *Right:* A German self-propelled gun moves up towards the fighting front. The only self-propelled mounting in service with the German Panzer forces at the beginning of the war had been AA guns, despite urgent requests from armoured commanders for mobile support weapons. By the end of the war production of self-propelled guns exceeded that of tanks.

Hungary had been cleared, and the Russians were advancing into Austria.

What of Woehler's performance? It has to be admitted that he had been presented with an impossible task right from the outset, and that his mission had been made even harder by his lack of resources and the nature of the terrain and weather. Nevertheless, he had fought his offensive battle with considerable skill. Only when the Russians themselves went over to the offensive did his lack of forethought reveal itself in the lack of defensive positions in his rear.

Field-Marshal Ferdinand Schoerner

As the Russians pressed on with their final offensives of the war, Schoerner's forces were gradually compressed into an ever-decreasing pocket in Czechoslovakia. To the end Hitler called upon Schoerner to break through to free Berlin from the last Russian drives.

An avowed Nazi, Schoerner was a man of considerable personal courage, but his real abilities are hard to assess: he was noted for driving his men, both officers and enlisted men, with the utmost ruthlessness, but this may have been the result of the fact that he was used only in the direst straits, when his support of Nazism would ensure that he obeyed Hitler's orders to the full.

At the last his courage deserted him, and rather than face capture by the Red Army, Schoerner abandoned his men and surrendered himself to the Americans.

Ferdinand Schoerner was born in Munich on 12 June 1892, and during World War I served in the Bavarian Infantry Regiment of the German Alpine Corps. On 24 October 1917, during the Battle of Caporetto in Italy, Schoerner won the coveted *Pour le Mérite* decoration in the same action as Erwin Rommel won his.

In the early stages of World War II the 6th Austrian Mountain Division was commanded by Schoerner, who then went on to command XIX Mountain Corps. In October 1943 Schoerner took up the post of commander of XL Panzer Corps in Russia. Schoerner's next appointment was on the staff of *Oberkommando des Heeres,* the Army High Command which ran the war against Russia under the supervision of Hitler himself. Whilst serving with OKH Schoerner was made acting commander-in-chief of Army Group 'A', an appointment that was confirmed in May 1944.

Two months later, however, Schoerner found himself moved to become commander of Army Group 'North', finally cut off by the Russians in Kurland. In this isolated pocket he conducted an energetic, although hopeless, defence.

From Army Group 'North' Schoerner was shifted to Army Group 'Centre' in January 1945.

Field-Marshal Ferdinand Schoerner

By the end of 1944 it was obvious to almost everyone that Germany would lose the war before the Western Allies and Russia would cease to be on friendly terms. However, Hitler and a small element of his entourage still hoped that they might cause a split between the two Allied groups, or by such firm resistance produce a casualty rate which was unacceptable to an attacker and so force him to negotiate with Germany.

But by the end of 1944 Germany had lost 106 divisions in the East, destroyed or disbanded, in a mere 12 months. She was cut off from her supplies of oil in Rumania, her armaments industry and communications were crippled and she had few generals whom Hitler regarded as sufficiently loyal by his deranged standards. As one general failed to hold back the Russians he would be replaced by another who would receive fantastic promises of new troops and arms and who under pressure from Hitler would give equally fantastic promises – although

neither could keep their word. By adjusting the age of entry and period of service Hitler had been able to rebuild his armies with 16-year-old boys and men in their late middle age. Now he looked for generals with fanatical wills to match his own.

One such general, Ferdinand Schoerner, seemed an unlikely man to fulfil this rôle. A heavily-built, bespectacled man, he had served with distinction in World War I and was a specialist in mountain warfare. Devoted to Hitler, he had proved a tough defensive fighter in the East and had risen rapidly, so that by the end of the war he held the rank of Field-Marshal.

Hitler, as always obsessed with oil, considered that it was vital to hold the oil shale areas of Hungary and the Vienna basin. Thus a major portion of the German army was deployed south-east of Berlin, covering Prague and the approaches to Austria. In the recently renamed Army Group 'Centre' which covered Czechoslovakia with its

armaments industries, some 20 infantry divisions, eight Panzer and *Panzergrenadier* divisions were faced by the 1st, 4th and 2nd Fronts. If the German units had been up to their paper strength, they could have made a coherent and effective defence, but now it was a game of fitting an impressive name to a nondescript unit – so that a party of middle-aged men on bicycles with *Panzerfaust* hollow-charge projectiles slung from the handle bars became a tank-destroyer unit.

No real army

On 16 January it was time for a change and Colonel-General Schoerner was ordered to leave his command in Army Group 'North' and take over Army Group 'A' or 'Centre' as it was renamed on the 26th. The promised reinforcements he received from the Replacement Army now under the command of *Reichsfuehrer* Himmler were a few poorly trained and equipped *Volksgrenadier* divisions, the staff and students from military schools and some policemen. With such men he was to cover Saxony, Sudetenland and the whole of Czechoslovakia. In fact for three days the army was without a commander, for it was difficult for Schoerner to quit his previous command in Army Group 'North'.

When he arrived he found that there seemed little for him to command: the staff of the 4th *Panzerarmee* had disappeared, for as far as anyone knew, it was fighting its own war somewhere beyond their front. The 17th Army and the 1st *Panzerarmee* were retreating from Konev's 1st Ukrainian Front in the area of the upper Vistula east of Krakow and in Czechoslovakia. Despite this pressure they had maintained their cohesion. Schoerner therefore sent the dubious reinforcements he had received to bolster the 4th *Panzerarmee*. During the withdrawal he lost the 1st Hungarian Army – it disbanded itself.

The army group stopped on a 300-mile front covering the Oder, and leaving his excellent cubordinates, General Schulz of

Grenade-throwing practice at an extremely sketchily camouflaged anti-aircraft gun site in Austria. But what the Germans needed at this stage of the war were large numbers of well trained men and heavy weapons to try to stem the Russian armoured advance.

the 17th Army, General Heinrici of the 1st *Panzerarmee* and General Graeser of the 4th *Panzerarmee* to watch their fronts, Schoerner looked to the rear areas. He was a believer in the 'Will to Win' and 'The Fight to the Last Breath' and was well known as a National-Socialist officer.

Adopting a motto of 'Strength through Fear' he succeeded in making many officers think that the punishment for retreat was more dreadful than the prospect of death in battle facing the Russians. He could still count on the faith of the soldiers and younger officers whom he wooed, portraying the *Fuehrer* as a common man much like themselves.

On 23 January the 1st Ukrainian Front reached the Oder and crossed it at two points near Brieg and in the area of Steinau. With no reserves available, Schoerner ordered the exhausted and understrength XXIV Panzer Corps and the Panzer Corps '*Grossdeutschland*' to destroy the bridgeheads. They tried and failed.

On 8 February Konev broke out from the Steinau bridgehead and punched a gap 40 miles deep and 95 miles wide, getting close to the Neisse and encircling 18,000 troops in the German forteess of Glogau. A week later the 5th Guards drove north-west from the Brieg bridgehead and in conjunction with the 6th Army moving from the Steinau bridgehead surrounded Breslau.

The defence of Breslau stands out as an epic in the defeat and disorder of the last days of the Reich. Two regular army infantry divisions were ordered to break out of the city when it was surrounded and so its garrison was merely the 609th Infantry Division – which had itself only been raised in Dresden a few weeks earlier from stragglers, *Volkssturm* soldiers and SS men. It had no tanks, but did possess 32 batteries of guns, captured in earlier campaigns in Russia, Poland, Yugoslavia and Italy. Under the professional leadership of General Hermann von Ahlfen und Niehoff and the political exhortations of Doctor Goebbels and *Gauleiter* Hanke, the city was still fighting when Berlin surrendered.

Schoerner ordered the 4th *Panzerarmee* to counterattack to clear the Berlin–Silesia railway and relieve the Glogau garrison. It failed to reach Glogau and the city capitulated on 18 March. After warding off this counterattack Konev paused, and then with ponderous strength moved again. On 15 March he attacked on both sides of the town of Oppeln, intending to clear Upper Silesia up to the Czechoslovakian border. By the end of the month he had fulfilled his intention.

On 6 April Schoerner received reinforcements. Three *Panzergrenadier* divisions were switched from Army Group 'Vistula', despite the protests of General Heinrici. The *Fuehrer* had an intuition that the Soviet offensive would not be directed against Berlin, but at Czechoslovakia.

On 15 April Hitler sent out his order of the day. It was to be his last, and reflected the way his brain had deteriorated. He told his men: 'For the last time, the deadly Jewish–Bolshevik enemy had started a mass

German artillery takes the Russians under high-angle fire.

attack. He is trying to reduce Germany to rubble and to exterminate our people. Soldiers of the East! You are already fully aware now of the fate that threatens German women and children. Whilst men, children and old people will be murdered, women and girls will be reduced to the rôle of barrack-room whores. The rest will be marched off to Siberia.' Now he was speaking the coarse parade ground language of an army corporal.

On 16 April the Russians launched their assault on Berlin and by the 18th, despite determined resistance and counterattacks by the 4th *Panzerarmee*, Konev reached the strongpoints of Cottbus and Spremberg. He was unable to take them, and pouring past Spremberg to the north and south he cut off Schoerner's Army Group 'Centre' from its northern neighbours, Army Group 'Vistula'.

In the midst of this crisis Hitler's 56 birthday dawned on 20 April and Schoerner called at the *Fuehrer* headquarters to congratulate his leader. It was a game of bluff, and Hitler appeared cheerful after the visit. Schoerner had assured him that counterattacks by the 4th *Panzerarmee* were being launched on the Russian breakthrough on the Oder. Hitler pressed that the Oder line be defended, though by now it was, to misquote him, 'merely a geographical concept'.

By the end of April Konev began to withdraw units from the Berlin front and direct them towards the south. On the 26th an excited Hitler telephoned Schoerner and urged his chief-of-staff Natzmer 'to bring the battle for the capital to a victorious end'. He dismissed the protests that their was neither the fuel nor the ammunition to attack over 125 miles: 'that is of no importance. Shortages must be filled, the battle for Berlin must be won.'

No surrender

On 7 May OKW contacted Schoerner's headquarters and ordered Army Group 'Centre' to cease fighting at midnight on 9 May. General von Natzmer realised that this meant he would be unable to save his troops from Russian prisoner-of-war camps, for it would be impossible to disengage from the front in the time allowed. Schoerner shouted that he would not obey the order and demanded that his commanding officers submit their opinions by nightfall.

They were rational men, however, and saw that continued resistance would put them beyond the law and make American commanders far less sympathetic to their surrender pleas. Their decision shocked Schoerner, who realised that he was in danger of being captured by the Russians – who had marked his name down on their wanted lists.

Natzmer suggested that the northern wing of the 4th *Panzerarmee* should be ordered to resist so that other units could then set in motion an 'organized flight to the west'. Inevitably men would be captured by the Russians, but the majority, particularly those with vehicles, would be able to make their escape.

On 8 May a small convoy set off from Schoerner's headquarters. The Field-Marshall intended to escape westward by light aircraft, and after some near brushes with

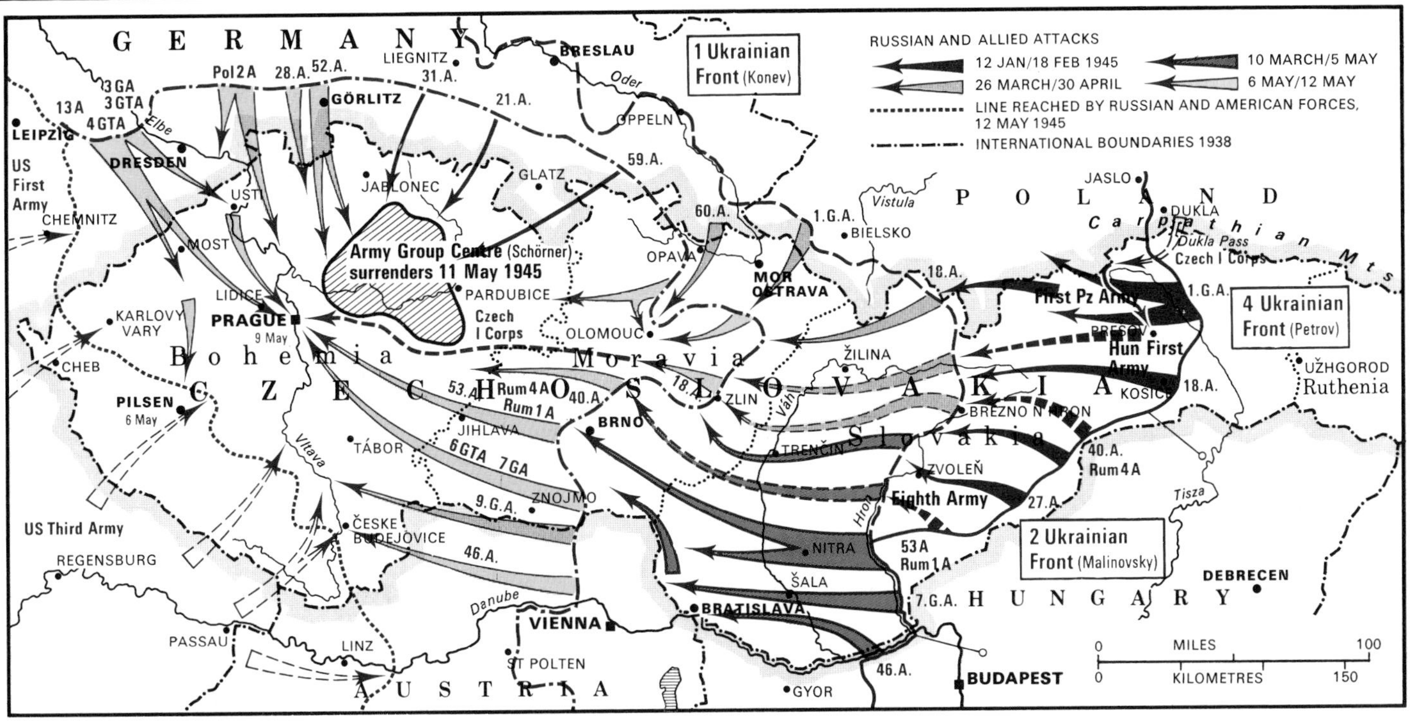

RUSSIAN AND ALLIED ATTACKS
12 JAN/18 FEB 1945
26 MARCH/30 APRIL
10 MARCH/5 MAY
6 MAY/12 MAY
LINE REACHED BY RUSSIAN AND AMERICAN FORCES, 12 MAY 1945
INTERNATIONAL BOUNDARIES 1938
G E R M A N Y
1 Ukrainian Front (Konev)
4 Ukrainian Front (Petrov)
2 Ukrainian Front (Malinovsky)
Army Group Centre (Schörner) surrenders 11 May 1945
P O L A N D
H U N G A R Y
A U S T R I A
Bohemia
Moravia
Slovakia
Ruthenia
C Z E C H O S L O V A K I A
Carpathian Mts
BRESLAU
LIEGNITZ
GÖRLITZ
LEIPZIG
DRESDEN
CHEMNITZ
US First Army
US Third Army
OPPELN
GLATZ
JABLONEC
USTI
MOST
LIDICE
PRAGUE
9 May
KARLOVY VARY
CHEB
PILSEN
6 May
TÁBOR
JIHLAVA
ZNOJMO
ČESKE BUDEJOVICE
REGENSBURG
PASSAU
LINZ
ST POLTEN
VIENNA
BRNO
ZLIN
OLOMOUC
PARDUBICE
Czech I Corps
OPAVA
MOR OSTRAVA
BIELSKO
JASLO
DUKLA
Dukla Pass
Czech I Corps
First Pz Army
PRESOV
Hun First Army
KOSICE
UŽHGOROD
ŽILINA
BREZNO N HRON
TRENČIN
ZVOLEŇ
Eighth Army
NITRA
ŠALA
BRATISLAVA
GYOR
BUDAPEST
DEBRECEN
Vistula
Oder
Elbe
Vltava
Danube
Váh
Hron
Tisza
Pol 2 A
28.A.
52.A.
31.A.
21.A.
59.A.
60.A.
1.G.A.
18.A.
13 A
3 GA
3 GTA
4 GTA
53.A
Rum 4 A
Rum 1 A
40.A.
6 GTA
7 GA
9.G.A.
46.A.
27.A.
40.A.
Rum 4 A
53 A
Rum 1 A
7.G.A.
MILES
KILOMETRES
0
100
150

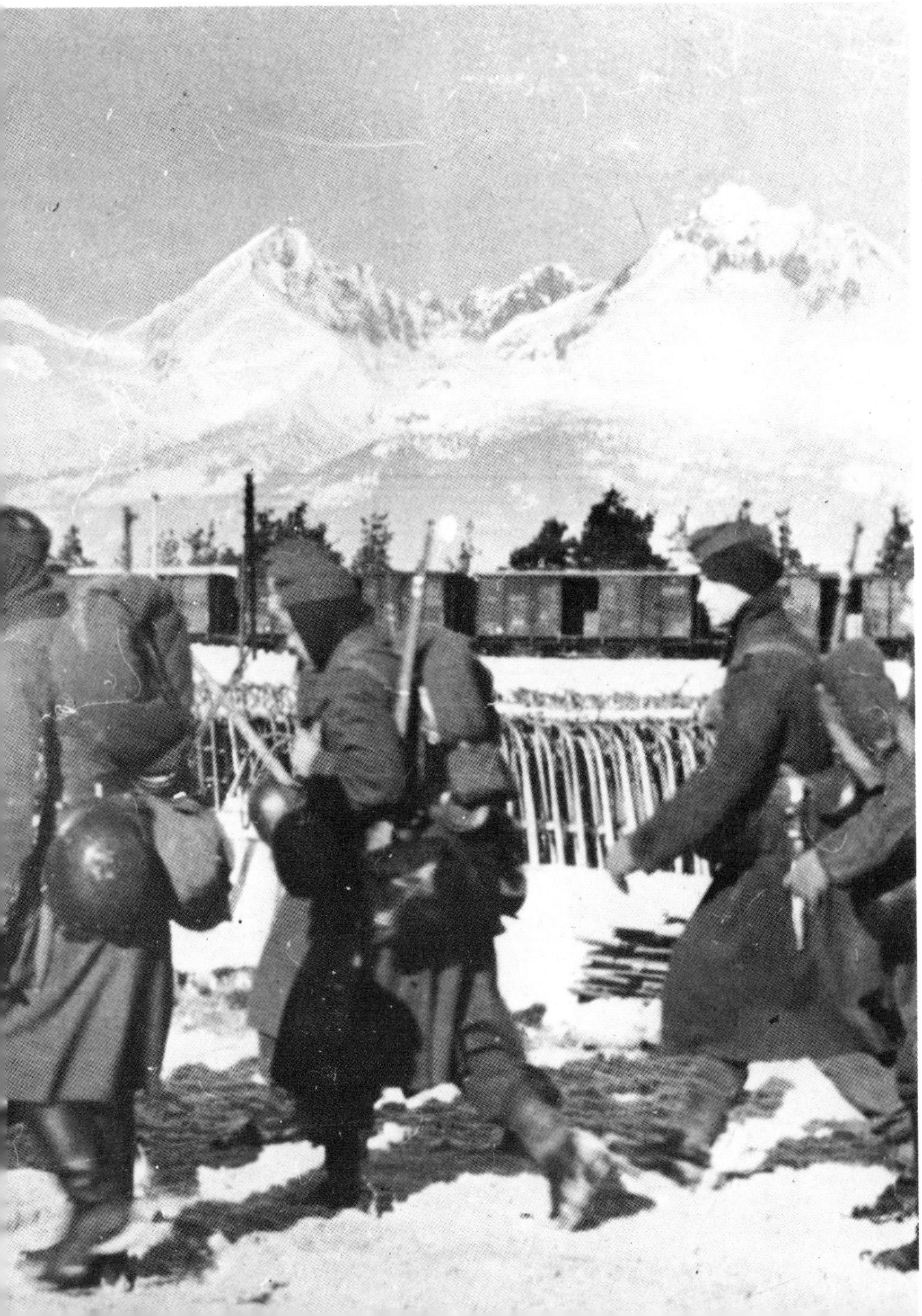

Above left: **Difficult fighting terrain in Slovakia, typical of the type of country in which Schoerner made his last determined, even fanatical, stand against the Russians.**

Above: **The final ebb of Nazi Germany's military ambitions – Field-Marshal Ferdinand Schoerner's hopeless attempt to hold Czechoslovakia against the Russians and Americans. When he realised that the cause was lost, he fled to the Americans in civilian clothes, abandoning the men he had terrorised into action.**

Left: **German infantry start their move up into the high Tatra mountains to try to form a bulwark against Russian advance into the southern half of Germany.**

advancing Russian troops he located the aircraft near Podersham. Here he summoned the local party chief and ordered some civilian clothes. To the consernation of a small crowd that had gathered he appeared in the green jacket and leather shorts of Bavarian traditional costume.

To the disgust of his chief-of-staff, Schoerner made his escape and crash-landed in Austria. As he fled westwards Schoerner did not hear that even in death the *Fuehrer* rewarded his loyal soldiers. In the Doenitz government the Field-Marshal was to head the army. He would be part of an executive which included men like Goebbels, Bormann and Seyss-Inquart. It was another promise that Hitler could never keep. Around 15 May he reported to the staff of the German 1st Army who, though prisoners, were now engaged in the dismissal of low-ranking German troops. The Americans handed him over to the Russians, as they did many of the men of his army group who reached the Allied lines.

Analysis-
Generalship against Russia

The story of Germany's war in the East is one of missed opportunities and, predictably, of Hitler's interference and indecision. Even before *Barbarossa* was launched there were three plans, and when the operation was under way Hitler changed the priority of Moscow making it as the main objective in the autumn of 1941. When the Germans fell back in the winter counter-offensive before Moscow they made sure that they would not win the war with Russia, and at Stalingrad in the following winter and Kursk in 1943 they made certain their defeat.

Whereas in their attacks in the West the Germans had faced enemies who had been reluctant to incur heavy casualties, the Russians had little compunction about the ruthless use of their manpower. The casualties in prisoners, dead and wounded suffered in the opening months of the war would have crippled any Western nation, but the Russians were prepared to trade not only space for time, but men as well. The shape of western Russia, which tapers from a narrow border to a broad interior, meant that the German and Axis forces were forced to thin their units to cover the whole front as they advanced eastwards. In an attempt to cover the front, satellite armies from Italy, Rumania, Bulgaria and Hungary were moved forward from their rear-area responsibilities. These units became the proverbial weak link in the chain of defences, and were singled out by the Russians for attack. There was, moreover, intense suspicion and ill feeling between Rumanian and Hungarian troops, engendered by prewar land-snatching by Hungary.

Russian tactics, like their men and equipment, were robust and simple, but very effective. They aimed to achieve a massive local superiority before an attack, and when they attacked it was pressed home with a fanaticism second only to that of the Japanese. Surrender was not regarded with the religious horror of the Japanese, but avoided by many men because by Soviet lights it constituted desertion, and action was taken by the authorities against the relatives of those who surrendered.

Besides this human enemy, the Germans faced many physical hazards in the East. The severe winter is well known, but the poor roads, broad-gauge railways, river barriers, woods and swamps made communications and logistic support extremely difficult. Most of the highly-bred European horses that the Germans employed for transportation died in the hard winters, and they were forced to use the smaller, but hardier Russian ponies.

However, besides these hazards and their enemy at the front, the Germans were increasingly troubled by partisans in their rear. Their long and ill-guarded communications made an easy target and many small groups of Axis troops were killed even before they reached the front.

The Germans were partly to blame for this because of their genocide policy in the East and because they regarded the Russians as 'Slavic sub-humans' fit only to be serfs. In 1941 many of the inhabitants of the Ukraine had welcomed the Germans as liberators from Stalin's centralised dictatorship, but the Germans tried to harness this good will only when the war had turned against them, and by then it was too late.

Left: **A German soldier doubles along a poorly constructed trench.**

Right: **German heavy artillery provides long-range fire support.**

Undoubtedly, however, the chief contributor to Germany's loss of the war in the East was the men who originated *Barbarossa*. Hitler, who had saved the army from rout in front of Moscow with his 'Stand and fight, no retreat' order, now saw this as the panacea against all Russian offensives. At Stalingrad he urged the 6th Army to hold on and await relief. It is interesting to note that at the time some Western observers thought that the Russians had committed a blunder and that the Germans would be able to hang on and tie up Soviet forces. After the Stalingrad defeat Hitler was shaken, but this did not last long and he was back to the old formula when the Russians launched their summer counter-offensive after Kursk. It was this desire to hold ground just for the sake of prestige that had produced the earlier massive Russian losses in 1941 and 1942. Now the rôle was reversed and German and Axis troops were being encircled because they could not retreat. Hitler's hatred of the thought of retreat, 'defeatism' in his vocabulary, meant that there could be no reasonable contingency planning and nor could work be done on fortifications in the rear because he said that his generals would simply wish to withdraw to these lines.

Spying the key

Mention should be made here of the Soviet use of spy rings in Germany. They employed two varieties, professional spies they had trained and introduced into occupied Europe and Germany, and amateur rings composed of anti-Nazi Germans. From these sources the Russians were able to build up a clear and very detailed picture of German plans and also of their economic and manpower strength. The Kursk attack (Operation '*Zitadelle*') was lost even before the first tank rumbled off or shell was fired, for the Russians had been provided with details of units, objectives and routes, and lacked only the exact date and time. They received this in time, however, to fire a counter-battery shoot at German emplacements – before the German guns had begun to fire.

The Russians must have had an agent placed somewhere very high in the German command structure, because they were kept informed of policy decisions taken by Hitler and his immediate circle. It is interesting that the third battle of Kharkov was fought by Manstein without direction from Hitler, and the German moves remained unknown to the Russians until the trap had been sprung on their two armoured groups. It was the information from Richard Sorge in Japan which enabled the Russians to move their Siberian troops from the Russo-Japanese border in time to launch the winter counter-offensive at Moscow. Moreover, the assurance that Japan would not attack Russia allowed Russia to draw on her vast pool of manpower in the Far East.

Training was not as long or thorough as Western nations and this also enabled Russia to use men from recently liberated areas of her western territories – they

might have been peasants or partisans, but if they could use a rifle they were fit to be soldiers.

This crude system of training even extended to tanks. The Germans once destroyed a group of British-made Valentine tanks crewed by industrial workers – operating instructions had been chalked in Russian on the inside of the fighting compartment.

Russian tanks and assault-guns, though poorly finished and without the elaborate optical equipment of western vehicles, were some of the best armoured vehicles to be produced in the war. The T-34 had thicker armour than any of the tanks with which Germany begun the war in the East, a maximum of 47-mm and a minimum of 20-mm, a speed of 32 mph and a 76.2-mm gun. Its broad tracks enabled it to travel over soft ground and snow despite its weight of 26 tons, while its well-sloped hull and turret presented fewer shot-traps for anti-tank shells. Having produced a war-winner the Russians concentrated on its mass production. The plants which produced this tank were situated beyond the Urals, far out of range of any German bomber. This meant that the Germans were confronted with hundreds of tanks which they had to destroy on the battle-field, rather than at their source in a factory.

In the battles of encirclement in 1941 and 1942 the Germans captured or destroyed vast quantities of Russian tanks, guns and trucks. In doing this, however, they assisted the Russians, for the Soviet high command was in the process of re-equipping its forces and the Germans had simply disposed of the obsolescent or obsolete weapons. The Russians produced their own tanks and most of their aircraft, but received a number of these from Britain and the United States. American trucks were an important asset when Russia moved onto the offensive since they enabled her to sustain the momentum of attack by allowing support and re-supply vehicles to keep up.

On 22 June 1941 Germany attacked an enigma. Soviet Russia had built a surprisingly effective security screen between herself and the west and the Germans had calculated that she possessed 155 divisions. In fact she had 230, and of these 170 were within striking distance of her western front. The Germans had based their analysis of Russian forces on the disastrous war with Finland in which the Soviet losses were about 200,000 killed, with 1,600 tanks destroyed. They also thought that the 1937 purges had destroyed the brains of the Red Army. A war in the East, according to Hitler's assessment, could be successfully concluded before winter. The Germans underestimated the courage of the average Russian, and they were unaware of the new industrial power of the Soviet Union. Combined with Stalin's ruthlessness and Zhukov's forceful leadership these elements produced an unbeatable enemy.

A 3.7-cm light anti-aircraft gun manned by the *Waffen-SS*.

199

Hitler and his High Command

Hitler inspects some of his elite troops – men of the *'Leibstandarte Adolf Hitler'*, which later became the dreaded 1st SS *Panzer* Division.

During the war years, and ever since then, the most famous German military word has also suffered misunderstanding and misuse: *Wehrmacht*. It has become popularly identified as the expression of German might and efficiency. It has been used as an alternative description of the German army. It has been wildly over-praised, and as hysterically vilified. But whenever it has been thus misused, the *Wehrmacht* has always been generally understood:

powerful, competent, the military weapon for the realisation of the ambitions of Adolf Hitler.

In fact *Wehrmacht*, pure and simple, was the word used for the armed forces – nothing more or less. It was composed of the Army *(Heer)*, the Navy *(Kriegsmarine)* and the Air Force *(Luftwaffe)*, each of which had a commander-in-chief of its own. The obvious problem in war was the co-ordination of these three entities into

the achievement of a common strategy. All combatant nations of World War II had to solve this problem in one way or another; the Allied solution, by no means invariably successful, was the Joint Chiefs-of-Staff Committee. Hitler's version, however, had first come into being as a result of his extension of his personal authority over the German military. Thus it never became a team of professionals working to get the cumulative best out of the three services in the field: it always remained a small military court, on the loyalty of whose permanent members Hitler could always depend.

In the early days of the Third Reich, the forces were the preserve of the Defence Minister, General von Blomberg. How Hitler engineered Blomberg's removal has been described elsewhere. In February 1938 a new command set-up was announced. This was the *Oberkommando der Wehrmacht* (OKW) or 'Supreme Command of the Armed Forces'. Hitler stood at its head, exercising the immediate command. Chief-of-Staff was the former chief of the armed forces office under Blomberg, General Wilhelm Keitel. Chief of Operations was General Alfred Jodl. These two men remained in their posts until the German collapse of 1945 – a remarkable fact in itself, when the ups and downs of other German generals are considered.

Hitler in command

This was Hitler's basic team. It was no part of Hitler's plan to have Keitel act as the chairman of an armed forces committee, in constant touch with the three services on all matters of joint concern. Keitel was in fact technically junior to the three forces commanders. It is essential to grasp the incredible fact that the chiefs of the German army, navy and air force hardly ever met in conference, and when they did it was in Hitler's presence. Rivalry among them was intense, particularly between the navy (Raeder) and the air force (Goering). The latter rivalry was the prime reason why the Third Reich never had a navy with an operational fleet air arm, mercifully for the British. The best co-operation between the services was to be found between the army and the air force, and then it was established at a lower level, between army group/army commanders and air fleet/air corps commanders.

This personal rivalry among the three leaders of the *Wehrmacht* lasted right through the war. It was not changed by Admiral Doenitz's replacement of Raeder at the end of 1942; it was not changed by Hitler's personal assumption of control over the army in the winter fighting of 1941–42, for even then he needed an army chief-of-staff and spent the rest of the war trying to find a suitably pliant candidate. (He never did.) But it was mirrored by an equally serious lack of understanding within OKW itself.

For the fullest details of this posterity is indebted to the evidence of General Walter Warlimont, Jodl's deputy. His main burden of complaint has been the total lack of mutual understanding between himself and Jodl. Warlimont is a lucky man: he has survived Keitel and Jodl, both of whom were hanged by sentence of the Nuremberg Tribunal after the war. He has himself admitted that had he not suffered severe injuries in the bomb attempt on Hitler's life in July 1944, he would have remained with the OKW entourage at Hitler's elbow and would almost certainly have ended up in the Berlin *Fuehrerbunker* in 1945. A good example of the sort of

work Warlimont did during the war was his memorandum of what should be done with Leningrad. (His recommended solution was to seal off the city, let as many of its inhabitants starve as possible, evacuate the survivors after the winter, and raze the city to the ground.) Callous though it sounds, this aspect of OKW's work is not relevant. Warlimont's evidence makes it clear that after the first three campaigns fought by the *Wehrmacht* in World War II – Poland, Scandinavia and the West – OKW lost any semblance of being a 'think-tank' of ideas for future operations. The ideas of junior officers wilted under the indifference of Jodl, who after the fall of France deliberately kept his better judgement subordinate to his faith in Hitler's genius.

An example of how the hero-worship of Hitler by both Keitel and Jodl sometimes did not matter was provided at the end of January 1940. Hitler's personal aide was Colonel (later General) Rudolf Schmundt, who was frequently entrusted with report-ing missions to the army headquarters at the front. Personal reports direct to Hitler would then bypass both the army high command (*Oberkommando des Heeres*

or OKH) and OKW. At the HQ of Army Group 'A' in Koblenz, Schmundt heard of the novel operational plan of the army group commander's chief-of-staff – a plan which had been repeatedly sat on by Brauchitsch and Halder at the head of the army, and which had never been submitted to OKW. This plan was enthusiastically adopted by Hitler as the *Fuehrer*'s own, and in due course was triumphantly revealed to OKW and the army. It was, of course, Manstein's 'Sickle' plan for the severance and destruction of the Allied armies in Flanders.

The whole mess reached its most confused state in the Dunkirk fiasco, another major controversy of World War II. By this stage Hitler, encouraged by success, was being tempted to meddle increasingly in the day-to-day conduct of operations, and Keitel and Jodl made no move to discourage him. As a result the army's decision to crash on to Dunkirk and destroy the trapped Allies there before they could get away was reversed, and a priceless opportunity lost.

One of the greatest criticisms levelled at OKW was that as the armed forces high command it should have prepared plans

Above: Hitler, who filled the triple roles of head of state, head of the government and commander-in-chief of the armed forces, watches the progress of operations in Poland during 1939 with members of his military entourage.

Left: A major-general (facing Hitler) explains one of the finer points to his *Fuehrer* with the aid of a map during the opening stages of Operation *'Barbarossa'*. The officer with goggles is Keitel.

for the eventuality of Britain's continuing the war alone – in other words, a blueprint for invasion. Hitler had already had this done without consulting either the army or the *Luftwaffe* when he made his decision to invade Scandinavia. The real reason why the possibility of an invasion of Britain was not seriously considered until July 1940 was quite simple: Hitler did not consider it necessary, and he was not alone. Jodl did not. Halder, who would have to work out the assault details and bear the direct responsibility for failure, certainly did not. It took six weeks of

indecision before Hitler issued his famous 'Directive No. 16' for Operation 'Sealion' and the great inter-services wrangle began. From start to finish of the debate, OKW never acted as a co-ordinating influence. In fact the fear of Raeder, whose navy (what was left of it after the punishing battles off Norway) would have the job of putting the troops ashore in Britain, sufficiently impressed Jodl for the latter to inhibit any tendency towards an early concrete decision. The army passed the responsibility to the navy and the navy to the air force, and all were happy when the blame finally settled on the failure of Goering's 'eagles' to make the invasion possible.

A definite achievement on the part of Keitel and Jodl was made when they argued Hitler out of an autumn campaign against Russia should the plan to invade Britain come to nothing. This won the approval of OKH and the planning for 'Barbarossa' proceeded with unaccustomed harmony. Before the offensive could begin on schedule, however, OKW had to issue snap orders for the reduction of Yugoslavia and Greece.

On 13 May 1941, Keitel issued one of the most notorious directives of the war – a limitation of the normal jurisdiction of army courts-martial with regard to the civilian population of Russia after the

Left above: The *Fuehrer* hands out the personal rewards of victory to some of the generals responsible for the triumph of German arms over those of Poland in September 1939. Here Hitler is seen awarding the Knight's Cross of the Iron Cross to Generals Halder, Guderian and Hoth (from left to right) at a ceremony at the New Chancellery on the 30th of that month.

Left below: Hitler in typical pose, engrossed in the information shown on a map. He liked the simplified form of information shown thus, but also had a phenomenon memory for the minutiae of military activity, such as returns on equipment and *matériel* strengths at divisional level. Hitler used this memory to strike back at generals who might appear to be getting the better of him in discussion of more important military matters: few generals knew, or needed to know, the number of 10.5-cm shells held in reserve by their corps or other formation.

Right: Hitler exercises his personal magnetism on some of his soldiers on 16 March 1941, when planning for Operation *'Barbarossa'*, which was to kill great numbers of them, was well advanced. Behind Hitler's left shoulder is visible Grand Admiral Erich Raeder, Commander-in-Chief of the German Navy, or *Kriegsmarine*.

invasion, providing for draconian maintenance of order in the occupied areas. This was one of the murkiest tasks of OKW, whose planners – men like Warlimont – never showed the slightest reluctance to work out the details of atrocity and submit them in memorandum form.

The blind faith of the top OKW officers in Hitler remained unshaken during the first year of campaigning in Soviet Russia, but there were plenty of fundamental disagreements between Hitler and OKH. Brauchitsch, army C-in-C, was a morally-broken man, as was proved by his order to Guderian not to bring up the subject of a drive on Moscow at the conference of 23 August. (Guderian ignored Brauchitsch, and Hitler turned down Guderian's representations.) Any signs of sympathy on the part of Keitel and Jodl with the increasingly depressing reports from the front were crushed by contemptuous tongue-lashings from Hitler.

Obsequious toady

By 1942, the year of the great turning-point for the Axis war effort, the rôle of OKW was firmly defined and never really showed any signs of modification. Keitel, the dim, obsequious toady, kept his place as the nominal head of OKW because of

his readiness with the right comment at *Fuehrer* conferences and also because he did not tell Hitler 'unpleasant things'. Jodl was the dominant partner. Unshakably loyal to Hitler, he was the man who mattered in OKW. Jodl suffered a traumatic shock in September 1942 when Hitler sent him down to the Kuban to find out why Army Group 'A' was being so slow. When Jodl came back and told Hitler that Army Group 'A' was doing all that could be done, Hitler raged and screamed and ordered Jodl's dismissal. This was never implemented, but Jodl never forgot the lesson. (He so far unbent as to tell Warlimont that 'a dictator, as a matter of psychological necessity, must never be reminded of his own errors'.)

Rubber stamp

Thus OKW remained as the official stamp on Hitler's military decrees. The direct control of operations was denied it: this control was exercised by Hitler himself. Keitel, Jodl and Warlimont, however, remained the trio who relayed the orders for atrocity to the fighting forces. Yet OKW was a large, if securely trussed, body. From the original four basic departments – operational orders, foreign intelligence, supply and general purposes – a forest of industrious sub-departments

grew. Staffed by professional officers, its work was nevertheless largely nullified by Hitler's increasing lack of touch with reality.

It must also be remembered that OKW, unlike OKH, was mobile. It had to be: it was an extension of Hitler's personal authority, and where Hitler was, there also were OKW headquarters. OKW had started its existence as a revamped war office, centralised on Hitler's orders: it ended the war as a travelling military court.

Genuine respect

Jodl undoubtedly deserves credit as the most able of the 'political generals' and was certainly the man for whom Hitler had the most genuine respect. It was no accident that Jodl's ascendancy made him the natural choice to sign the instrument of surrender in May 1945, rather than Doenitz, Hitler's designated successor. But apart from Keitel, Jodl, Warlimont and Schmundt other generals deserve the description of 'political'. Among that handful without hope who committed suicide in the Berlin *Fuehrerbunker* in 1945 there was General Wilhelm Burgdorf. He was head of the army personnel department and armed forces adjutant at OKW HQ; and it was Burgdorf who carried the ultimatum of suicide or disgrace to Rommel in October 1944. General Hans Krebs, a shrewd and adaptable character cast in the same mould as Jodl but without the signs of the latter's ability, became Hitler's last chief of the army general staff and surrendered Berlin. The *Luftwaffe*, too, produced its own 'political' generals, men such as General Korten (chief of the *Luftwaffe* general staff, and killed by the 'July Plot' bomb), and Koller, who replaced him. Then there was the confirmed Nazi, General Ritter von Greim, who was summoned into the hell of Berlin to be promoted field-marshal

Hitler and part of his immediate circle pose for the camera at Fuehrer headquarters. From left to right in the front row are Otto Dietrich, press chief for the Nazi Party and the state, Keitel, Hitler, Jodl, Martin Bormann, Hitler's second-in-command of the party, and Colonel Nicolaus von Below, Hitler's *Luftwaffe* adjutant. Between Bormann and Below, in the second row, is Heinrich Hoffmann, Hitler's personal photographer, who took many of the colour photographs we now have of the early days of Nazi power. It is very noticeable that there are few senior officers of the armed forces present – Hitler preferred to keep his immediate circle restricted to party functionaries such as Bormann and junior officers such as adjutants and liaison officials.

Left: **Hitler gets to know some of the young officers, with seniority dating from 1938, who will lead his men in war. Introducing the officers at this presentation in the New Chancellery on 18 January 1939, is Colonel-General Walther von Brauchitsch, Commander-in-Chief of the Army. Few young men who met Hitler before the war came away from the meeting with anything other than total belief in the *Fuehrer*'s personality.**

Above: **Hitler reviews the military situation with *General von Artillerie* (General of Artillery) Ritter von Leeb. In typical pose, looking over his master's shoulder, is Field-Marshal Keitel.**

and be appointed commander-in-chief of the *Luftwaffe* by the crazed *Fuehrer* in 1945.

Throughout the disastrous months of 1943 and 1944, the pattern of OKW remained much the same in defeat as it had done in victory, with the small, permanent group of trusties manning the key posts. Forming an 'outer circle' were a group of equally obsequious generals who had found out how to keep in Hitler's good books. It was left to the last campaign of the war in Europe, the battle of Berlin, for Hitler to do the one thing he had never brought himself to do: unite OKW with OKH. It was in any event an acknowledgement of hard facts, for the tiny compressed pocket of German soil

left to the German armed forces was now so small that the two headquarters had been intermingled anyway. It was a symbolic gesture which gave Keitel, for a few meaningless hours, the latitude to exercise, as far as he was able, the actual powers of command which Hitler had always denied him, before the inevitable end.

The depressing story of OKW and the 'political generals' reveals not the strength but the basic internal weaknesses of the Third Reich. The 'political generals' were professional officers who had pinned their faith, and their personal careers, on one man: Hitler. They were a unique body of men in that all their training and background before the advent of Hitler went by the board. Closest of all to the core of Hitler's magnetism, they genuinely felt that they were doing their duty as best they could in assisting the German war effort. Labouring under this delusion, they out of all the men of the German officer corps shouldered the most opprobrium and blame for the evil which Hitler's Germany unleashed on Europe. They proved that to get on in the Third Reich it was advisable to adapt. But whatever condemnation they merited for their toadying to Hitler and their delinquencies as officers – let alone as human beings – their main defence at Nuremberg still merits consideration. Even if they had been advisers, instead of opting to become courtiers and sycophants; even if they had spoken out against the wrongdoing they helped to implement, it would have made little difference. They of all people in the Third Reich knew how easily they could be replaced. It was so much easier for them to convince themselves that they would do more good by staying.

Field-Marshal Wilhelm Keitel

During the war Keitel did little but 'rubber-stamp' Hitler's orders and turn them into intelligible military orders. He did, however, keep his job throughout the war, and ratified the final German surrender on 7 May 1945.

Keitel was tried for war crimes before the International Military Tribunal at Nuremberg, sentenced to death, and hanged on 15 October 1946.

Hitler once said of Keitel that he had 'the brains of a cinema usher'. He was a big, impressive man with little real ability, but remained useful to Hitler as a military show-piece for public occasions and when dealing with difficult generals. In the latter capacity he could be relied upon always to echo the *Fuehrer*'s will.

Wilhelm Keitel was born in Helmscherode near Brunswick on 22 October 1882, and joined the army as an artillery officer in 1901. Keitel was promoted to captain shortly after the outbreak of war, and given command of a battery on 11 November 1914. In March 1915, however, Keitel became a staff officer, at divisional and corps level until he joined the Great German General Staff on 21 December 1917.

After the end of World War I Keitel stayed in the army, rising to lieutenant-colonel in various staff and regimental posts by February 1929. Keitel's career moved ahead slowly until he attached himself to Hitler. On 1 April 1934 Keitel was promoted to major-general, and on 9 September 1935 he was appointed to the *Wehrmachtamt*, being given the job as its head just under a month later. At the beginning of 1936 Keitel was again promoted, to lieutenant-general. Elevated to general on 1 August 1937, Keitel reached the pinnacle of his career on 4 February 1938, when he was given the post of chief of the *Oberkommando der Wehrmacht* (High Command of the Armed Forces). Further promotion, to colonel-general on 1 November 1938 and field-marshal on 19 July 1940 after the fall of France, followed.

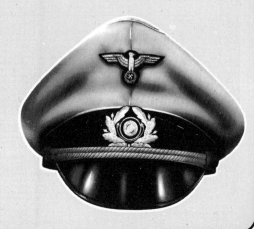

Field-Marshal Wilhelm Keitel

In 1940 the soldiers came home from France, and the Germans thought they had won the war. Britain would come to terms, indeed the *Fuehrer* had offered them a 'Final Appeal to Reason' and translated versions of his speech had been dropped from aircraft over England. It was a time for self-congratulation and promotions.

Hitler made up nine of his generals to the rank of Field-Marshal, and after the ceremony they posed for a photograph in the Reich Chancellery with the *Fuehrer* and *Reichsmarschall* Goering. All of them had proved their worth in the battle of France, except one man who stood a little apart from the group. The photographer caught the look of withering disdain on the face of

Field-Marshal von Rundstedt as he glanced with disgust at the chief of the OKW, Wilhelm Keitel.

In his rôle of head of the High Command of the Armed Forces, Keitel was a party to all the major decisions taken by Hitler in the prosecution of the war, yet he exercised no real influence in the planning or choice of these operations. Guderian commented after the war that Keitel 'soon fell under the sway of Hitler's personality and, as time went on, became less and less able to shake off the hypnosis of which he was a victim. He preserved his Lower Saxon loyalty until the day of his death. Hitler knew that he could place unlimited confidence in the man; for that reason he allowed him to retain his

position even when he no longer had any illusion about his talents as a strategist. The Field-Marshal exerted no influence on the course of operations.' Guderian is generous to his former colleagues. Indeed, after listing the faults and failings of Keitel and Jodl he adds: 'For all that – they were my comrades.'

Keitel is described as 'lacking the strength to resist Hitler's orders when such orders ran contrary to international law and to accepted morality. It was only this weakness on his part that permitted the issuing to the troops of the so-called "Commissar Order" and other notorious decrees.' Once more Guderian is generous. Keitel was not weak; he was totally subservient to Hitler and served only to put the military rubber stamp on the *Fuehrer*'s dreams and plans. There is no record that he attempted to divert Hitler from the invasions and expropriations which the Germans made throughout Europe.

Keitel fell under Hitler's spell in 1938. On 27 January, after Field-Marshal von Blomberg had departed in disgrace for Italy, Hitler summoned Keitel. At that time Hitler did not know his new Chief of the *Wehrmachtamt* and addressed him as 'General von Keitel', which aristocratic appellation must have delighted the middle-class soldier. The *Fuehrer* complained that he was becoming ever lonelier and that Keitel would have to endure with him the changes which were taking place in the armed forces. Keitel, uncomplicated, found himself touched by this confidence and from that moment was Hitler's man.

Intermediary

As head of OKW his signature ratified Hitler's orders and instructions. He was under the *Fuehrer*'s spell and a scribbled 'Keitel' at the foot of some sheets of typescript seemed nothing. He signed for the destruction of Poland, Denmark and Norway, France and the Low Countries, much as a soldier signs for the kit with which he is issued as a recruit. He even signed for the destruction of Britain, but at the end of 1940 OKW informed units on the Channel in the autumn of 1940 that the '*Fuehrer* has decided that from now on until the spring,

Keitel emphasises the point to a pensive Hitler, watched by Jodl. Keitel's position as head of the *Oberkommando der Wehrmacht* was an unenviable one, and well suited to the mediocre gifts enjoyed by Keitel. Had he possessed a more aggressive and self-confident personality, combined with abler military thinking, Keitel would not have held his job long.

preparations for landing in England will be maintained purely as a military and political threat.

It was a meaningless gesture, for on 18 December 1940 Keitel initiated a document of fatal importance. Nine secret copies of *Fall Barbarossa* had been circulated among the heads of the services; Germany would invade Russia and defeat her before she had finished with Britain.

Low intelligence

Hitler imagined that Russia would be torn apart by political upheavels when Germany attacked and Keitel supported his master's view. 'The war has been won already; it has only to be terminated,' he told diplomats in Italy and Finland. It sounded like the brave words he had uttered before the attack on Poland in 1939. Hitler had told him: 'We cannot expect a repetition of the Czech affair. There will be war. Our task is to isolate Poland.' Thrilled by the prospect of a real war he told the doubters at OKW, who prophesied that this would lead to a world war for which Germany was ill-equipped: 'France is too degenerate, Britian too decadent and America too uninterested to fight for Poland.'

Yet he had his doubts. Beck had told him that the new army Germany was building would not be a reliable military instrument before 1942 or 1943. Keitel even reached the point of offering his resignation to Hitler,

but as usual the *Fuehrer* refused to accept it.

To the surprise of the general staff, the campaigns in Poland and in the West went well and it was not until the halt before Moscow that Keitel began to feel uneasy again. On 1 December Bock reported that the troops were exhausted and would need to go onto the defensive for the winter. In the discussion which followed Keitel suggested that it might be better that the troops withdraw to a winter line.

Hitler turned on him and dismissed the suggestion as one coming from a '*Strohkopf*', crude slang for a man with a low IQ. Deeply hurt, Keitel turned and left the room. Jodl found him in his quarters writing out his resignation with a pistol on his desk. Jodl quietly took the pistol away and tried to persuade Keitel to remain. He gave in and stayed in service.

This reputation of being the servant of Hitler, his military showpiece, had now become public knowledge. Keitel was always hovering near his master on public occasions and the Berliners with their sharp humour dubbed him '*Lakaitel*' or 'little lackey'. It was not far from the truth. Keitel had begun to climb the back stairs to promotion before he met Hitler. In 1937 he married the youngest daughter of Field-Marshal von Blomberg. Three years later he showed off his talents for gross flattery at the *Fuehrer*'s headquarters. Hitler had paid tribute to OKW for its training and leadership, for the Battle of France was clearly

Above: **Keitel and *Reichsmarschall* Hermann Goering compare notes at the *Wolfsschanze* in the summer of 1941, at the time of '*Barbarossa*'.**

Above right: **Keitel in conversation with the Hungarian Minister of War.**

Right: **The crucial conference of 9 May 1942 at which Hitler decided to strike at Stalingrad. At the right are Keitel and General Paulus.**

going Germany's way and her troops had just captured Abbeville. In front of a large gathering of generals Keitel begged to differ: 'No, no, my *Fuehrer*, to you alone are due these magnificent achievements.'

He backed Hitler even when his judgements seemed to others to be at fault. When the Canadians suffered their disastrous defeat at Dieppe, Keitel saw this as an immediate threat to France. Even though there were protests from Halder and Jodl two divisions, the '*Leibstandarte Adolf Hitler*' and '*Grossdeutschland*', were withdrawn from the Eastern Front, although fortunately the latter unit was still at its railheads when the Russians attacked. Liddell Hart thinks that if both these divisions had been employed they might have turned the scales at Stalingrad.

Understandably a man who did so little to further the war, and who in the pre-Nazi era would never have risen above his

majority, earned a name in the army. He was 'knick-Keitel' 'nodding Keitel' the *Fuehrer*'s yes-man. The contempt in which he was held extended, perhaps unjustly, to Jodl. Speaking to Liddell Hart after the war, General Hasso von Manteuffel was more generous: 'Keitel, Jodl and Warlimont had never been in the war. At the same time their lack of fighting experience tended to make them underrate practical difficulties, and encourage Hitler to believe that things could be done that were quite impossible.'

But just as he despised Keitel in 1940, Field-Marshal von Rundstedt, the aristocratic professional still loathed him at the end of the war. In 1944, in a telephone conversation from the Normandy front, Keitel had a gloomy report from Rundstedt. It was uncommon for Rundstedt to speak direct to the head of OKW. Such was his dislike he normally arranged for Blumentritt, his chief-of-staff, to undertake the unpleasant duty. Keitel complained about the way the fighting was going, and Rundstedt snarled over the line: 'If you think you can do any better you had better come down here and lead this filth yourself.' A few days later there was a similar exchange. Cherbourg was about to fall and Keitel was on the line again: 'What shall we do? What shall we do?' This time the answer came in a cool, impassive voice: 'What shall we do? Make peace you idiots! What else can you do?'. The line went dead as Rundstedt quietly hung up.

Keitel's tragedy was that despite such epithets as 'the brains of a cinema usher' he was not without intelligence. Free of Hitler's spell, he saw Germany's mistakes quite clearly in his postwar interrogation. Recalling the interview, Milton Shulman writes: 'Second guessing, after it was all over, Field-Marshal Wilhelm Keitel nodded in agreement with history's verdict.

'"Instead of attacking Russia," he said, "we should have strangled the British Empire by closing the Mediterranean. The first step would have been the conquest of Gibraltar."'

Expanding on this theme he said: 'One of the biggest occasions we passed by was El Alamein. I would say that, at that climax of the war, we were nearer to victory than at any time before or after.'

Wilhelm Keitel never had a moment which was truly his own. He won no battles and took no momentous decisions. After five years of service to Hitler he was left by the *Fuehrer* to tidy up the mess that remained in 1945. Despite his protests that he alone enjoyed the right to lead, Hitler evaded the responsibility of ending the war when he committed suicide. On 8 May 1945, at the headquarters of the Russian 1st Belorussian Front with Admiral Friedeburg and Colonel-General Stumpff, Keitel ratified the unconditional surrender of the Third Reich. Impeccably dressed, with his cap, gloves and marshal's *Interimstab* baton, this was Keitel's finest moment. This time his signature marked the end of a war.

The body of Field-Marshal Keitel after his execution by hanging on 16 October 1945. He was condemned to death for war crimes by the International Military Tribunal.

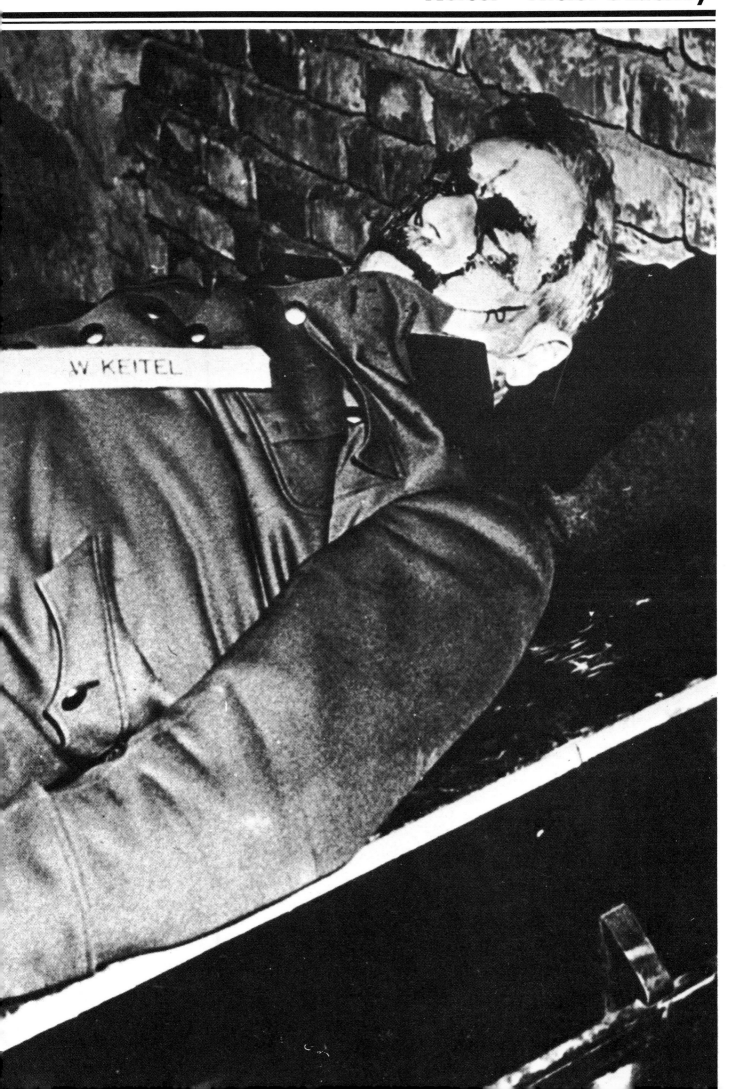

Colonel-General Franz Halder

Hitler, but gradually mellowed into a half-hearted acceptance of Germany's position. He remained Chief-of-Staff during the Polish and Western campaigns, and was promoted to colonel-general on 19 July 1940.

Halder's army career ended on 24 September 1942, when he was transferred to the reserve as a result of Hitler's anger at his 'mismanagement' of a mission to spur on German efforts in the Caucasus.

On the day after the July Plot, Halder was arrested by the Gestapo. Just over six months later, on 31 January 1945, he was dismissed from the army, and soon found himself in Flossenburg concentration camp. On 7 April 1945 he was moved to Dachau camp, where he was found by the Allies.

A man of decidely conservative leanings, with an outstanding brain and tireless energy, Halder had not the strength of character to stand up to Hitler.

Franz Halder was born in Wuerzburg on 30 June 1884, and joined the 3rd Bavarian Field Artillery Regiment on 14 July 1902. Despite his training as an artillery officer, Halder soon gravitated towards staff work, and throughout World War I served in a number of posts as a staff officer on the Western and Eastern Fronts.

Halder remained in the army after the war, serving principally as an adjutant, tactics instructor frond battery commander. Later he became second-in-command of the Directorate of Training. On 1 October 1934 Halder was promoted major-general; just over a year later he became commander of the 7th Division. On 1 August 1936 Halder was again promoted, this time to lieutenant-general, and in November of the same year he became the department head of the army general staff. October 1937 saw the elevation of Halder to the post of Director of Training, and 1 February 1938 further promotion, to general. On the 10th of the same month Halder was appointed Director of Operations, under General Ludwig Beck.

When Beck resigned on 27 August 1938, Halder took over as Chief of Army General Staff, being confirmed in this post on 1 September.

Halder was at the time against

Colonel-General Franz Halder

On 1 September 1938, Halder replaced Beck as Chief of the Army General Staff. He was then aged 54, a man of wide intellectual interests including botany and mathematics, and the first Bavarian to hold the position.

Beck, who opposed Hitler's policy of aggression, had recommended Halder as his successor when he resigned because he was convinced Halder shared his views and would act with those who sought to overthrow the Nazi régime. The Chief of the Army General Staff was a key figure for the conspirators to have on their side, but Halder soon found himself in a dilemma. He was a devout Catholic and consequently suffered crises of conscience over supporting Beck and the conspirators – which he felt was the right course of action – and his oath of allegiance to the *Fuehrer*, his supreme commander. His first orders were to hasten the preparations for the invasion of Czechoslovakia, whereas Beck had operated a go-slow policy. Halder therefore vacillated and

made excuses to the conspirators, saying that nothing could be done against Hitler whilst he was so popular, and that they must wait until the Nazis suffered a defeat. On one occasion, Halder made the tenuous distinction that he could support an assassination attempt, for one could not be loyal to a dead *Fuehrer*, but that he could not support a coup at time of war.

He did nothing more than warn Hitler of the folly of his aggression.

Poland

Together, Halder and Field-Marshal Walther Brauchitsch, commander-in-chief of the army, worked on the plans for the invasion of Poland, and pondered on the forces the British and French could muster if they decided to support Poland. There is no record – even in the invaluable diary kept by Halder – of anyone questioning Hitler on the rationale behind the proposed attack. Halder did not speak out against Hitler and in later years he claimed he never believed Hitler would actually go to war, and he

certainly did not believe that Great Britain would fight. Only one voice was raised in protest at the military conference at Obersalzburg on 14 August 1939, and that belonged to General Thomas, head of the economics and armaments branch of OKW, who said that Hitler's attack on Poland would start a world war. At a further conference on 22 August, Hitler adopted an arrogant and uncompromising attitude which made it impossible for those present to challenge his statements. In his monologue, he assured them that conflict with Poland was inevitable, that Germany had nothing to

Colonel-General von Brauchitsch, Commander-in-Chief of the Army, salutes the welcoming party on his arrival by air to report on the progress of operations in Poland. Watching, with his left hand behind his back, is General Halder, the army chief-of-staff.

Halder — 'the Peevish Professional'

lose and must act immediately. Whether Britain fought or not, he said, was irrelevant – 'our enemies are little worms'. Halder knew well enough what Hitler was up to over the negotiations with Poland, but he did nothing. He knew that Hitler would 'raise a barrage of demographic and democratic demands ... The Poles will come to Berlin on 30 August; on 31 August, the negotiations will blow up; on 1 September, Germany will use force.'

Halder also knew the implications of Hitler's 'final solution' for the Jews in Poland. Hitler had instructed his generals to confine themselves to military matters only. SS commissars would be stationed in each military district and would carry out the required exterminations. Halder accepted that there would have to be these commissars, in order to keep the army out of the exterminations. He also knew of Hitler's plan to drive the Poles from their territory, but he still could not find the strength to join the conspirators.

War in the West

Warsaw fell after 17 days of siege. Hitler immediately requested plans for continuing the war in the West. Halder told him that only defensive plans existed. Hitler, inflamed by his Polish victory, thought that France would fall just as easily and took no notice of Halder, who commented that the techniques of the Polish campaign were no recipe for war in the West, against a well-knit army. Hitler wanted a lightning strike through Holland and Belgium on a very wide front that Britain and France would not be able to stop. Halder, Brauchitsch and several other generals attempted to prove to Hitler that an offensive was impossible, that it would take many months to equip the army appropriately. But Hitler was longing for battle, and his Directive No. 6 showed an amazing grasp of history, strategy and tactics. Halder and Brauchitsch saw three courses of action open to them: first, go ahead with the attack in the West; second, wait and see; and third, remove Hitler. Brauchitsch did not care for option three (a 'man of straw', Hitler called Brauchitsch) and they decided to try to work further on changing Hitler's mind, although now after Poland, Halder must have known there was little hope of this. But he could not bring himself to act against Hitler without superior orders, and Brauchitsch was not giving any.

On 27 October, Hitler told his generals in no uncertain terms that the attack in the West would definitely take place, so they should plan accordingly and stop arguing. Halder felt quite battered after Hitler's tirade and from then on showed dutiful enthusiasm for the offensive whilst, inside, he was filled with gloom. Politically and militarily, he was a defeatist.

Hitler presents the Knight's Cross of the Iron Cross to Halder, Guderian and Hoth (from left to right) on 30 September 1939. Standing behind Hitler is Colonel Rudolf Schmundt, the *Fuehrer*'s *Wehrmacht* adjutant and a key figure in the inner circle of the *Fuehrer*'s entourage.

On 5 November, Brauchitsch complained to Hitler of his interference in the Polish campaign and requested that OKH should be solely responsible for any future campaign. Hitler went into a fury. This was the first occasion on which he truly abused his generals, calling them disloyal, cowardly and defeatist.

On 20 November, Hitler issued Directive No. 8 for the conduct of the war, ordering maintenance of an alert to 'exploit favourable weather conditions immediately'. Fed up with the criticism of the generals, and with what he regarded as the 'stiff-necked attitude' of the general staff, Hitler again addressed them on 23 August, telling them his plans were unchangeable. No one, he said, had ever achieved what he was about to achieve: 'I will shrink at nothing . . . I shall annihilate anyone opposed to me.' There is no record of any general expressing the doubts most of them felt at this time, or questioning the immorality of attacking through Holland and Belgium. From this point on, Hitler considered his political and military judgement to be superior to that of the generals, and henceforth would hardly ever listen to advice, let alone allow criticism. His outburst put a real damper on any thoughts the generals might have had for overthrowing him, and Halder was certainly not the man to stand up to the threat of being 'annihilated'. He was fast losing independent thought.

Operation 'Sealion'
After the fall of France and the evacuation of the BEF from Dunkirk, Hitler declared 'England's situation is hopeless. The war has been won by us.' In July 1940, planning began in earnest for the invasion of Britain – Operation 'Sealion'. Hitler, however, had decided on the invasion before he knew the inherent difficulties of an overseas landing and at a time when he was also beginning to concentrate on his proposed attack on Russia.

OKH looked forward to a war of movement on the island and Halder, always methodical and meticulous, concerned himself with details such as the difficulties of landing troops where they were supposed to be, and how to convey enough horses for the offensive on limited means of transport. The navy soon revealed the wide margin that existed between the army's requirements for the land war and its own capabilities of conveying these requirements. Halder remarked that if this was so, planning might as well cease, but of course he did not tell Hitler this, and work on the plans continued even though fresh drawbacks were discovered almost daily. Irreconcilable differences arose between the army and navy concerning the length of the front. The army wanted a wide landing front so that it could secure a number of beach heads at an early stage, while the navy felt itself capable of landing troops only on a narrow front. This seemed to Halder like 'feeding the troops into a sausage machine'. Originally, Hitler had stated that he intended hurling 40 divisions across the Channel, but detailed planning showed that only nine could be sent in the first wave with two airborne divisions in support, and that it would take 11 days to land them. Reinforcements would only arrive at the rate of two divisions every four days.

As the dangers and difficulties of an amphibious operation became obvious to Hitler – Admiral Raeder did his best to persuade the army that 'Sealion' was out of the question, at least in 1940 – he began to hesitate, and it seems that his interest waned, probably because of his concentration on Russia. At the same time, however, he continued to hope that something would turn up to make the invasion possible before the bad weather. With all the delay, Halder requested that the forces concentrated on the Channel coast be dispersed as they presented a sitting target to the RAF. Hitler allowed this and then called the operation off in October.

In this instance, everyone concerned had been loathe to tell Hitler that his ambitions were not possible and so they continued planning regardless. Hitler was than at his zenith.

Operation 'Barbarossa'
Hitler intended to attack Russia in the spring of 1941 – 'The sooner Russia is smashed, the better.' Halder and his staff went to work on the plans in August 1940. Halder's diary reveals that he was full of enthusiasm for the task. The German army, with the successes in Poland, Norway, Denmark, Holland, Belgium and France behind it, appeared invincible.

Planning for the invasion of Russia – Operation 'Barbarossa' – had to take careful note of the climate: the short, hot summers and long, extremely cold winters, which necessitated a German victory within a single summer offensive not more than five months in duration. The Germans were not equipped for winter warfare. The spring thaw and autumn rains which turned the roads into impassable quagmires added a further limitation to the timetable.

Hitler and his generals agreed to trap and destroy the main Soviet forces as near to the border as possible, but Halder and Brauchitsch disagreed with Hitler over the means for the final Soviet defeat. They favoured a march on Moscow, where the roads were best and where they believed Russia would commit its last strength to defend the capital. Hitler retorted 'Moscow is not important', and in his directive of 18 December 1940, he provided for simultaneous advances towards Leningrad, Moscow and Kiev.

Then came Hitler's decision to invade Yugoslavia, which meant that 'Barbarossa' had to be put back four weeks. Hitler did not consult OKH, and this decision later meant that deep snow and sub-zero temperatures hit German troops three or four weeks short of what they needed for victory.

Right from the beginning of the German invasion of Russia, OKH underestimated Russian ability and overestimated their own. During the first weeks, Hitler meddled nervously with the plans and attempted to impose on the battlefield his own tactical conceptions.

When the Germans reached Minsk, Halder hoped that the front would become so fluid that it would outrun Hitler's ability as a tactician – but no, Hitler was about to take over completely. Now the row about whether the German advance should be to Moscow blew up again. On 19 July, Hitler completed a directive about which OKH had not been consulted, restating that Moscow was not the primary target. Army Group 'Centre', the strongest of the three army groups in Russia, was to continue towards Moscow with its infantry alone and was to divert its armour to help the Army Group 'North' thrust towards Leningrad and the Army Group 'South' conquest of the Ukraine. Hitler overruled many generals over this, including Guderian. Halder noted that Hitler was obsessed with the capture of Leningrad and Stalingrad. Hitler called Halder and OKH 'men with minds fossilised in out of date theories' when Halder vainly pointed out that in accordance with Clausewitz, Moscow should be the main aim.

The march on Moscow restarted on 2 October, but it was too late. Victory appeared within Germany's grasp, and then the autumn rains started at the end of October. The army was 50 miles from Moscow, halted by oozing, muddy roads. It moved off again in mid-November but ground to a halt within sight of Moscow, where the Russians counterattacked throughout the winter.

Halder lingers on

In December, Brauchitsch retired and Hitler took over as commander-in-chief himself. He had always longed to be a general and to show off his military genius properly. Halder stayed on, but the army's last vestige of existence as an independent service was wiped out. Hitler ignored Halder's advice and ordered the armies in Russia to stand fast. There would be no retreats. Halder observed that the generals were now merely Hitler's postmen, conveying his orders, based on his own conception of strategy. The winter crisis of 1941–42, however, gave Hitler a personal triumph. Against the generals' advice and entreaties, he had ordered the armies to remain where they were, and they had done so. His confidence in his own military ability was further enhanced.

Plans for Operation 'Blau' – the 1942 summer offensive – were drafted by Halder and his staff in accordance with Hitler's detailed instructions. Hitler was now in complete command. The directive called for a full scale offensive on the southern flank of the Eastern Front, towards the River Don, Stalingrad and the Caucasus oilfields. Hitler's fanatical determination to take both Stalingrad and the oilfields was a bad mistake. In the end, he gained neither objective and suffered a humiliating defeat. Halder tried in vain to warn him of the danger of leaving the northern flank of the 6th Army so dangerously exposed along the line of the upper Don for 350 miles from Stalingrad to Voronezh, where only three, weak satellite armies were thinly deployed. Hitler, however, was convinced the Russians were finished and paid no attention, although the Don flank was the key to maintaining the 4th and 6th *Panzerarmee* at Stalingrad and Army Group 'A' in the Caucasus. Should this flank collapse, the troops at Stalingrad would be threatened with encirclement

and those in the Caucasus cut off.

Halder then suggested that the offensive against Stalingrad be called off, as it was losing its momentum. Hitler flew into a blind fury and dismissed Halder on 24 September 1942, saying he was no longer up to the 'psychic demands of his position'.

Halder commented in his diary that Hitler's decisions 'have ceased to have anything in common with the principles of strategy . . . They are the product of a violent nature following its momentary impulses which recognise no limits to possibility and which make its daydreams the father of its acts.'

Conclusion

By the summer of 1942, the chief-of-staff had no power or authority. Hitler was in absolute control of the war in the East. Even the day-to-day battle moves were controlled from his desk. Halder merely had the task of presenting the *Fuehrer*'s requirements in a logical and rational way.

Halder's mind was often confused, and his will to action paralysed. He could not bring himself to task risks. He stood up to Hitler in the early days to a certain extent, then went along with him, always hoping (vainly) he could prevent things becoming too terrible. His main trouble was he could not choose between his duty as a soldier and his patriotic and moral convictions.

Above: **Hitler congratulates Field-Marshal von Brauchitsch on his 60th birthday, on 4 October 1941. Looking noncommittal, as usual, is Keitel; Halder appears even more glum than was his custom.**

Left: **Halder in conversation with General Franz Ritter von Epp, Reich Governor of Bavaria.**

Colonel-General Alfred Jodl

Alfred Jodl was born on 10 May 1890 in the town of Wuerzburg in Bavaria, and served as an artillery officer in World War I.

After the signing of the Treaty of Versailles in 1919, Jodl decided to stay in the *Reichswehr*, or army of the German republic, and rose slowly but steadily via a succession of staff appointments.

In June 1935 Jodl, by that time a colonel, was appointed head of the Home Defence Department of the Reich Defence Council, and in October 1939, by which time he was a lieutenant-general, head of the Operations Staff of the High Command of the Armed Forces (*Chef der Wehrmachtfuehrungamt,* later *Chef der Wehrmacht-fuehrungstab),* a post he was to hold throughout World War II.

During 1940 Jodl was promoted general, and in 1944 colonel-general. His last act in the war was to sign the surrender of the German army to the Allies at Rheims on 7 May 1945.

Like Keitel, Jodl was arraigned before the International Military Tribunal at Nuremberg for war crimes, sentenced to death, and hanged on 16 October 1946.

Jodl was a highly competent staff officer who fell under the personal magnetism of Hitler and was used to translate some of the *Fuehrer's* military dreams into workable operational plans. His diaries are of great importance in the assessment of Hitler's command decisions just before and during the course of the war.

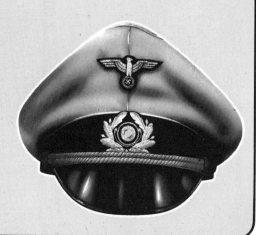

Colonel-General Alfred Jodl

When Hitler decided to invade Russia he had a special headquarters built in the woods of East Prussia. With his peculiar Gothic imagination he called it the '*Wolfsschanze*' – the Wolf's Lair. In the permanent shadow of the woods and camouflage nets, and confined to log huts and concrete bunkers behind belts of barbed wire and minefields, the staff and aides soon developed a prison psychology. Some visitors landing at the special airfield or coming in on the secret railway branch-line felt the place was like something out of a fairy tale from Grimm or some peculiar Wagnerian opera – with Hitler as the king of a Nazi court.

Among the courtiers who had fallen under Hitler's spell was the chief-of-staff of OKW, Colonel-General Alfred Jodl. Liddell Hart dismisses him as the able clerk to the chief clerk, Keitel. But since Keitel exercised little real control over the prosecution of the

war, it was up to Jodl to see that Hitler's ideas and dreams were transformed into some sort of order and instructions for the men on the ground. Guderian, who had little love for restrictive superiors or incompetent subordinates, does not treat Jodl so harshly. Jodl 'had in fact controlled the operations of the combined armed forces ever since the Norwegian Campaign of April, 1940 . . . originally he too had fallen under Hitler's spell, but he had never been so hypnotised as was Keitel and therefore never became so uncritical.'

In 1935 Jodl had been made head of the Department of National Defence, and had worked hard to build it into what was really an operations department of the Reich War Ministry. General von Fritsch regarded him as an exceptionally able officer, but also noted that he suffered from almost pathological personal ambition. It may have been

this characteristic that attracted Hitler. Although Jodl admired Hitler, he did have reservations, however, unlike his superior Keitel. After the war Jodl explained to an American doctor at Nuremberg that as the son of a middle-class military family he found Hitler's outbursts against the officer corps and middle-class rather offensive. There were moments during the campaigns in the West when Jodl doubted the *Fuehrer*'s judgements of the situation, and there were also times when he imposed considerable burdens on OKW, calling on them to change

Below: A typical gathering at the *Wolfsschanze,* with the addition of of Benito Mussolini.

plans and operations at very short notice. At the operational conferences there was the carping tone of the south German corporal who had made good teaching the German professionals how to make war. It was not until the war with Russia, however, that this behaviour became so intolerable for Jodl that he clashed with his master.

In 1942, after their defeat before Moscow, the Germans struck in southern Russia. Hitler told his generals that it was for economic reasons, and baffled them with talk of the coal and iron of the Donets basin and the oil of the Caucasus. Oil had always been an obsession with Hitler, and he had pressed for the capture of the Crimea so that its air bases could be eliminated as a threat to the Rumanian oilfields. Hitler's Directive No. 41 stated that after Rostov had been secured Stalingrad would be the main objective, but then Hitler changed his mind. He would not merely cut off Russia from her oilfields in the south – he would capture

them. Halder noted bitterly in his diary: 'His persistent underestimation of the enemy's potential is gradually taking on grotesque forms and is beginning to be dangerous.'

In Directive No. 45, transmitted to Army Group 'A' under Field-Marshal List, he stated that 'following the annihilation of the enemy force south of the Don the main task of Army Group "A" is the seizing of the entire eastern coast of the Black Sea, with a view to eliminating the enemy's Black Sea ports and Black Sea Fleet . . .

'Another force, to be formed by the concentration of all remaining mountain and *Jaeger* divisions, will force a crossing of the Kuban and seize the high ground of Maykop and Armavir . . .'

But in addition Operation '*Edelweiss*' called for fast formations from the army group to cut the Ossetian and Georgian Military Highways and drive along the Caspian to Baku. One of these objectives

alone would have been enough for List, and he admitted afterwards that he could only assume that OKW had secret information to indicate that enemy forces in that region were severely weakened or under strength.

Assuming that OKW had this information, List set about allocating his forces for their objectives. One of his problems was that his *Jaeger* troops had not seen action in mountains, and had been employed in conventional fighting in the steppes of Russia – they were out of training for their specialised rôle. More disturbing was the fact that the Russians were no longer allowing themselves to be cut off and encircled. Instead they were withdrawing into the vast plains south of the Don.

The steppe south of the Don is rather like the desert in North Africa. Split up by watercourses which made excellent stop lines that could be held by light forces, it is 300 miles deep. To the south-east the River Manych forms the border between Europe

and Asia. The Germans were not only in a new territory – they were in a new continent.

Stalin was a Georgian and the area had seen considerable improvements in farming and irrigation. Dams and canals added to the natural obstacles which confronted the invaders. The Manych had been dammed at several points to form lakes, which were in some cases over a mile wide. In addition to these obvious barriers, the Russians exploited the terrain. The vast sunflower fields, which seemed to stretch like a sea of gold as far as the horizon, offered excellent cover for small groups to ambush despatch riders and patrols.

On 28 July the Germans scored their first major victory over their elusive enemy. At Martynovka on the River Sal the 3rd Panzer Division fought a confused short-range duel with a Soviet motorised corps. At the end of the fighting the Germans had destroyed 77 tanks, a mere handful compared with their earlier victories.

A month after the start of operations, Army Group 'A' and the 4th *Panzerarmee* had driven a deep wedge into the Caucasus and by 29 July were within 70 miles of the Caspian Sea. Now Hitler transferred the 4th *Panzerarmee* to Stalingrad to assist the 6th Army – but he still expected Army Group 'A' to reach its objectives. On 9 August they captured the oil wells at Maykop, but only after the Russians had set them on fire.

With the thermometer at 55 degrees centigrade, the Germans advanced through clouds of white dust. On 12 August they captured Elista, the only important town in the Kalmyk steppes and the same day men of the 3rd and 23rd Panzer Divisions caught their first glimpse of the Caucasus. These mountains abut onto the Middle East and Hitler's long-term plans envisaged a link up with the *Afrika Korps* and the capture of the Arabian oilfields which supplied Britain. But it was from this area that the Russians were now drawing their supplies. American

Left above: Hitler and Brauchitsch leave a command bunker after an inspection visit. Such bunkers were built in most *Wehrkreise* (military administrative districts) for use in war, and the one seen here was located in Gross Born, near Neustettin in Pomerania. Note the *Fuehrerstandarte* (Hitler's standard) at the left.

Above: Hitler visits the headquarters of Army Group 'South' in August 1941. Hitler's party, which includes Colonel Schmundt (behind the *Fuehrer*'s left shoulder), has just been met by Field-Marshal Gerd von Rundstedt (right), the army group's commander. It was after a similar visit to List in 1942 that Jodl all but lost his job as Keitel's deputy.

trucks loaded with rations and equipment were being driven overland from Persia. Along with Jeeps and scout cars, they would give Russian troops a new mobility. Meanwhile, at the end of a supply line which stretched for over 1,000 miles, the Germans were being forced to use the local dromedaries pulling requisitioned peasant carts.

By 1 September Army Group 'A' had crossed the River Terek and even reached the highest peak of the Caucasus, Mount Elbrus; but it had run out of energy and run into increased opposition. The advance was almost at a halt and the Germans had neither cleared the Black Sea, nor captured the oilfields of the Caspian.

On 7 September Hitler ordered that Jodl should visit List at his headquarters at Stalino and find out why Army Group 'A' was making no progress. He was to discover why the port of Tuapse on the Black Sea had not been taken, though it was less than 50 miles away, and to re-emphasise Hitler's orders.

Away from the claustrophobic atmosphere of Hitler's new Russian HQ near Vinnitsa in the Ukraine, Jodl met the soldiers who were doing the fighting. General Walther Warlimont described to Liddell Hart after the war what happened when Jodl returned that evening to report.

'Jodl reported to Hitler that List had acted exactly in conformity to Hitler's orders, but that Russian resistance was equally strong everywhere, supported by a most difficult terrain. Hitler, however, kept on reproaching List with having split up his forces instead of breaking through with concentrated power.'

Hitler's anger

List had in fact been wanting to regroup his forces, but was carrying out his orders as best he could. Enraged by Hitler's implications that he had been duped by List, Jodl repeated in a loud voice the very orders that Hitler had given, which had forced List to advance on so wide a front.

It triggered the biggest crisis that the German high command had suffered since the beginning of the war. With his face discoloured by rage, Hitler rounded on Jodl: 'You're lying, I never issued such orders – never!' He stormed out of the meeting and it was some hours before he returned to his quarters, still clearly suffering from shock.

The truth had hurt. This time there was no one to blame for the failure. Hitler was not the genius he thought he was, and his grand strategy was not invincible. However, Hitler had to shift the blame and so he sacked Colonel-General Halder, his chief-of-staff, and List. There were indeed also rumours that he would dismiss Keitel and Jodl and replace them with Field-Marshal Kesselring and General Paulus – which would have meant that men with active service experience would have been in command might have been able to avoid the disaster of Stalingrad.

Keitel and Jodl did not go, but instead a stenographer was added to the staff. Every word uttered in conference with his generals was now to be recorded. There were other changes: the *Fuehrer* no longer ate lunch and dinner with his entourage but dined alone

in his quarters with the sole company of Blondi, his Alsatian bitch; and he never left his hut in daytime, not even for the daily briefings on the military situation, which were now delivered to him in his own hut with a small circle of friends and aides.

Warlimont said that Jodl reached the conclusion that these changes were attributable to the special character of a dictator. By a process of spurious logic he decided that the dictator must never be reminded of his own errors 'in order to keep up his self-confidence, the ultimate source of his dictatorial force'. In other words he must be treated to the lies and flattery once the preserve of an 18th century monarch.

Warlimont came to a more reasonable conclusion that 'Hitler, when confronted with the actual situation at the end of the second offensive against Russia, suddenly grasped that he would never reach his goal in the East and that the war would eventually be lost.' So, like a spoilt child which is denied its wishes, he had a good howl and went out to sulk, and like indulgent parents Keitel and Jodl made sure that they did not pain him with further direct statements but tried instead to plead or persuade.

Above: Hitler salutes his men as they march past him towards the front in Poland.

Right: An *alfresco* conference at the *Wolfsschanze* at Rastenburg in East Prussia. Seated at the table with Hitler is a Major Christiansen; on the right is General Karl Bodenschatz of the *Luftwaffe*, Goering's chief-of-staff; holding the papers is General Jodl; watching is Field-Marshal Keitel; and on the left of Keitel is *SS-Brigadefuehrer* Julius Schaub, one of Hitler's SS adjutants. It was Schaub who destroyed those of his papers that Hitler wanted burning in the final grim days in the *Fuehrerbunker* in Berlin as the Russians closed in during April 1945.

The Political Front

Colonel-General Kurt Zeitzler

better defensive line before Moscow and Leningrad. Zeitzler also played an important part in the planning of the last German offensive in Russia, Operation 'Zitadelle'.

Zeitzler became increasingly unwell during 1943, and this made it all the more difficult for him in his efforts to moderate Hitler's wild strategic orders.

Zeitzler was sacked as OKH chief-of-staff on 20 July 1944, and at the same time discharged from the army.

A little-known figure of World War II, Zeitzler was a surprise selection as Halder's replacement, but did perform creditably. He was a highly competent staff officer and an expert in armoured strategy. A master of detail, he was responsible for solving the supply problems of the 1940 Ardennes push. His one major 'failing' was that he lacked the seniority to deal with other German commanders.

Kurt Zeitzler was born in 1895, and served throughout World War I, remaining in the army after the conclusion of hostilities. He showed a penchant for staff work, and rose gradually in rank.

By 1938 Zeitzler was on the *Oberkommando der Wehrmacht* planning staff, with the rank of lieutenant-colonel. Here he was primarily responsible for the preparation of *'Fall Gruen'*, the directive for the political occupation of Czechoslovakia, dated 30 May 1938.

By the beginning of World War II, Zeitzler had been given the command of an infantry regiment with the rank of colonel, but by the time of the Western campaign in 1940 he was a corps' chief-of-staff.

In the early stages of the invasion of Russia, Zeitzler was chief-of-staff to Kleist, who commanded first a *Panzergruppe* and then a *Panzerarmee*. He was again shifted to the West in 1942 as chief-of-staff to the Commander-in-Chief West, with the job of reorganising the defence of France.

On the dismissal of Halder as Chief of Army General Staff on 24 September 1942, the post went unexpectedly to Zeitzler, who was promoted to general straight from major-general. After the defeat of the 6th Army at Stalingrad, Zeitzler persuaded Hitler to pull.back to a

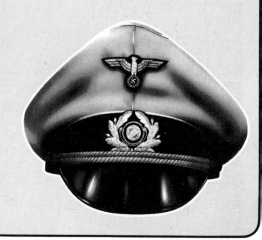

Colonel-General Kurt Zeitzler

On 2 September Kurt Zeitzler, who had been a general officer less than a year, replaced Halder as chief-of-staff at OKH. This promotion astonished everybody. Although the new man had earned the reputation of being alert, energetic and physically active while the chief-of-staff of Army Group 'D' in the Low Countries, it was widely felt that his lack of status, seniority and experience, particularly on the Eastern Front, would rule out his candidature for the post. But apparently Hitler decided that he preferred more hustle and bustle in OKH in contrast with the supposedly woolly intellectualism of Halder. As a result of this appointment, Zeitzler in

theory assumed control of the most powerful section of the army, the Army General Staff. Despite his inexperience, Zeitzler soon demonstrated that he was not prepared to be the yes-man that Hitler might have assumed. During the first few weeks of his appointment he successfully engineered a realignment in the structure of power and authority in the German high command, which was to produce significant effects on the future of campaign planning.

The army had, for a long time, been disgruntled at the influence of the Operations Staff at OKW (Jodl) over the formation of *Fuehrer* directives, many of which dealt with tactical aspects of the campaigns on the

Eastern Front and had little strategic content. This annoyance had intensified after Hitler became Commander-in-Chief of the Army as it had the effect of reducing the army staff to the position of a second personal staff.

Zeitzler, at the time a captain in rank, as a staff officer at the *Reichswehrministerium* (War Ministry) in Berlin during 1934. He later became one of Germany's abler staff officers during World War II.

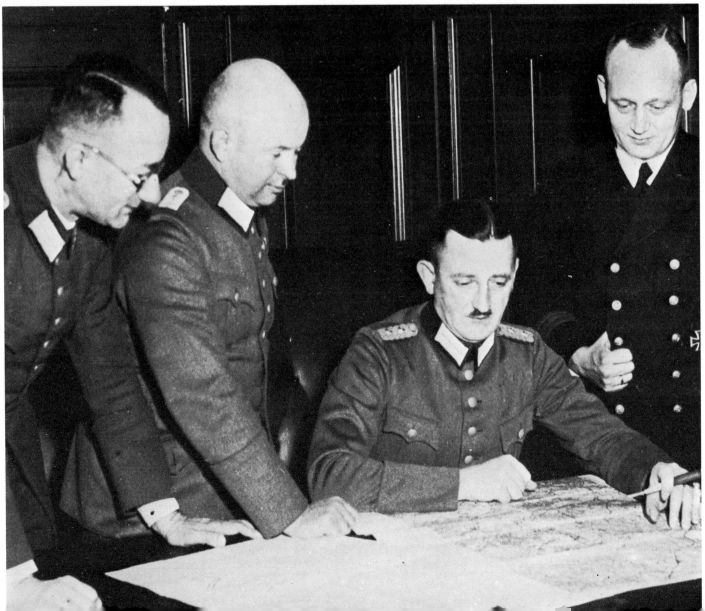

Almost immediately after his appointment Zeitzler approached Hitler and demanded that OKH should assume responsibility for Hitler's campaign directives applicable to the Eastern Front, to the exclusion of the meddling Jodl and his Operations Staff at OKW. His demand was finely timed, for Jodl had recently incurred the displeasure of Hitler by his support for the apparently incompetent List. Hitler agreed to Zeitzler's request and henceforth the former's directives were issued as 'operations orders' through OKH. Subsequently Zeitzler was able to prevent OKW gaining access to detailed information about Eastern Front affairs.

But how far did the change in general staffs alter the situation facing the German armies, and to what extent was Zeitzler able to influence Hitler in the formation of policy? These two interrelated questions will be examined by reference to the events on the Eastern Front in general and at Stalingrad in particular.

Hitler's plans for the summer of 1942 included the taking of the Caucasus oilfields, the Donets industrial basin and Stalingrad

on the Volga. On 23 August, before Zeitzler was appointed, the 6th Army under Paulus reached the Volga just north of Stalingrad. By 4 October, much of this strategic goal had been achieved. The Volga was closed and half of the town was under German control. The rest of Stalingrad was under fire. But Russian resistance was total and the German advance halted. At this stage, it would have been wise to consolidate the position. Yet Hitler was furious at the breakdown of the offensive, and despite vociferous criticism from Zeitzler and others at supreme headquarters, he was determined to occupy the rest of Stalingrad, taking it, if necessary, street by street and building by building. The 6th Army commander had no choice but to continue the bloody battle.

Zeitzler took it upon himself to prepare a long and detailed report on the situation in the hope that a factual and statistical analysis might make Hitler realise the futility of the continued offensive. The Germans simply did not possess the men, arms, ammunition, tanks or transport to achieve their objectives. The Russian resources were superior in all departments. Zeitzler con-

cluded his report with four basic postulates which had to be acted upon if the Germans were not to be routed. These he formulated as follows:

'1. Owing to the summer offensive, the territory to be occupied in the East no longer corresponds to the size of the occupying army. In a word, there are too few soldiers for too much ground. Unless this is adjusted, a catastrophe must occur.

'2. The most perilous sector . . . is undoubtedly the long, thinly-held flank stretching from Stalingrad to the right boundary of Army Group "Centre". Furthermore, this sector is held by the weakest and least reliable of our troops, Rumanians, Italians and Hungarians. This danger must be eliminated.

'3. The flow of men, equipment, weapons and ammunition to the Eastern Front is entirely insufficient. Each month losses exceed replacements. This must have disastrous consequences.

'4. The Russians are both better trained and better led in 1942 than they were in 1941. This fact should be realised and taken into account.'

Zeitzler – 'the Last of the Old Breed'

Hitler received the report with uncharacteristic patience, and gently chastised his chief-of-staff for being too pessimistic. He minimised the conclusions almost to the point of insignificance. Zeitzler's only recourse was to reiterate his remarks over and over again in the hope that some of them might stick in the *Fuehrer*'s mind. He continually impressed upon Hitler that a withdrawal westwards from Stalingrad was the only option open. In this he had the support of both Paulus and his own chief-of-staff. But Zeitzler found himself in the awful situation where he could envisage impending disaster but do absolutely nothing about it. Hitler would not withdraw from Stalingrad; his frustration had overcome his reason. Zeitzler's war of words with the *Fuehrer* had begun in earnest, but time was of the essence.

The Russians had considerable offensive potential. The problem for German intelligence was to predict where the counterattack would occur. It was not long before they found out. In freezing conditions, the Soviet attack, which combined the 5th Tank Army and the 21st Army, was launched on

19 November. It hammered the whole of the Rumanian 3rd Army front north-west of Stalingrad. Zeitzler succeeded in convincing Hitler that the reserve, Panzer Corps H (XLVIII Panzer Corps), must be released and sent to Army Group 'B'. The Russians meanwhile had broken the Rumanian front at two points and the Panzer corps was sent to counterattack these advanced units. Zeitzler kept Hitler constantly informed about the situation and urged him to withdraw from Stalingrad before the 6th Army became encircled. An irate *Fuehrer* took no notice.

The situation continued to deteriorate as the Panzer corps itself was attacked by the advancing Russian armour. The possibility of a successful counterattack quickly diminished. Again Zeitzler recommended that the 6th Army should break out and establish a solid front to the west and attack the Russians who had broken through the Rumanian position. Hitler rejected this situation out of hand. Disaster became increasingly inevitable. Two conferences were held at which Zeitzler put forward the views of the general staff, Army Group 'B' and the

Left above: A good proportion of the Axis high command gathered together, and looking not much the worse for wear after the 20 July bomb plot against Hitler's life. From left to right are Mussolini, Bormann, an unidentified officer, Grand Admiral Karl Doenitz (commander-in-chief of the navy), Hitler, Goering, and in the foreground *SS-Gruppenfuehrer* Hermann Fegelein (SS liaison officer at Hitler's headquarters) and Colonel-General Bruno Loerzer of the *Luftwaffe.*

Above: An open-air discussion. Amongst those present with Hitler are Zeitzler (right foreground), Keitel (visible over Zeitzler's cap) and Albert Speer (between Hitler and Zeitzler), the *Reichsminister fuer Bewaffnung und Munition* or Reich Minister for Armament and Munitions, a key post which Speer filled with very considerable ability.

231

Zeitzler – 'the Last of the Old Breed'

6th Army. Again he urged a withdrawal. Hitler lost all self-control and thundered 'I won't leave the Volga! I won't go back from the Volga!'

On 20 November the Russian 57th and 51st Armies launched the second attack, on the Rumanian VI Corps south of Stalingrad. They broke through very rapidly, and the Rumanian corps disintegrated. The 6th Army was now faced with the almost inevitable prospect of encirclement from both flanks. It was only a question of time before the Russian pincers met and the Germans' escape route became blocked. A message was sent by General Paulus on 22 November informing the high command that his army had been cut off. The worst fears of Zeitzler and the army commanders had been realised. Some 250,000 troops were isolated in 'Fortress Stalingrad'.

Hitler's decision to keep the 6th Army in the city was based on two dubious assumptions: firstly that an operation could be planned to relieve the German forces, and secondly, that the army itself could be effectively maintained by air supply. Zeitzler was not deceived by either assumption and in his daily meetings with Hitler urged, vainly, that the order be given to the 6th Army to carry out a fighting withdrawal.

Despite the bombastic assurances of *Reichsmarschall* Goering, the air-supply failed. The required tonnage of supplies to meet the needs of 250,000 men could not be delivered. Meanwhile, Manstein was appointed to the command of Army Group 'Don' with orders to co-ordinate the counter-attack for the relief of Stalingrad with General Hoth and the 4th *Panzerarmee*. Manstein, like Zeitzler, protested vigorously to Hitler that the 6th Army should break out to meet his own relief army and form a new front further to the west. But Hitler remained adamant and stuck to his original

Hitler and Zeitzler watch as a factor in the situation on the Eastern Front is pointed out to them.

scheme for the relief of the 'fortress'.

The attack commenced on 12 December. By the 21st, Hoth's troops were only 30 miles from Stalingrad. But here, the offensive ground to a halt as the exhausted 4th *Panzerarmee* met an unbreachable Russian front. The very last chance of saving the 6th Army had vanished.

Manstein and Zeitzler once again did all that was possible to convince Hitler that he should sign the directive to break out. Zeitzler in particular spent several hours every night trying to make the *Fuehrer* see reason, but to no avail. However, on 26 December, Paulus reported that the cold weather, hunger and the large number of casualties meant that his army could not break out unless a supply corridor was opened. By now this was also impossible.

At the beginning of the new year, the 6th Army was starved and exhausted. Relief supplies were totally inadequate. The final Soviet offensive aimed at destroying the 'fortress' began on 10 January after General Paulus, on the orders of Hitler, had rejected a Russian ultimatum to surrender. After suffering fierce bombardment, Paulus sent a message on 20 January stating that he could not hold Stalingrad for more than a few days. The tragedy was drawing to its close. On 24 January, the Russians again demanded surrender. Zeitzler, despite presenting Hitler with the cold facts of the numbers of dead and wounded, could not persuade him to order a capitulation. Paulus was to continue.

Stalingrad falls

On 28 January, the 6th Army commander stopped issuing rations to the wounded in order to maintain the troops still capable of fighting. The final collapse came early on 2 February when the remnants of XI Corps surrendered.

The horrific battle had ended. But it is easy to imagine a much less fateful finale had the 6th Army been allowed to withdraw its 20 divisions from Stalingrad, as advised by

The last authenticated photograph of Hitler, taken on 12 April 1945 as he inspected and decorated with the Iron Cross members of the *Hitlerjugend,* none of them more than 16 years old, for bravery against the Russians.

Manstein and Zeitzler. The colossal defeat was due more to Hitler's incompetence and refusal to listen to reason than to Russian tactical awareness.

The chances of Zeitzler significantly influencing the course of the war in the East were never very great. Hitler probably wanted a man who would be subservient and unquestioning. With that aim, he appointed Zeitzler, a very junior general, to a very senior position, which had the effect of down-grading the post to an executive level. As a result, Hitler gained tighter control of the command apparatus of the army. Zeitzler was also handicapped in the early stages by a lack of knowledge of the situation in the East. But he quickly mastered his subject and refused blindly to follow the whims of the *Fuehrer*. Hitler's aim for an acquiescent chief-of-staff did not materialise – instead he ignored Zeitzler's advice.

So Zeitzler's rôle in the Stalingrad débâcle was not one noted for its conspicuous success or great achievements. Although he had ability, worked with great energy, fought hard in the defence of his opinions and was not afraid to stand up to Hitler, he did not wield inordinate influence through his staff office. He was unable to persuade the *Fuehrer* to change his attitude over Stalingrad, but on the other hand, it is unlikely that any man could have done so. Russian victory was facilitated by Hitler's obstinate policy of 'fortress-building' – a policy which Zeitzler could not reverse. During the course of his appointment he offered his resignation five times and on each occasion it was refused. He was finally dismissed in July 1944 after the plot to assassinate Hitler.

Analysis–
Hitler and his High Command

The rôle in which Adolf Hitler always fancied himself most was that of supreme commander and omniscient warlord, a fact that bedevilled the professional officers at the head of the German army throughout the short life of the 'Thousand-Year Reich'. As an embittered ex-infantryman from the trenches of World War I, Hitler retained a lasting contempt for 'these stuffed-shirt gentlemen in their red-striped trousers',

as he called the generals. Nevertheless he needed them to fight his wars for him. For their part, the generals were not averse to fighting a war, but they wanted to do it their way – and this Hitler never tolerated. In the beginning, of course, he had a very good argument in his favour: every time the generals had prophesied disaster between 1935 and 1939, Hitler had been right and they wrong. The *Fuehrer* found

it very convenient to give his generals an inferiority complex about their real abilities and thus get them to try all the harder to prove their worth. But this discounting of professional ability, although justified in the short run, led him to disaster in the end.

The war opened with a lopsided chain of command. At the top, commanding the operations of all three arms, was OKW,

presided over by Hitler with the obsequious Keitel and Jodl as his chief executives. The army case was pleaded by the C-in-C, Brauchitsch, and the Chief-of-Staff, Halder, the service chiefs of OKH.

The Polish campaign of September 1939 went smoothly enough, but the real trouble started when Hitler subsequently told OKH that he wanted to attack in the West that November. Brauchitsch failed completely to get an assurance from Hitler that OKH would be allowed to direct land operations in future campaigns. They fell back on delaying tactics for the Western campaign, obstructing Manstein's suggestions for a concentrated drive through the Ardennes. They knew that this campaign would almost certainly win the war and they did not want it launched prematurely.

Great annoyance

Hence their fury when Hitler sprang the news of the Scandinavian campaign on them. This was planned rapidly and secretly, with neither the army nor the *Luftwaffe* being informed. Although the army added to its laurels with its speedy

victory in Denmark and Norway, it did the army leaders little good in the long run, confirming Hitler's belief that he was a natural general.

The campaign in the West of May–June 1940 proved that neither OKH nor OKW had fully grasped the tactical truth that armour, having broken through, must not wait for the infantry to close up before pushing on. OKH ordered such a halt after Guderian's brilliant crossing of the Meuse; Hitler, on the other hand, temporarily lost his nerve and 'raged and screamed' about a non-existent French threat to the southern flank of the 'Panzer corridor'. Neither lapse was serious because Guderian, the Panzer commander on the spot, ignored the restrictive orders he got from his superiors and drove through to the Channel anyway. Then came Dunkirk. Who was right? There were two logics behind the decision to halt the armour on 24 May. The decisive battle against the French army certainly still had to be fought; on the other hand, the victory in Flanders would be a hollow one if the British army escaped. The resulting compromise allowed the British to escape but did not save the French army.

Brauchitsch's order for Rundstedt rather than Bock to administer the hammerblow at Dunkirk had been the correct one as far as the envisaged destruction of the encircled British was concerned.

It was after the battle of France that the total failure of OKW to plan ahead stood revealed, for no detailed plans to invade and conquer Britain had been prepared. This, the ultimate in all-forces operations, was an astonishing oversight. It was easy enough for OKH to do their part: all Halder had to do was to insist on having the assault troops land on as wide a front as possible, as Montgomery did when he saw the first tentative plans for the invasion of Normandy in 1944. The fact that the navy and *Luftwaffe* could not

Hitler with his new field-marshals in September 1940. From left to right these are Wilhelm Keitel, Gerd von Rundstedt, Fedor von Bock, Hermann Goering, Hitler himself, Walther von Brauchitsch, Wilhelm Ritter von Leeb, Sigmund Wilhelm List, Hans von Kluge, Erwin von Witzleben and Walter von Reichenau.

guarantee an unopposed passage was not the army's fault. What was amazing was the speed in which Operation 'Sealion', the final invasion plan, came into being in July and August. It showed what Hitler's military experts could do when they had to.

Now came the awesome revelation that the next victim would be Soviet Russia – and for this, the decisive land operation of the war, OKH gave its full and detailed attention. But the operative word was detailed. Operation '*Barbarossa*' was an open-ended lunge into the void, with no definitive halt-line, relying entirely on the destruction of the Red Army in the initial battles. Brauchitsch and Halder set their team of planners to work on the details of maintaining the advance with their eyes, as ever, fixed on the short-term problems. It was all that they could do in any case. Hitler simply refused to believe such army warnings that the Red Army was armed with a tank superior to the battle-tested Panzers of the German army.

Against this background, the refusal of OKH and OKW to concentrate on North Africa after Rommel's bewildering first success against the British was hardly surprising. Nor, in view of the Russians' winter counterattack and the near-total collapse of the Eastern Front, was it any more surprising that Rommel got little attention until the summer of 1942. By that time, what remained of the withered authority of OKH had vanished. Hitler had assumed personal command of the army during the Moscow counter-offensive and had overridden all advice from his generals to retreat – a decision which events proved entirely correct. Brauchitsch went; Halder stayed on as chief-of-staff until Hitler replaced him with Zeitzler in September 1942. This was the final turning-point in the day-by-day conduct of the German war effort on land. Down to the battle of Moscow the campaign had been conducted largely in the old style, with OKH carrying out orders from OKW. From Zeitzler's appointment onwards, the army chief-of-staff got his orders at daily conferences at OKW. Zeitzler lasted until July 1944, when he was replaced by Guderian, the one man in the German army, perhaps, who was never afraid to bellow back at Hitler when the *Fuehrer* went into one of his rages. Hitler never did get what he wanted as chief of the army general staff – a yes-man who did not tell him unpleasant truths – until General Krebs took over from Guderian at the close of March 1945, when the war was lost.

No cental command

With Hitler determined to run the war himself, and totally unpredictable as to when he was prepared to listen to reason, it is hard to see how the staff generals in the army and *Wehrmacht* high commands could have done a proper job. Keitel, Jodl and Krebs were certainly pliant toadies, but they were professionals; and they, too, often felt the rough edge of Hitler's tongue for that very reason. Hitler's obsessive belief that all staff generals were

hidebound fogies never weakened, although his sanity and his grip on reality did. The whole story, in fact, might very well be summed up as the struggle of the professionals to do their job. They were certainly capable enough, yet constantly reduced to impotence. What, for example, was the value of the excellent work done by General Gehlen's intelligence staff, when Hitler refused to believe the real figures of the Red Army's strength right from the beginning of the campaign in Russia?

The one thing Hitler could never bring himself to do was to scrap the former system of an independent army command and centralise the whole *Wehrmacht* command set-up. At the very least this would have accelerated the flow of orders. But another of the 'unpleasant things' which he could never bear to accept was that he was not '*der groesster Feldherr aller Zeiten*' – 'the greatest commander of all time'. He needed his staff generals to do the work for him – but the only leeway he would allow them was the short-term resolution of details. At the top of the pyramid, the leadership of the German war machine was carried out in a stifling atmosphere caused by the reaction of megalomania against professionalism. The real victims were the commanders and troops in the field.

Above: Hitler assesses the air situation over Poland in September 1939 with the aid of a map while visiting a forward *Luftwaffe* airfield. Not content with issuing general strategic instructions, a field in which he had considerable natural abilities, Hitler was too prone to dabble in the day-to-day running of campaigns, which greatly disturbed the efforts of the generals professionally trained to deal with such matters.

Above right: A discussion in progress between Hitler, Jodl (on the left), Keitel and a Major Deyhle.

Right: The end of the road for the military ambitions of the Third Reich as Field-Marshal Wilhelm Keitel signs the surrender of the German armed forces at Karlshorst outside Berlin, in the presence of Marshal of the Soviet Union Georgi Zhukov, the man who perhaps more than any other Allied general had been responsible for the humbling of Nazi Germany.

German Generalship in World War II

For an overall assessment of the standard of German generalship between 1939 and 1945, it is necessary to grasp the fact that right down to the autumn of 1941 the men of the German army and their commanders were learning the technique of modern mechanised warfare. This considerable period – from the invasion of Poland to the commencement of the giant pincer movement of Kiev – taught many lessons which could be learned in no other way by the generals in the field.

The question 'Who was the best German general of World War II?' is a meaningless one, and the only possible reply is 'Best at what?' The basic building-block of the German army, as with every other, was the division. Above that came the corps, above that the army, and above that the army group. All these levels were commanded by generals and a further basic distinction must be made between infantry and armoured troops, the command of which required very different qualities.

The Panzer tactics as brought to perfection by the German army in World War II were the vital ingredient of success. Two names automatically stand out as brilliant Panzer divisional commanders: Rommel, for his superb performance with the 7th Panzer Division in the Western campaign of 1940; and General Hermann Balck, a veteran Panzer general who served on all fronts apart from North Africa and Italy, eventually rising to the command of Army Group 'G' in the West. Perhaps Balck's finest hour was his counterattack with the 11th Panzer Division in the winter of 1942–43, after the Soviet encirclement of the 6th Army at Stalingrad, when his division broke the Soviet drive towards Rostov.

Corps commanders

Moving up the chain of command to the level of Panzer corps commander, it is easy to pick out Guderian, Kleist, Reinhardt and Hoepner, all of whom rose to higher commands. It is almost certainly true to state that Rommel's true operational 'ceiling' was that of a Panzer corps commander, a rôle in which he could still exercise his brilliance as a front-line leader. In addition, Rommel was well served in Africa by a series of able commanders for the *Afrika Korps*, the most famous Panzer corps of World War II. These included Cruewell, Nehring and Bayerlein.

In the first two years of the war, the Panzer divisions went into action as *Panzergruppen* (Panzer Groups), upgraded to the status of *Panzerarmee* (Panzer Army) in the winter of 1941. As a *Panzergruppe* commander, Rommel's record was patchy. He got himself defeated in his first set-piece battle in the 'Crusader' fighting of November–December 1941, bounced back brilliantly to recover Benghazi in January 1942, and won his greatest victory at Gazala and Tobruk in May. He then failed to keep the initiative at El Alamein and was forced to fight against hopeless odds there in October and November. His withdrawal of the survivors of *Panzerarmee Afrika* to Mareth was masterly, and so was the strategy behind his attack at Kasserine in February 1943. Both

Left: A German assault gun on the Italian front, in the Cassino sector. Great hopes had been pinned by some Allied generals on a swift advance through Italy towards Austria during 1944, but determined German defence, combined with generalship of a high order, had thwarted these plans.

Below: The Russians celebrate the fall of Berlin on the steps of the *Reichstag.*

of the latter two operations, however, were fought with considerably depleted forces and were offset by his resounding defeat at Medenine on 6 March 1943.

By contrast, there was genuine brilliance behind the partnership of Hoth and Guderian during the invasion of Russia, with Hoth going on from strength to strength with the 4th *Panzerarmee* whilst Guderian went into the eclipse of temporary disgrace. Kleist, too, did well with the 1st *Panzerarmee,* most notably in the spectacular advances across the Kuban steppe in 1942.

The infantry were the unsung heroes of the German army in World War II, and their story is summed up by General Heinrici, an unglamorous master of defensive infantry tactics who rose to army command and was entrusted with the thankless job of defending the Oder front in March–April 1945. The top infantry generals at the close of World War II had one thing in common: they had spent years of trying to do the impossible in Russia, holding out against impossible odds when any defence seemed out of the question. One of the most notable defensive feats occurred during the Soviet winter offensive of 1941–42, when 100,000 men of II Corps, 16th Army, commanded by General Graf von Brockdorff-Ahlefeldt, survived complete encirclement from 8 February to 21 April. Further to the south, a combat group under Major-General Scherer, around 5,000 strong, held out from 28 January to 5 May, by which date Scherer's effective combat strength was down to 1,200 men.

The name which always hit the headlines were those of the army group commanders, and of these it is fair to say that the most able men did get to the top in the end. These were the dour, hard-core professionals whom Hitler could never really do without – men like Bock, Leeb and Rundstedt, Busch and Kuechler, Weichs and List. For sheer longevity – not to mention the number of times Hitler sacked and reinstated him – the prize must go to Rundstedt. But two army group commanders stand out above the rest: Manstein and Kesselring.

A sound Panzer corps commander in his own right, as he proved with Army Group 'North' during the opening stages of 'Barbarossa', Manstein was the man who had originated the revolutionary 'Sickle' plan which sliced open the Allied front in the West. As an army commander in the Crimea, he earned his field-marshal's baton by taking Sevastopol in July 1942. But his chief claim to fame was the discovery of the only form of strategy which gave the German army a chance in Russia: yielding the initiative to the Red Army and then slicing decisively at the tentacles that broke through the German front. His finest hour was certainly the retrieval of the near-catastrophic situation created by the Stalingrad breakthrough in the winter of 1942–43, when he not only halted the German retreat but launched a breath-taking counter-offensive which was halted only by the spring mud. All his gains were then jeopardised, despite his pleadings, by the ill-advised offensive against the

Kursk salient in July 1943. In 1940 the adoption of Manstein's thinking had led to one of the greatest victories in German history. Had his strategy for the Eastern Front been adopted, the German army would almost certainly have been able to hold its gains in Russia west of the Dniepr river line.

Kesselring was unique in that he was the only *Luftwaffe* general who was entrusted with extensive land operations. Down to the end of 1941 he had been commanding his *Luftflotte* (Air Fleet) in support of army groups. His rôle in the Mediterranean started as air commander and chief supply officer to support Rommel in Africa. In this capacity he was able to secure Tunisia for Rommel's retreat, and build up a complete army there in the winter of 1942–43. He refused to throw away German troops in a futile defence of Sicily; and his success in defending southern and central Italy kept the Allies out of the Po valley for 19 months. Kesselring's war ended in chaos: Hitler pulled him out of Italy and made him Commander-in-Chief West, when the Allied rampage across western Germany had already broken loose. But he had certainly earned full respect for his initiative and flexibility in apparently desperate situations.

Model was another remarkable army group commander in that he was one of the few generals whom Hitler trusted. His nickname was 'the *Fuehrer*'s fireman' because of the number of appalling situations, from the battle of Moscow onwards, which he managed to retrieve. A typical case was the speed with which he reacted to Operation 'Market Garden', the airborne attack on Arnhem, in September 1944. Model's end was sad: trapped in the vast Ruhr pocket in April 1945, he shot himself rather than surrender.

Against all this professionalism, however, there were many cases where key field appointments were placed disastrously in the wrong hands. Perhaps the most notorious has to be Paulus, the commander of the 6th Army, who surrendered at Stalingrad. Paulus had proved himself a capable staff officer and his spell of field command was only intended as a prelude to an even more senior staff command. His appointment to the 6th Army for the Stalingrad offensive gave him the strongest command on the Eastern Front, which he thoroughly misused. Paulus was by no means the only general in modern warfare to be foxed by the problem of taking a city street by street, but he had plenty of capable subordinate

commanders who told him where he was going wrong. He may also be excused for taking at face value the promise that the encircled 6th Army would be adequately supplied. But nothing can excuse his shilly-shallying, his refusal to accept that the 6th Army was not going to get the supplies so lavishly promised, and not making the decision to fight his way out before it was too late. Desperately, Hitler made Paulus a field-marshal, clinging to the historic fact that no German field-marshal had ever surrendered; but Paulus made his inevitable capitulation within 48 hours of his last promotion.

Nazi court politics were responsible for the most disastrous – not to say ludicrous – appointment of the war: *Reichsfuehrer*-SS Heinrich Himmler to command the optimistically-named Army Group 'Vistula' holding the Oder front in March 1945. Himmler was totally unfitted for military command on all counts, and his mismanagement of the front was retrieved in the nick of time only by Heinrici with a brave but doomed defence on the Oder when Zhukov and Konev attacked on 16 April.

Mention must also be made of the youngest and most specialised army of the *Wehrmacht*: the airborne forces. These forces, whether landed by transport plane or glider, or dropped by parachute, ended the war with an impressive record of aggressive dash. In General Kurt Student (who also collaborated with Model to win the battle of Arnhem) the German airborne arm had a decisive and forceful leader who understood his job and did it well. Outstanding among the divisional commanders of the airborne arm was General Heidrich, whose paratroops did so well in the long defence of Monte Cassino. And another general of the highest calibre was the German army's top mountain-warfare specialist, Colonel-General Dietl, victor at Narvik in 1940. Dietl spent his war well out of the limelight, commanding the German troops in the Far North. This was a decided oversight on the part of OKW. Dietl's talents would have been put to far better uses in the Caucasus or in Tunisia, while Kesselring would have found him invaluable in Italy.

Napoleon was wont to complain that having raised his marshals to the peak of their profession they were more concerned with their new-found riches than with serving the French Empire. In general, Hitler could not have levelled this accusation against his generals in World War II but there was certainly one glaring exception:

Field-Marshal von Kluge, a sound enough army commander who rose to army group command. A touchy and pompous man, Kluge was not above accepting substantial monetary rewards from Hitler – a fact which the members of the anti-Hitler conspirators on his staff used to jog his conscience as they tried unsuccessfully to get Kluge to help them. After the failure of the 'July Plot' of 1944, Kluge committed suicide after penning a note, protesting his loyalty, to Hitler. By this time he had already fallen from favour because of his inability to check the Allied break-out from Normandy, and he knew full well that the Gestapo would be on his trail once they started rounding up others in the conspiracy. A strange, complex man, Kluge stands apart from the other generals who secretly favoured the idea of getting rid of Hitler but refused to act against the *Fuehrer*.

Hitler's rage

All the names mentioned above, and every single general on the active list right down to divisional level, knew that they all had one thing in common. None of them was exempt from the nerve-cracking insults with which Hitler constantly belaboured the German officer corps. This could take the form of a face-to-face screaming-match, a contemptuous dressing-down, or even dismissal by telegram. There were no exceptions.

Another devastating weapon which Hitler used against his generals without any scruple was his fantastic memory. This gift extended to the most remote levels. If a general protested that such-and-such a task was impossible, Hitler would retort by asking him what his shell stocks or fuel supplies were – something detailed, which any general would normally leave to his staff to worry about. Hitler would then produce the actual figure out of his memory and usually, by the implication that the general was not up to his job, get his way.

In general, Hitler's generals tried hard to serve their country well and loyally. This caused constant trouble for the anti-Hitler conspirators, who knew that they would stand no chance without the backing of the field commanders. Most generals genuinely believed that it would be disloyal to act against Hitler, not so much because of the 1934 oath of loyalty but because the enemies of Germany were still in arms – and, after the Casablanca Conference of January 1943, holding out for 'unconditional surrender'. Thus Hitler's sneers and contemptuous insinuations that the army did not want to fight, and that the generals were a pack of contemptible cowards, were particularly unfounded. 'Loyalty up' from the generals to Hitler therefore left little that could be desired; but the fate of Rommel showed how even a general who was a national hero could be driven to his death by the *Fuehrer*.

Left: Germany was let down partially by prewar failure to appreciate the amount and quality of *matériel* that would be needed. When shortages were met, therefore, captured weapons and vehicles, such as this Czech tank, were used.

Rommel was no Nazi; before the war he had had to give up the job of supervising the military training of the Hitler Youth because of his inability to work with the Hitler Youth leader, the arrogant and foolish Baldur von Schirach. But when war came he served his country well. During the Polish campaign he commanded Hitler's bodyguard, and then moved on to command the 7th Panzer Division (an interesting commentary, incidentally, on Panzer appointments in the early months of the war, since Rommel's World War I experience had been with the infantry). By July 1942, newly-promoted field-marshal, he could do no wrong in Hitler's eyes. No wrong, that is, until he tried to point out the hopeless case of the *Panzerarmee* at El Alamein. Hitler sent Rommel a 'stand fast' order concluding: 'As to your troops, you can show them no other road than that to victory or death.' After the initial shock of this callous blow, Rommel then experienced 18 months of increasing disillusionment which did not prevent him giving his all, and suffering a near-fatal wound, in the fruitless defence of Normandy. Implicated in the 'July Plot', Rommel was brought Hitler's offer of honourable suicide and a state funeral rather than a public trial by two brother generals, Burgdorf and Maisl. He chose to take poison. It was announced that he had died of the wounds suffered in Normandy.

A famous axiom of generalship holds that 'no commander can be considered a great

Above: German armour in the Western Desert, almost Germany's 'forgotten theatre of war'.

Left: A German reconnaissance party scans the desert from a Volkswagen *Kubelwagen* light utility vehicle. Although always vital for the success of military operations, reconnaissance was even more important in the desert, with its difficult terrain, than in most other theatres. Yet as a result of the speed of advance Rommel tried to keep up, such reconnaissance was quite difficult for the *Deutsches Afrikakorps.*

general who has not had to conduct a dangerous retreat'. The turning of the tide certainly gave Hitler's generals plenty of opportunity to display their skill in that direction after 1942. Rommel's retreat from El Alamein to Mareth remains a classic; so does Kesselring's steady withdrawal up the Italian peninsula. But Hitler tended to give his generals little or no chance to act correctly in the face of hopeless situations. Carried away by the success of his 'stand fast' order during the battle of Moscow, which alone kept the Eastern Front in being, he tended more and more to the hysterical belief that the panacea for avoiding defeat was never to retreat. Thus in November 1941 he sacked Rundstedt for pulling out of Rostov to the Mius river line and replaced him with Bock, who promptly completed the withdrawal. The 18 surviving divisions of Army Group 'North', retreating through the Baltic States on their long retreat from Leningrad, were badly needed on the Oder front; Hitler refused to bring them out by sea when they got cut off in Kurland. The most latitude he ever allowed was to the favoured few such as Model or Manstein on their sudden appointment to 'disaster fronts' – sectors which would never have been in such a serious state if Hitler had let the original commanders use their initiative. Hundreds of thousands of irreplaceable troops were thrown away between the summer of 1943 and the end of the war, hopelessly cut off in surrounded pockets or what Hitler loved to call 'fortress' positions (the latter being towns which Hitler could not bear the thought of losing without a fight).

How did Hitler's generals, gifted as they were in their individual ways, work as a team? Personality had a lot to do with it. Lasting enmities were made by the friction of the early campaigns between the Panzer generals, who chafed at being tied to the infantry, and the infantry generals, who resented being left to do all the heavy fighting while the Panzers dashed on into the blue. The enmity between Guderian and Kluge was a case in point. Kluge's abrasive personality also offended Rommel in the summer of 1944 when the former took over as C-in-C West, fresh from Russia, and breezed into the latter's HQ in the middle of the battle of Normandy saying that now Rommel would have to get used to taking orders. But Kluge was, as we have seen, an exceptionally complex character. In general the system worked well enough. The top generals – Manstein, Model, Rundstedt and Kesselring – never had any trouble in holding the professional respect and loyalty of their subordinates. And all field commanders had a common bond of sympathetic loyalty against the toadies at OKW, which also helped.

In the last analysis it is safe to say that the combined armies of Great Britain, the British Dominions and Empire, the United States and the Soviet Union put together failed to produce so rich a crop of highly talented generals as boasted by the German army alone. The achievements of Hitler's generals in the field were formidable enough. That they managed to achieve anything in the face of Hitler's megalomania was positively astonishing.

Picture Credits

The publishers wish to thank the following photographers and organisations
who have supplied photographs for this book.
Photographs have been credited by page number. Where more than one
photograph appears on the page, references are made in the order of the
columns across the page and then from top to bottom.
Some references have, for reasons of space, been abbreviated as follows:
Bapty & Co, London: Bapty
Blitz Publications, London: Blitz
Imperial War Museum, London: IWM
Süddeutscher Verlag GmbH, Munich: Südd.

12: Südd. **13 (top)**: Time-Life; **(bottom)**: JG Moore Collection, London.
14–15: Südd. **16**: JG Moore Collection. **18–20**: Südd. **21**: IWM. **22–24**:
Südd. **26–27**: Südd. **28**: Blitz. **31–33**: Südd. **34**: IWM. **35–39**: Südd.
40–41: JG Moore Collection, London. **43**: Südd. **44**: Bapty. **45**: Südd.
47: Bapty. **48–49**: Südd. **50**: Blitz. **51**: Bapty. **52–54**: Südd. **55**: JG Moore
Collection, London. **56–57**: Bapty. **57**: IWM. **58–59**: Bapty. **60**: US Army,
Washington. **61**: Bapty. **62–64**: Südd. **65**: Blitz. **66**: Südd. **67**: IWM.
68–71: Südd. **72–73**: IWM. **74–75**: Südd. **76–77**: Südd. **79**: Südd.
81: Blitz. **82–84**: Südd. **84–85**: Bapty; Blitz. **86–87**: Südd. **88–89**: Bapty.
89: Südd. **90–92**: Südd. **93**: Bapty. **94**: Südd. **96–97**: Bapty. **96**: Bapty.
98–100: Südd. **101**: Blitz. **102–104**: Südd. **105**: Bapty. **107**: Südd.
108–109: Blitz. **110–112**: Südd. **112 (top)**: Bapty. **113**: IWM. **114–115**:
Südd. **116–117**: Südd. **118–120**: Südd. **121**: Bapty. **122–123**: Südd.
124: Bapty. **125**: Blitz. **126–128**- Südd. **129**: Blitz. **130–133**: Südd.
134: IWM. **135**: Südd. **136–137**: IWM. **138–140**: Südd. **140 (bottom)**:
IWM. **141**: Bapty. **142–144**: Südd. **145**: IWM. **146–147**: Südd. **148**: IWM.
149–150: Südd. **151**: IWM. **152 (top)**: Bapty. **(bottom)**: Blitz. **153**: Blitz.
154–155: Südd. **155**: IWM. **156–157**: Bapty. **158–160**: Südd. **161**: Bapty.
162–163: Südd. **164–165 (top and bottom)**: Bapty. **166–167**: Südd.
168: Bapty. **169**: Blitz. **170–186**: Südd. **187**: IWM. **188**: Südd. **189**: Blitz.
190–196: Südd. **197**: Blitz. **198–204 (top)**: Südd. **204 (bottom)**: Bapty.
205–222: Südd. **223**: IWM. **224–237**: Südd. **238–239**: Novosti Press
Agency, London. **239**: IWM. **240–242**: Südd. **243**: Blitz.

59372088550192   FTBC

I0646977

WORN, SOILED, OBSOLETE

AR!

AR 2.8
.5 pts
Q# 166460.

Also by David McKee:
Elmer and Rose
Elmer and Snake
Elmer and Super El
Elmer and the Big Bird
Elmer and the Birthday Quake
Elmer and the Hippos
Elmer and the Rainbow
Elmer and the Whales
Elmer's Christmas
Elmer's First Counting Book
Elmer's Opposites
Elmer's Special Day

American edition published in 2014 by Andersen Press USA,
an imprint of Andersen Press Ltd.
www.andersenpressusa.com

First published in Great Britain in 2014 by Andersen Press Ltd.,
20 Vauxhall Bridge Road, London SW1V 2SA.
Published in Australia by Random House Australia Pty.,
Level 3, 100 Pacific Highway, North Sydney, NSW 2060.

Copyright © David McKee, 2014.

All rights reserved. No part of this book may be reproduced, stored in a retrieval system,
or transmitted in any form or by any means—electronic, mechanical, photocopying,
recording, or otherwise—without the prior written permission of Andersen Press Ltd.,
except for the inclusion of brief quotations in an acknowledged review.

Distributed in the United States and Canada by
Lerner Publishing Group, Inc.
241 First Avenue North
Minneapolis, MN 55401 USA
For reading levels and more information, look up this title at www.lernerbooks.com.

Color separated in Switzerland by Photolitho AG, Zürich.
Printed and bound in Malaysia by Tien Wah Press.

Library of Congress Cataloging-in-Publication data available.
ISBN: 978-1-4677-4200-9
eBook ISBN: 978-1-4677-4201-6
1 – TWP – 2/28/14

ELMER
and the
MONSTER

David McKee

Andersen Press USA

Elmer, the patchwork elephant, had just started
his morning walk when he heard a terrible roar.
"Look out, Elmer," the birds and small creatures
called out as they came hurrying past him. "There's
a monster!"
"A monster?" thought Elmer. "*Really?*"
He continued his walk.

A little while later there was another roar. "Don't
go that way, Elmer," said the monkeys, swinging
through the trees. "There's a monster!"
Then they were gone.
"A monster again," said Elmer. "Very interesting."

Before long there was a third roar.
"Was that you roaring, Tiger?" asked Elmer,
as Tiger raced towards him.

"Certainly not, that was a monster!" said Tiger, and
he disappeared into the jungle.
   "Fascinating," murmured Elmer, and he went on
      his way.

When the next roar came, Elmer was ready for it.
"Was that a monster?" Elmer called out to the crocodiles
as they fled past.
"Yes, a pretty monstrous one by the sound of it," said the
crocodiles. "Turn back, Elmer!"
"Or go on carefully," said Elmer to himself.

Soon after that there was another huge roar and Lion ran by.

"Nice roar, Lion," said Elmer.

"It wasn't me," said Lion. "That's the roar of a decent sized monster. I'm off to see where everyone's gone," he explained as he ran off.

Almost at once another roar split the air. "Come with us, Elmer," called the elephants as they stampeded past. "There's a monster!"

"I have never seen a monster," said Elmer.
"You don't have to *see* it. Just imagining it is horrible
enough," said an elephant as he vanished after the others.

Elmer walked on. The next roar was very close.
It shook the trees and sent leaves flying. Cautiously
Elmer moved forward, ready to flee at any moment.
He peeped through the trees and then pushed himself
through into a clearing.

There, on a rock, sat a furry creature in tears.
"Hello," said Elmer. "Did you hear that roar?"
"That was me," sobbed the creature. "I do that when
I'm frightened."
"Why are you frightened?" asked Elmer.
"I'm just passing through on my way
home," sniffed the blue animal.
"But I keep hearing
monsters."

"Come with me," said Elmer. "I'll look after you."

Riding on Elmer's back, the furry creature chatted
happily until they reached the other animals.
"Hello, Elmer," said an elephant. "Thank goodness
you're safe. Who's your friend? Did you save him from
the monster?"
"This is Bloo-Bloo," said Elmer. "Go on, Bloo-Bloo,
show them."
Bloo-Bloo opened his mouth and . . .

The animals almost jumped out of their skins in shock. "Friendly, furry Bloo-Bloo is the monster you've been frightened of," said Elmer, laughing. "And these

friendly fellows, Bloo-Bloo, are the monsters *you* were frightened of. You've all been rather silly, but it's quite funny really."

So, laughing at their own silliness and sometimes whispering Boo! to each other, the animals happily accompanied the monster Bloo-Bloo on his way.